Everyman Revived

THE COMMON SENSE OF MICHAEL POLANYI

Drusilla Scott

Foreword by Lesslie Newbigin

*"In our search for a reasonable
world view, we should turn in the
first place to common sense."*
MICHAEL POLANYI

WILLIAM B. EERDMANS PUBLISHING COMPANY
GRAND RAPIDS, MICHIGAN / CAMBRIDGE, U.K.

ACKNOWLEDGEMENTS

I SHOULD LIKE to thank, without laying any responsibility upon them, some of those who have helped or encouraged me, Professor T. F. Torrance, Robin Hodgkin, Joan Crewdson, Walter James, Professor W. T. Scott and not least my husband without whose support the book would never have been completed. The late Arthur Koestler read my manuscript and encouraged my undertaking; this I valued particularly since he was a friend and long associate of Michael Polanyi.

I shall always be grateful to Michael and Magda Polanyi for their long and generous friendship.

© 1985 Drusilla Scott
First published 1985 by
The Book Guild Limited, Lewes, Sussex

This edition published 1995 by
Wm. B. Eerdmans Publishing Co.
255 Jefferson Ave. S.E., Grand Rapids, Michigan 49503
P.O. Box 163, Cambridge CB3 9PU U.K.

Printed in the United States of America

00 99 98 97 96 95   7 6 5 4 3 2 1

Library of Congress Cataloging-in-Publication Data

Scott, Drusilla, Lady, 1911-
Everyman revived : the common sense of Michael Polanyi /
Drusilla Scott.
p.   cm.
Originally published : Lewes, Sussex, Great Britain : Book Guild Ltd., 1985.
Includes bibliographical references and index.
ISBN 0-8028-4079-5 (pbk.)
1. Polanyi, Michael, 1891-1976.   I. Title.
B945.P584S36   1995
192—dc20
95-19182
CIP

The author and publisher gratefully acknowledge permission to
quote material from the sources listed on page 216.

CONTENTS

FOREWORD

I AM very thankful that Drusilla Scott's admirable introduction to the work of Michael Polanyi is again to be available after a period in which it was out of print. I believe that Polanyi's work is of great importance, not least to those who are trying to commend the Christian faith to a sceptical generation. But his major work *Personal Knowledge* is not easy reading, and Lady Scott has given us the essentials of his thought in a form which is much more accessible to the reader who is not a trained scientist. Polanyi was not, of course, writing a work of Christian apologetics: he was concerned about the threat to the future of our culture, and to the future of science in particular. But his work is of the greatest significance to Christians.

One of the most widely read books of the 1980s was Alan Bloom's *The Closing of the American Mind,* with its picture of an intellectual world from which the concept of truth had disappeared, a world where one speaks only of 'What I feel', of 'experience' rather than of truth, of what is the case. How does one commend the Gospel as truth in a world from which the very idea of truth has disappeared? Polanyi, as a scientist engaged in fundamental research, was forced to face this issue by his encounters with scientists of the USSR during the 1930s. They regarded science as simply a necessary instrument for gaining the power to implement their social programme. The idea that the scientist is concerned about the truth for its own sake was ridiculed as a piece of bourgeois ideology. Polanyi had to ask the question: What are the grounds for affirming that the findings of science are not merely useful but true? He saw that current views of the nature of science gave no satisfactory answer to this question, and that, if this question was evaded, science itself could collapse. At a time when such far-sightedness was remarkable, Polanyi foresaw not only the nemesis which must follow for Soviet science and culture, but also the loss of confidence in science, and the threat to western culture as a whole which must follow if the element of personal responsibility in the work of the scientist was not recognised.

Polanyi traced the source of the trouble in a false ideal of 'objectivity', in the illusion that there could be a kind of knowing from which the knowing subject — a human being shaped by historical, cultural and psychological factors — is eliminated or ignored. The effect of this false ideal was to relegate a vast amount of what human beings know to the realm of the 'subjective'. Polanyi, as a working scientist rather than a philosopher of science, knew well the personal factors which shape all scientific work — the necessary apprenticeship to a long tradition of scientific work, the learning of skills, and the personal gifts of intuition, imagination, judgement, courage and patience without which scientific advance would never happen.

In the preface to his major work he gives a succinct description of his central concern. After speaking of the personal participation of the knower in the act of knowing, he goes on: 'But this does not make our understanding *subjective*. Comprehension is neither an arbitrary act nor a passive experience but a responsible act claiming universal validity. Such knowing is indeed *objective* in the sense of establishing contact with a hidden reality, contact that is defined as the condition for anticipating an indefinite range of as yet unknown (and perhaps yet inconceivable) true implications. It seems reasonable to describe this fusion of the personal and the objective as "Personal Knowledge"' (*Personal Knowledge* pp. vii-viii). To put it briefly, all knowing of any kind involved personal commitment and the acceptance of personal responsibility for one's beliefs.

It follows that Polanyi unmasks the illusion that science is a separate kind of knowledge, sharply distinguished from the vast areas of our everyday knowing which we do not call 'scientific'. His message, as Drusilla Scott charmingly shows in the present book, is addressed to Everyman, with the assurance that we do not need to be intimidated by the claims of some populariser of 'science' to represent a superior kind of knowledge by which all the rest of our knowing is to be tested and judged. There is no way of arriving at the truth except by being willing to take the risk of being mistaken. We must recover the confidence to affirm what can be doubted as a step on the way to contact with reality.

I warmly commend this fine book. It will help the reader to enter into the thought of a profoundly original and important thinker.

DECEMBER, 1994   LESSLIE NEWBIGIN

FOREWORD

I HAVE read this book with increasing delight. It is a very faithful, clear and elegant discussion of Michael Polanyi's thoughts. It has been done in a way and in a style that makes for very easy reading and understanding, even by those who have not been familiar with the deep changes going on in science. This is a fine piece of communication to the wider public and will be widely received.

THE REVEREND PROFESSOR T. F. TORRANCE

PREFACE

WHY don't they read Polanyi? I find myself asking when I read arguments on a range of subjects which fairly frequently come under discussion – such subjects as creation versus evolution, free will or determinism, faith and reason, the validity of the truth of art and poetry, 'artificial intelligence', science and religion. No one else talks such convincing wisdom on these and many other subjects as Polanyi.

Michael Polanyi lived from 1891 to 1976, and is perhaps still too close to us to be seen in his full stature. To a growing number he is one of the very great minds of our time, yet he has been strangely ignored by much of the academic world and is largely unknown to the public.

'Michael walks alone' a fellow student warned his mother when he was a boy of sixteen. 'He will need a strong voice to make himself heard.' Telling this story Michael commented wryly, 'Today at seventy-five my voice has not carried far; I shall die an old man as an infant prodigy'.

Though he loved what he called the 'conviviality' of intellectual co-operation which he had enjoyed as a scientist, when he turned to philosophy he pioneered a lonely path. I suppose the trouble was that he belonged to neither camp. In recognising the bodily, intuitive and traditional roots of our knowledge, the moral and aesthetic elements in all our understanding, he made himself suspect to the philosophic establishment, yet he did not attract the anti-science rebels, for he was not at all tempted by any pseudo-mysticism such as gives up intellect to live by feeling. He was an austere truth-seeker as well as a deeply committed, feeling human being. Perhaps what set him apart was his faith that these two things belong together.

I have subtitled my book The Common Sense of Michael Polanyi, and have said that he wrote for Everyman. 'Common Sense?' some readers of *Personal Knowledge* might exclaim – 'Written for Everyman? But Polanyi is so difficult to read.' In some ways, yes. *Personal Knowledge* is a difficult book in two ways. First the task it attempts is difficult. It is no use marching against the battalions of the scientific outlook with a little tin sword, and Polanyi brings to bear a formidable array of arguments from science, law, politics and other fields as well as from everyday experience. Not many can match the breadth of his knowledge and follow them all. Secondly, it is difficult because Polanyi is advocating such a U-turn in accepted ways of thinking that the experience of reading him can be disorientating. The reader may keep grasping at supposed certainties which are being swept out of sight by the change of direction. "On one level the undertaking of the book seems senseless," wrote one student of *Personal Knowledge*, "but on another perhaps inarticulate level the text keeps intimating a new kind of sense." This two-way pull may be exasperating, as we leave hold of what we are accustomed to and catch at something that seems strange – and yet – is it what we have really believed all along?

Some readers do not feel this second difficulty, but walk joyously into Polanyi's philosophy as into a long-lost home. This is how I felt myself, although the first difficulty remains, for I have to admit there is a very great deal of the scientific evidence that I cannot understand. This may be an advantage of a sort, if I can show that without much science it is possible to get an idea of what Polanyi is after and how it could change our outlook.

One kind of difficulty Polanyi's writing never had: that of the jargon and mystification of a pseudo-science which the reader is not expected to understand too clearly in case he should find the matter too simple, and so not think the writer as learned as he would like to be thought. Polanyi sometimes stated his ideas more simply for the general reader, sometimes in greater depth for the more knowledgeable, but never with more complexity than the matter demands. He always wrote with wit, style and humour, always with faith in Everyman and determination to set him free to use his own wisdom and common sense.

What I have tried to do in this book is to introduce some of his main ideas as simply as possible so as to show their value and meaning in today's world. I think it is time that Everyman's heirs, that is, you and I and all who urgently want some light on the real world, should claim Polanyi as our philosopher.

Too human for the intellectual establishment, too rational for the rebels, he speaks to Everyman's need with the authority of a true tradition of learning and the creativity of the true pioneering rebel. To simplify is to risk misrepresenting, and I can only hope that I have not too seriously misrepresented Polanyi's intentions.

CHAPTER I
THE POWER OF IDEAS

FACES distorted by terror and hate – shots and screams and blood – no, it was not the real thing; we were watching on television the re-enactment of some recent terrorist attack. But it had really happened, and such things do happen, so often that we get accustomed to these sights; they are almost commonplace. Perhaps we stop asking – Why? How can it be that, not just in some back-water of tyranny where there is no other way of redressing wrongs, but in the most modern, democratic and humane societies, young men and women devote themselves to fanatical cold-blooded brutality, with total contempt for human life and society? It is not any ordinary criminal motive that inspires them but an ideal, however twisted.

Terrorism is only one of the symptoms of the strange contra-dictions in our civilisation; a civilisation so clever, so humane, so rational and progressive; yet so stupid, so cruel, so lost and despairing. Anyone who thinks and feels about the world we live in must be to some degree aware of these incompatible aspects.

Psychologists, philosophers, sociologists and historians have claimed this or that as the root of the trouble, and the causes must be complex. To most of us it would seem an unlikely idea that philosophy itself could be a main cause; that the ideas of philosophers about the way we know our world could so disastrously affect the way it is.

But to Michael Polanyi this conclusion became more and more compelling, as he traced what had led to the disasters of Europe in this century. He came to believe that a terribly mistaken under-standing of what science is has distorted our whole outlook and alienated men from their own powers of understanding the world. Polanyi, himself a scientist, found himself driven to question this scientific world view.

Who then was Michael Polanyi and how did he come to this search? Growing up in Hungary in the years around the turn of the century, in a brilliant European civilisation whose outlook seemed tolerant, free and full of hope, he saw this Europe torn apart and destroyed in two world wars, in revolution and terrorism and the totalitarian tyrannies of Bolshevism and Fascism. Recalling, years later, the days when in 1909 he entered the University of Budapest, he told of "an almost forgotten past of peace, of bold intellectual and artistic enterprise, and of continuous progress towards liberal ideals. And then, after a mere six years of this life full of confidence, I see years of destruction and fear, extending substantially up to this day". "I can relive," he said, "how the possibility first dawned upon us that the great hopes intrinsic to our every thought might fail us; that we might actually be witnessing the destruction of Europe. I remember how this hitherto inconceivable thought gradually took possession of our minds, and finally faced us as a fact."[1]

It was his determination to search out the causes of this destruction and descent into violence that sent him exploring in the 'high country of the mind' about which Robert Pirsig wrote in his intellectual adventure story.[2] Polanyi opened up some new trails in that high country and showed that the old maps were dangerously misleading.

He was not by training a philosopher. He qualified first in medicine, but was strongly drawn to science, and became a student of physical chemistry. From an early age he showed an active, confident, original mind, and at twenty-one he wrote a paper about the Third Law of Thermodynamics which his professor sent to Einstein. It came back with Einstein's comment – "I like this paper of your Mr Polanyi very much". "Bang – I was created a scientist," says Polanyi,[3] and when the paper was published he waited for general acclaim – but he was young and unknown and nobody paid any attention. He went on writing original papers on scientific subjects and corresponding with Einstein, meanwhile serving as a medical officer in the war. While ill in hospital in 1916 he finished one of these papers, on the adsorption of gases, and submitted it as a thesis for a PhD at the University of Budapest.[3] "The Professor of Mathematical Physics, to whom my paper was assigned, had never heard of my subject matter. He studied my work bit by bit and then asked me to explain a curious point; my result seemed correct but its derivation faulty. Admitting my mistake, I said that surely one first draws one's conclusions and then puts their derivation right. The professor just stared at me." He got his doctorate – but later in Polanyi's life a number of philosophers may have shared the professor's emotions.

Polanyi moved to Berlin in 1920 to work at the Fibre Chemistry

Institute, and later at the Physical and Electrical Chemistry Institute. These were years of widening scientific interest for him and of research and discovery in a stimulating collaborative group. But here, in the days of Hitler's rise to power, be became increasingly concerned at the way things were going, revealed for instance in the dismissal of Jewish professors. He resigned his post in protest, and in 1933 he accepted the offer of the Chair of Physical Chemistry at Manchester, and left his work and friends for a new start in England.

Since this book will not be concerned with Polanyi's scientific work, it needs only to be said at this point that he was in fact a most distinguished scientist, the list of whose honorary degrees and Fellowships attest his world reputation in physical chemistry. His contributions "were widely spread yet centred principally on three subjects: adsorption of gases on solids, X-ray structure analysis of the properties of solids, and the rate of chemical reactions".[4] What concerns our story is that so much of his work was brilliantly original in theory and inventive in method, and made lasting impacts in his several fields. It is also relevant, since this theme was part of his philosophy of knowledge, that much of it was done in close collaboration with others, where he experienced what he called the 'conviviality' of intellectual work, with its climate of mutual trust and criticism.

In Manchester "he quickly established a world-famous school of physical chemistry, forward-looking and most stimulating for those in it".[5] But here, in thirteen years of teaching and research, he found himself less and less able to live in an ivory tower of scientific study, ever more deeply concerned about the way science relates to the rest of life, how a free society and a true practice of science depend on each other, and the immense evils springing from a false scientific outlook. "I believe," he said, "that the doctrines derived from our erroneous scientific world view have in our days shattered our culture, casting much of the world into mindless servitude, while afflicting the rest with basic confusion."[6]

Dr Polanyi was back to diagnosis again, but the study he needed for this diagnosis was philosophy, not medicine. After his new field of interest emerged clearly with the publication of the lectures *Science, Faith and Society* in 1946, Manchester University was enlightened enough to create a new Chair for him, without obligation to teach, so that he could work out his ideas into the Gifford Lectures (1951-2) which later became his major philosophic work – *Personal Knowledge*. "I believe," he wrote later, "that I came into my true vocation in 1946 when I set out on the pursuit of a new philosophy to meet the needs of our age. My way of starting off with little or no schooling was wholly beneficial here. For a sound knowledge of philosophy makes the necessary radical advances extremely difficult. One must shoot here first and ask questions afterwards, as I have always done."[7] Perhaps it is not surprising that this frontier method has been sooner appreciated in America than in England, where philosophy is more set in its ways. Now, however, it seems as if in many countries awareness is growing of the sureness of Polanyi's aim from the hip.

Shoot first and ask questions afterwards – draw your conclusions and then find the reasoning to support them – these two half-jesting remarks about his own methods tell something important about Polanyi, besides his impish enjoyment of an 'enfant terrible' role. He did not start from formal reasoning leading to conclusions, but from a few conclusions to which his own experience led him inescapably. He was a practising scientist and he knew from the inside what it is like to make scientific discoveries, and how the most original scientists actually work. No abstract reasoning according to accepted logical rules was going to make him believe that scientific knowledge was something quite different from what he knew it to be. But he needed a philosophy that would back up his understanding of science and show its wider implications. Here he had the advantage of being a man of exceptionally wide-ranging interests and knowledge, who could use his acute mind in one area of ideas after another, bringing each to bear tellingly on his argument. He could find the supporting reasons well enough when he set about it. What came first was his sureness, which could be called faith, in the independent reality of truth – scientific, moral, aesthetic or religious. What he said was never a philosopher's juggling with words but was rooted in experience and human concern, and in this faith. Words his friends used of the young Polanyi, 'gentle' and 'reverent', describe him all through his life, and this puts his jesting description of his methods in the right perspective.

He has told the story of an event which crystallised his unease and sent him off to explore the theories of what science is and what knowledge is. He was in Moscow in 1935 and he asked Bukharin, then a leading theorist of the Communist Party, what was the future of pure science in the Soviet Union. Bukharin replied 'that pure science was a morbid symptom of a class society; under socialism the conception of science pursued for its own sake would disappear, for the interests of scientists would spontaneously turn to the problems of the current five year plan'.[8]

So "the comprehensive planning of all research was to be regarded merely as a conscious confirmation of the pre-existing harmony between scientific and social aims".[9] In 1935 this sounded mere dialectical rubbish, but very soon it became only too real in the State control of biologists in the USSR, the persecution and death of Vavilov and State support of Lysenko's theories.

Polanyi was challenged in his whole outlook by this attitude, and astonished that a socialist theory which claimed to be scientific could so misunderstand science, denying the reality of independent scientific thought. The 'scientific' outlook had produced a dogmatism in which there was no room for science as he knew it. It was not that he despised applied science, or research directed to finding solutions to practical problems; far from it, he had taken part in such research himself and fully respected it. But he knew that room must be left also for the original scientist to choose freely his own problems and follow his hunches. A directed programme of research could never foresee where the next breakthrough might come; it could not avoid nipping off the buds of truly creative discovery. "This is why the initiative to scientific inquiry and its pursuit must be left to the free decision of the individual scientist; the scientist must be granted independence because only his personal vision can achieve essential progress in science. Inquiries can be conducted as surveys according to plan, but these will never add up to new ideas."

Of this Polanyi was sure, and he worked in England with Dr John Baker in the 'Freedom in Science' movement to prevent the Soviet style of control of science being introduced there, as Bernal and some others attempted to do. In 1940 in a letter to Baker – "We cannot," he asserted, "defend the freedom of science unless we attack . . . collectivism. If the community acting through the power of the State is to be the sole judge of what is bad for men living in society, then it has to claim also supremacy over what is to be considered true and what untrue. Science cannot be free in a state formed as sovereign master of the community's fate, but only under a state pledged to the guardianship of law, custom and of our social heritage in general, to the further advancement of which – on the lines of the universal ideas underlying it – the community is dedicated. I have recently read Rauschning's book *Hitler Speaks* and was impressed by the fact that Hitler and Himmler use exactly the same terms about the necessity of subordinating science to collective aims as the Bolsheviks . . . Democracy is the form of public life by which a community, dedicated to certain universal ideas, cultivates these ideas and develops its institutions under their guidance. The adventure of scientific research, undertaken regardless of the possibilities to which it may lead, is only *one* of the ideas to the service of which our community is pledged; and it cannot retain its claim on society by defending its title in isolation from the other ideas similarly endangered by the absolutist state."[11]

Yet Polanyi found he could not answer the Marxist view of science with a solidly based view of his own, either from the scientists' own accounts of what they were doing or from what the philosophers said the scientists must be doing. He had only his own sure belief that creative discovery in science is rooted in freedom, and freedom itself rooted in faith in certain fundamental values. He had to find a reasoned justification of this belief to show its validity in face of the Marxist denial. The search was urgent because the reasoning underlying Bukharin's denial of the independence of thought seemed to underly also the violence, oppression and inhumanity that he saw destroying Europe. Only a metaphysical base for his faith would do.

Violence and oppression are not new; they have always been part of the human story. But what seemed new to Polanyi was the combination of a ruthless *contempt* for moral values such as truth, compassion and justice with an unbounded *moral passion* for utopian perfection. These two seemingly incompatible extremes appeared in conjunction both in nihilist or terrorist individuals and in political systems such as Soviet communism. It was as if the whole rational way of thinking, which produced modern science and brought such incalculable benefits to the Western world, had at some point gone off course, while the high ideals deriving from the Christian ethic, released from their religious channel and turned to secular improvement, had likewise suffered a pathological change. Could these two great streams of reason and of moral ideals, that had flowed from Socrates and from Christ, and had nourished European civilisation for so long, have produced, by some strange modern fusion, a new and deadly poison?

Polanyi gave up science and turned to philosophy to find the answer. "It seemed to me then," he said, "that our whole civilisation was pervaded by the dissonance of an extreme critical lucidity and an intense moral conscience, and that this combination had generated both our tight-lipped modern revolutions and the tormented self-doubt of modern man outside revolutionary movements. So I resolved to look into the roots of this condition."[12] He embarked on a long search for understanding of 'how we know', and in his book *Personal Knowledge* he worked to free our minds from distorting assumptions about the impersonality and certainty of scientific knowledge, and the belief that anything outside this framework is unreal. These assumptions devalue man's moral values, spiritual powers, affections, responsibilities and judgments. Yet, as we see in modern terrorism and fanaticism, the power of moral ideals remains, but it is power let loose from moral control, denatured and deadly.

Polanyi felt that Britain, his adopted country, had happily escaped the worst effects of this disastrous dissonance, partly because of our national habit of not taking theories too seriously. Typically, we produced in the eighteenth century the most devastatingly sceptical critic of man's powers of knowing, who admitted that he could only live his own life by not paying too much attention to his own theories.

"Carelessness and inattention alone can afford us any remedy," said David Hume, and by carelessness and inattention plus some kindliness and commonsense – and religious movements like Wesley's which kept religion in touch with common people and common needs – by all these means we have avoided the full logical consequences of the way our philosophers have taught men to think about knowledge. But when we exported their teaching to countries where there is less inattention, more logic and perhaps less traditional kindliness, the full logical consequences arrived and blasted with destructive ideologies the lives of thousands.

Nor can we assume that, in times of stress, carelessness and inattention would always save us. "Today," Polanyi wrote, "our moral judgments are quite generally without theoretical protection. . . . It is dangerous to rely on it that men will continue indefinitely to pursue their moral ideals within a system of thought which denies reality to them." There are more ominous signs, since Polanyi wrote, that the full logical consequences of the ideas of our philosophers, assembled abroad, are being re-exported to this their country of origin.

It is becoming more and more apparent that the 'scientific' world view applied to the whole of life is devastatingly inadequate. Many people have said this and many thinkers have tried to wrestle their way out, but it is not so easy. Some hold on to this world view from fear, reminding us of that well-known moral for children –

And never leave ahold of Nurse
For fear of finding something worse.

Nurse 'Science' is pretty difficult but she's safe, not like those will-o'-the-wisps Intuition and Emotion who will lead you into the swamps. You had better learn to get along with Nurse, many people say, even if she takes away all the things you love.

Bertrand Russell expressed this fear, and this desperate belief in science, in his book *The Scientific Outlook*. All through the book he extols scepticism and the scientific method in his usual dry, sarcastic, nose-in-the-air style. He welcomes particularly the findings of Pavlov on the mechanisms of stimulus and response in animals; hopes and believes that by such methods we shall soon know all the physical causes of human thought and action, and give up our foolish belief in free will. But in the last chapter he makes a moving lament for all he cares about, for beauty, tenderness, happiness, hope; for all that scepticism destroys. But he saw no way out, for as he said – "While science as the pursuit of power becomes increasingly triumphant, science as the pursuit of truth is being killed by a scepticism which the skill of the men of science has generated. That this is a misfortune is undeniable, but I cannot admit that the substitution of superstition for scepticism . . . would be an improvement. Scepticism may be painful, and may be barren, but at least it is honest, and an outcome of the quest for truth . . . no real escape is possible by returning to the discarded beliefs of a stupider age".[14]

That's an icy, stoic courage which is in some sense admirable – but terrible. It leaves men's values and beliefs subjective, unsupported. But it puts the issue fairly before us. Is this dilemma real – honest scepticism or dishonest comfort? Can anyone answer Russell's stoic despair with an honest hope? Can we in the end evade the destruction by reason of all we care about, all that makes us human, without giving up our faith in reason?

Polanyi came to this task with the great advantage of being a highly respected scientist. It is a good position from which to attack the scientific world view; you cannot be accused of woolly romanticism. He was able to show with authority that it is a false idea of science to which we cling, that science cannot be accounted for by the 'scientific' view of knowledge, that the idea of completely certain, impersonal, testable knowledge is a will-o'-the-wisp itself. He can say this without scepticism, however, because he believes in man's powers of understanding the world he lives in, and can show how knowledge, though not guaranteed by any cast-iron test, can be valid. His is no cosy retreat from reason into old beliefs, nor a stoic acceptance of scepticism, it is a gospel of responsible hope.

Some people may still object that Polanyi's whole diagnosis is too intellectual. There are plenty of other causes than philosophy for the disasters of Europe. Not all that many people read philosophy any way – how can it matter so much? But look at Karl Marx for example. "Less than a hundred years ago, there he was, an intellectual in his fifties, living in Hampstead with his wife and family, devoting his days to reading and writing, little known to even the educated public. And in under seventy years of his death a third of all the human race . . . had adopted forms of society which called themselves by his name."[15]

It is not necessary that so many people should read the philosophers for their ideas to prevail. Deadly viruses produced in the 'high country of the mind' can get into the streams, run down and be picked up by the plants below; the sociologists and psychologists, the imaginative writers, novelists and poets, who grow them into edible form on which thousands unwittingly feed.

The philosopher Whitehead wrote, "The nearest analogy is to be seen in the history of some species of animal, or plant, or microbe, which lurks for ages as an obscure by-product of Nature in some lonely jungle, or morass or island. Then by some trick of circumstance it escapes into the outer world and transforms a civilisation, or destroys an empire or the forests of a continent. Such is the potential power of the ideas which live in the various systems of philosophy".

If you are unconvinced of the power of ideas, watch for the scientistic assumptions lurking in what we read or hear every day. Among the statements that reveal such assumptions, these are examples that have recently appeared in the newspapers – that the decline of religion is due to the fact that there is no room for God in the universe revealed by modern science – that the connection of sanity with responsibility is meaningless, because sane and insane thought are both equally the product of causality, therefore a sane man is no more responsible than an insane man for his actions. That it is a waste of time to discuss some moral scruples, since all moral and political beliefs can be conditioned in precisely the same way as salivation was conditioned in Pavlov's dogs.

Popular books on evolution tell us we are the accidental result of the chance interactions of atoms, which have somehow produced us as vehicles for the survival of genes. Popular books on artificial intelligence tell us that computers will soon outstrip man, taking all the necessary decisions faster and better than we can. The odd thing is that books of this sort are not written as terrible prophecies of doom, they are cheery best-sellers. It seems we enjoy being told we are robots blindly programmed for survival, or that we are inferior to robots and will soon have to hand over to them.

There are examples everywhere of the use of 'science' to undermine confidence in any other way of knowing. "More research is needed" – "Statistics tell us" – "Laboratory tests have conclusively proved" – this kind of phrase is common and builds up the assumption that if you don't know in a scientific way, you don't know. Any judgment of value, any intuitive wisdom, is banished to the realm of fantasy or whim, while any statistical or scientific type statement gets an automatic endorsement. Studies that are not scientific start to cringe, and try to ape science, however inappropriate. The effects are felt disastrously in education, where for instance the study of human nature is more likely to mean sociology and psychology than literature and history; where the psychologist is likely to feel more authentic and confident the more he works in laboratories, the less he deals with actual people. Subjects are distorted, values destroyed, by this pseudo-scientific masquerade, yet how hard it is to stand against it, since the underlying false assumption is that science is truth, all else is self deception.

The devaluing of personal judgment is a self-fulfilling principle, since any faculty that is unused tends to decay. Many people have in any case less opportunity for using their personal judgment than men had in the past, and when they are consistently told it is unreliable and irrelevant, they use it even less, and it becomes unreliable and irrelevant. We wait for 'science' to pronounce.

Polanyi expressed it like this – "Backed by a science which sternly professes that ultimately all things in the world – including all the achievements of man from the Homeric poems to the *Critique of Pure Reason* – will somehow be explained in terms of physics and chemistry, these theories assume that the path to reality lies invariably in representing higher things in terms of their baser particulars. This is indeed almost universally regarded today as the supremely critical method, which resists the flattering illusions cherished by men about their nobler faculties".[17]

Such assumptions, about what is real and what is not, must and do affect men's behaviour. Lately an Archbishop of York made a comment to this effect about vandalism. "We look," he said, "for reasons why young people, not necessarily poor or deprived, should smash and destroy their expensive surroundings." He quoted from Bertrand Russell a phrase about the accidental, purposeless nature of the universe, and suggested the violence and destruction might be a shout of anger at the meaninglessness of life. "Only a very old philosopher or a very young vandal could live in such a world," he said.

A shout of anger – or perhaps the very young vandal is merely being what the very old philosopher tells him we all are. Compare these two quotations:

(a) Bertrand Russell wrote – "The problem which Pavlov successfully tackled is that of subjecting to scientific law what has hitherto been called voluntary behaviour . . . The more this achievement is studied the more important it is seen to be, and it is on this account that Pavlov must be placed among the most eminent men of our time".[18]

(b) *"Heavily Armed Children Prowling Los Angeles"* says a recent headline. The juvenile court judge said about these children, brought before him for shooting into crowds of people they did not know, and setting fire to an old woman, "They show no sense of empathy for their victims. It's almost like they are programmed robots out on the prowl to kill".

Isn't that what 'the most eminent men of our time' say we are?

It has become clear that if we are to escape from these numbing and dehumanising assumptions, our thinking about how we know has to be shaken out of the rigid and outdated 'scientific' habits which modern science itself finds inadequate. What we find real depends on how we know, and is a matter of life or death.

"It may appear extravagant," Polanyi wrote, "to hope that these self-destructive forces may be harmonised by reconsidering the way we know things. If I still believe that a reconsideration of knowledge may be effective today, it is because for some time past a revulsion has been noticeable against the ideas which brought us to our present state. Both inside and outside the Soviet empire, men are getting weary of ideas sprung from a combination of scepticism and perfectionism. It may be worth trying to go back to our foundations and seek to lay them anew, more truly."[19]

Other countries have their destructive thinkers to deal with; we produced Hume and Russell and their contemporary followers, and we have to deal with their intellectual vandalism. It is ironic that Russell is so widely revered as a philosopher and a worker for peace. He has the prestige of his superb intellect and his fierce passion for peace, yet he may in fact have done more to keep us from real peace than can at present be realised, simply by being obstinately wrong about how we know.

I was once reading to a small girl Edward Lear's nonsense limericks. I read –

"There was an old man of Hongkong
Who never did anything wrong.
He lay on his back
With his head in a sack . . ."

"But that *was* wrong, wasn't it?" the child interrupted sententiously. Yes, it was, I now mentally reply, thinking of Russell so determined to do nothing wrong in his logic that he shut himself up in a sceptical sack and told us everything outside it was illusion. This lie affects us all.

Notes to Chapter I

1. Address to FPG meeting 1968
2. *Zen and the Art of Motor Cycle Maintenance* Bodley Head 1974
3. Contribution to *Mid-Century Authors* 1966
4. E. P. Wigner in *Biographical Memoirs of Fellows of the Royal Society* vol 23, December 1977, p.417
5. Memoir by Norman Burkhardt (in *Memoirs and Proceedings of the Manchester Literary and Philosophic Society* 1975–6, 118)
6. Nuffield Lecture to the Royal Society of Medicine, 'Science and Man' *Proceedings of the Royal Society of Medicine* vol 58, September 1970, p.969–76
7. Contribution to *Mid-Century Authors* 1966
8. *The Tacit Dimension* p.3
9. *Science, Faith and Society* p.8
10. *Knowing and Being* p.82
11. Quoted in the Royal Society Biographical Memoir of Polanyi (*Biographical Memoirs of Fellows of the Royal Society* vol 23, December 1977)
12. *The Tacit Dimension* p.4
13. *Personal Knowledge* p.234
14. Russell – *The Scientific Outlook* p.104
15. B. Magee, *Popper*, Fontana Modern Masters, Collins, 1973, p.94
16. *Adventures of Ideas* (Cambridge 1933), p.186–7
17. *The Study of Man* p.64
18. *The Scientific Outlook* p.56
19. *The Tacit Dimension* p.60

CHAPTER II

EVERYMAN AND KNOWLEDGE

*Good deeds and Knowledge helped Everyman
in his trouble. Was it dishonest comfort they
gave?*

*Knowledge busy in her laboratory is no
longer Everyman's friend. Is honest despair
all she can give?*

SOON after I saw that terrorist incident on television, I watched another re-enactment. This one was a performance of the mediaeval 'mystery play', *Everyman*. The story of Everyman crept into my thoughts about Michael Polanyi, who surely wrote for and about the Everyman of today, as he searched out the reasons for terrorism and violence. The connections became clearer as I reflected on the play, and I thought of using the story as a guideline through Polanyi's thought.

Everyman, in the play, is an ordinary sort of fellow who enjoys good company and the pleasures of life. When he is suddenly summoned by Death to present his life's account to God, he turns desperately to his friends for help. His 'friends' in the play are personifications of his qualities and possessions. He goes first to Fellowship, then to his Kindred, then to his Goods, but they all excuse themselves and leave him when they hear where he has to go. His Discretion, Strength and Beauty seem at first willing to help, but they too abandon him as Death draws near, and even his Five Wits depart. Only Good Deeds and her sister Knowledge go with him to the end. It is Knowledge who says to him –

Everyman, I will go with thee and be thy guide
In thy most need to go by thy side.

Centuries have passed, the whole frame of thought has changed, since the play of *Everyman* was acted in the streets of our towns. There is not much talk now about the Day of Judgement or the Wrath of God. Yet the old play still has a powerful and curiously modern impact as an evocation of the human spirit facing mortality. The sense of agony and despair does not go out of date. The urgent need of a man suddenly cut off by a great calamity, or under intolerable stress, to know something sure about the meaning of his existence – this comes through to us. The explicit answers given to Everyman in the play may belong to the outdated certainties of its religious framework, but what gives the play its enduring power is the emotional force and truth with which the questioning is conveyed. The play is about values, and its strength is not that of a formal moral tale but that of an agonised search for values that can stand and endure in the face of suffering and death.

The questioning remains true, but the answers are suspect; the more I thought about it the more I suspected them. It was the priests who dictated these answers. The Church recognised Everyman's pain and despair, and offered him comfort. But was it honest comfort, or did the Church play on his anguish and fear to persuade him to walk in her narrow way?

For the explicit moral of the play was that Everyman's 'friends', his qualities and endowments, were nothing but hindrances to a holy life. The answer he got was narrowly moralistic. Good Deeds was what the priests thought he ought to do; Knowledge was what the priests told him to believe, and all the rest of his 'friends' were rubbishy rascals who would let him down. In the end, all the counsel he got from Knowledge was to go to the priests and do penance for his sins.

Yet what kind of Knowledge, what kind of Good Deeds, could there be without those discarded 'friends', without Beauty, Strength, Five Wits, Fellowship and Discretion?

The questions of the play still assault the Everyman of today. But if, in the old play, Knowledge was the mouthpiece of the priests, Knowledge today is often the mouthpiece of a no less narrow and authoritarian 'scientific world view'. The priests did at least recognise Everyman's pain and fear, but exploited these in order to control his thoughts and actions. Modern 'scientism' does not even recognise Everyman as a person. Like the priests, scientism discredits many of his qualities and skills as hindrances to knowledge, and thus reduces his full reality.

Polanyi often spoke of the parallel between the old authoritarian control of thought by the churches and the present domination of scientism. Scientism, he declared, 'fetters thought as cruelly as ever the churches had done,' and he thought of his own work as being aimed, 'to re-equip men with the faculties which centuries of critical thought have taught them to distrust'. In other words, to bring back into the pursuit of Knowledge those old 'friends' without whom Everyman cannot be fully real and human – the sense of Beauty, Discretion (which we might call judgment or Mind), Strength, Fellowship and all the rest. We shall see how some of them are reinstated as necessary to Knowledge, in Polanyi's thought.

Everyman has exchanged one tyranny for another (the tyranny of faith for the tyranny of scepticism) although this was not how it seemed at the dawn of the scientific era, when the scientific revolution and the freeing of Knowledge from the dead weight of Authority brought not only immense material benefits but great liberation of the human spirit. Yet it brought also in the end a new alienation, the rift between Knowledge and Everyman.

In pre-scientific days there was no such rift. From early times men had learnt how to do what was needed; to sow and reap; to build a boat, to rear a child; learnt by tradition and slow change. Everyman and his knowledge belonged within their world, as in some primitive societies they still do. Knowledge grew gradually from within such traditional skills, pushing ahead here, lagging there, found and lost again, rising to peaks of achievement and sinking back into ignorance, but never so far as we know reaching such sharp discord with Everyman the knower. That belongs to our modern age.

A great deal of Everyman's knowledge was of living things and the processes of life. He recognised a thousand forms of plants and animals useful or dangerous to him. He knew about health and sickness, birth and death, growth and maturity, loving and hating, intelligence and stupidity. All these things were familiar to him before they could be clearly expressed, much less scientifically classified. When such knowledge began to be the sciences of botany, biology and so on, these sciences were only clarifying and enlarging the tacit understanding of living things which Everyman already had; they described a world that he knew, and his knowledge of it gave the sciences their subject matter, as indeed it still does.

But it did not go this way with the sciences of inanimate nature. Before the development of modern physics man had relatively little acquaintance with the non-living world. Stone and metal he knew as materials that could be fashioned into tools, but had little intrinsic interest. "Few inanimate objects were known that puzzled men by their distinctive shapes or behaviours. Nothing suggested the hidden beauty of the gas laws, of thermodynamics, optics and acoustics; of the potential presence of atomic spectra; of a thousand elementary particles and a million organic compounds; of Newtonian mechanics, of quantum theory and relativity."[1] Before science revealed these beauties, the most intriguing features of the inanimate world were the stars, the sun and moon with their curious motions; and these did draw men's interest, but here a monumental mistake distorted knowledge for thousands of years.

There is an ancient Egyptian papyrus which shows Nut, the sky goddess, arching herself over mankind. Her toes touch the earth at one side and her fingers at the other, and her body, studded with stars, makes the roof that keeps us all safely sheltered. For many many centuries this sort of picture must have given an essentially cosy feel to the universe, where Everyman had the steady earth under his feet, and overhead the arch of Nut's kindly body. Later on it was the arch of the crystalline spheres that carried the stars and the

sun and planets round the central earth. Some of the early Greek
thinkers did wonder and speculate about this framework, but after
Aristotle had tidied it all up and the questioning had fallen silent,
this was the picture of the universe that Knowledge upheld, and this
was the way Everyman saw it. If anyone asked 'How do we know?'
the answer would be 'Aristotle says so', or 'the Church says so' – for
Christian theology had twined itself firmly round this seemingly
unshakeable structure and confidently located its Heaven and Hell
within this framework.

But it was wrong, basically wrong about the central earth and the
circular motion of all about it. And so the Copernican revolution
which showed Everyman that instead of standing steady at the centre
of the universe he was being whirled through empty space on a
spinning ball, swooping round the sun with the other planets, was
extraordinarily upsetting.[2] So much emotional capital had been
invested in the old picture. Of course, Everyman's newly revealed
situation was not really changed, but it felt so; a bit like the Polish
peasant near the Russian border when the authorities proposed to
move the border to the Polish side of his house and he protested that
he would not be able to stand the Russian winters.

Religion and Authority shut their eyes to the new understanding,
punished Galileo for saying the earth moves, and refused to listen; so
the credibility of Religion and Authority was undermined. But also,
Everyman's confidence in his power to understand the world in
terms of his ordinary perceptions was shattered. What he had seen,
through the centuries, was an optical illusion! While scientific
knowledge of the *living* world grew from Everyman's pre-scientific
knowledge, in physics and astronomy the new science made its
impressive progress by turning *away* from traditional knowledge and
denying it. It was as though Knowledge said to Everyman – 'You're
no good, you've got it all wrong. Your Five Wits have deceived you'.
Everyman faltered. "He agreed henceforth to accept unconditionally
the scientific view of things, however absurd some of it might appear
to him,"[3] says Polanyi, tracing to this catastrophic change some of
our excessive veneration for science. "Cowed by the experience of
the Copernican revolution, we dare not trust the testimony of our
senses to contradict the teaching of science."[4]

As the new science developed, it said many things that seemed
absurd, yet it had to be believed; it was so powerful and successful
that it must be right. Its way of knowing must be the true way. But
what *was* it? What was the secret of science? What made this new

Knowledge, which leant on no authority nor even on the evidence of the senses, so sure, so confident and powerful?

Philosophers puzzled over this. Some like Descartes set out to get rid of all vagueness and uncertainty in our knowledge, for if this strange implausible new knowledge did not rest on authority it had to be sure in itself; it had to be clear and distinct and inevitably convincing like geometry. It had to proceed by a reliable impersonal method. This involved emphasising the difference of Mind from Matter; here was the enquiring Mind, and there was the lifeless universe of Matter, surveyed and grasped by Mind's perception of clear, necessary truth.

You can see why this separation of Mind and Matter seemed so necessary. Too easily Everyman had seen the whole universe in human terms, personifying the sun and planets, explaining the movements of inanimate objects by attributing human desires to them, or piously accepting that things are the way they are because God thought that the best way for them to be. The new science got on so well because it did not have that outlook but set out to discover how things actually work, looking at them as purely material objects obeying physical laws. To do this, Everyman had to learn to keep himself out of the picture, to be simply an observing Mind. And Matter had to be simply Matter, not mixed up with Mind or desires or any ideas transferred from animal life; once let these in as explanations and you stop seeing what is actually happening and what is physically causing it.

With Sir Isaac Newton's great discoveries the prestige of science and its methods became overwhelming. It seemed to Everyman that Knowledge was now revealed in her true form, and that up to that time she had been only a fumbling infant. She was going to give him power over the whole world. Reading the history of philosophy you see philosophers trying to come to terms with the new Knowledge, and you see how various assumptions embedded in their understanding of it led to an impasse.

"During the fifty years or so following Newton's publication of his *Mathematical Principles of Natural Philosophy* a rather extraordinary state of affairs developed. Man became sure, on the one hand, that science had at last been put upon a secure basis and that we would soon be rolling in a knowledge of Nature such as we had never dared to dream of before – and on the other hand that knowledge (except of our own ideas) was impossible." [5]

Various features of the new way of knowing were picked out to explain its success. Its impersonal, laboratory, weigh-and-measure methods which could be tested and checked; the necessity for the mind to be passive, simply receiving impressions like a photographic plate; the need for all ideas to be clear and distinct like geometry so that reasoning could be as sure as experiment; the idea that to analyse anything into its least elements is the way to understand it – all these were partly true features of the new knowledge, seized on and distorted as the whole explanation of its success. From these grew the rigid view of scientific knowledge which gradually became a tyranny as great as ever the tyranny of Aristotle or the Church had been. The theory of Laplace, often quoted by Polanyi as the epitome of this view, was that an intelligence which knew at one moment of time the position of all atoms, and the forces operating on them, would know everything in the universe, past, present and future. Such a picture of the universe as a vast assembly of atoms moved relentlessly on its path by impersonal inevitable forces, seized the imagination of man and dominated it. This was what the Universe was really like, it seemed, and what Knowledge could really know. So when this Knowledge turned her cold analytic eye on to Everyman, and saw that he too was part of the world of matter, made of atoms, obeying the same laws as the planets; she could not recognise her sister Good Deeds nor her friend Everyman. Life, thought, moral values – they could not be known in these ways, so they were not real.

"This," says Polanyi, "is how a philosophic movement guided by aspirations of scientific severity has come to threaten the position of science itself. This self-contradiction stems from a misguided intellectual passion – a passion for achieving absolutely impersonal knowledge, which, being unable to recognise any persons, presents us with a picture of the universe in which we ourselves are absent. In such a universe there is no-one capable of creating and upholding scientific values; hence there is no science."[6]

David Hume, our bland 18th century sceptic, exposed this impasse of thought in which Mind and Matter both disintegrated and Knowledge lost all respectability. It did not bother the scientists, who were intent on their exciting discoveries and went on discovering, but it made things most uncomfortable for Everyman. Immanual Kant's heroic work began to show a way forward, in which mind could be creative *and* objective, in which science *and* moral values could be real. But even he did not free us from Hume's scepticism, it returns and haunts our world, producing strange distorted theories of knowledge.

Strange indeed they are, the theories of knowing that the thinkers worked out in their quest for certainty. Here for example is the full rigour of the "scientific" position stated by Karl Pearson.[7]

"The scientific method is the sole path by which we can attain to knowledge. The very word 'knowledge' indeed only applies to the products of the scientific method in the field. Other methods . . . may lead to fantasy as that of the poet or metaphysician, to belief or superstition, but never to knowledge. As to the scientific method, we saw that it consists in the careful and often laborious classification of facts, the comparison of their relationships and sequences, and finally in the discovery by aid of the disciplined imagination of a brief statement or formula, which in a few words resumes a wide range of facts. Such a formula is called a scientific law."

A formidable statement, which seems to imply that no one knew anything before the scientists got going. But at least, one might think, by following this strict method men can get to understand how the physical universe works. Not a bit of it; Pearson had discovered that the scientists were finding that they couldn't be as certain about the physical universe as they first thought. So he has gone back to Hume. The one thing we can be certain about is our own sense-impressions.

So[8] – "The law of gravitation," Pearson goes on, "is not so much the discovery by Newton of a rule guiding the motion of the planets, as his invention of a method of briefly describing the sequence of sense-impressions which we term planetary motion". Sense-impressions! This means that after all that careful laborious work we can never get beyond our own eyes and ears and the feelings we have in them. All we can do is to make rules about what sort of feelings usually come together or follow each other, and call these "the law of gravitation" or "planetary motion". "It is idle," Pearson admonishes sternly, "to postulate shadowy unknowables behind that real world of sense impressions in which we live." He compares the scientist to a man living in a telephone exchange, reading the messages coming in, but having no way of knowing that there is a real world of subscribers living outside.

It seems absurd to Everyman, this way of talking, and it is absurd. However did philosophers come to paint themselves into a corner like this, shutting themselves into a theory of knowledge supposed to explain how science is possible, but actually making science and even life crazy and impossible?

You may think such an idea out of date, but it is still around in many forms. Here is an example, unimportant in itself, but showing how these strange assumptions hang on. A fairly recent book[9] purports to explain in simple terms what we now know of the workings of the physical universe. This it does in a moderately interesting way. But it is prefaced with the recital of Hume's sceptical creed. To make our world view, the author explains, we mentally chop up our experience into bits called percepts. You have to imagine a baby doing this. Then, "Somehow the child comes to notice that certain sets of percepts are approximately constant . . . Each such set is mentally conjoined to form a single concept. After a time the different percepts that have been mentally conjoined to form a single concept come to be considered as being the different perceptual aspects of a much realler *thing*". But we grown-ups have got to remember that baby is wrong. "For us, any conceptualised *thing* is simply a mental shorthand symbol standing for the total set of all the possible perceptual experiences we have conjoined into the concept. Nothing is logically or pragmatically gained by adding to our postulates that of a primary world of real *things*."

Yet the rest of the book is not much affected by this preliminary incantation. The author goes on to describe the workings of the universe just as if they were really going on around us. Galileo and Newton and Einstein certainly thought they were talking about a real world, and an intelligent baby knows a real mother from a set of percepts. Any theory which explains that away is no explanation but a mystification. How could babies or scientists get excited over working out which percepts usually come after which? Babies and scientists make their discoveries through faith in the real though mysterious world they find themselves in, assuming that being real it will make sense if they keep on working at it. Scientists have given up their claim to certainty, and hold to their faith in a real world, which they can progressively understand, though not completely or certainly.

But the craving for *certainty* even if it means discarding the real world, still has a sinister power over us. The preposterous Karl Pearson model, which has to be maintained to get certainty, reminds me of the Solar Topi, that hideous sun helmet which was worn by all white men in tropical climates for years and years, and was supposed to be quite indispensable. Albert Schweitzer wrote about the men he had seen struck down by fatal fevers because they took off their topis for ten minutes, even towards sundown – the rays of the setting tropical sun, he said, are the most dangerous of all. Then in the last war some soldiers stopped wearing the cumbersome thing with no ill effects at all, and everyone discovered it was quite unnecessary. It continued to be worn however by some very minor local officials who thought it gave them the prestige of the colonial administrators who used to wear it. Similarly Science doesn't bother to wear its sceptical hat but new disciplines aspiring to the prestige of science, non-scientists trying to ape or explain science, still cumber themselves with its rigours.

The Solar Topi, though hideous and uncomfortable, did no actual harm, but the Karl Pearson model does, for it makes it impossible to judge whether one system of ideas is more true than another. This does little harm to scientists since on the whole they disregard it, but some intellectuals still maintain this debilitating dogma about politics or social subjects, undermining judgment by asserting that it is not allowable, by their strict criteria, to say that one theory is right and another wrong. For how can this be known, if there is no reality beyond sense impressions?

These strange ideas were part of the attempt to think out how Mind in the shape of Everyman could know about Matter. Since the universe was to be looked at as a lifeless world of Matter out of which all values had been taken, and Everyman was part of it, how could there be value in him? Everyman has been progressively dismembered and explained, as the sciences of the lifeless world took him to pieces. But then, how about the sciences of life which we saw building on the tacit knowledge of life which Everyman already had? Could not these sciences save him? No, by and large, they surrendered. The sciences of non-life were so successful and prestigious that the sciences of life tried more and more to use the same methods: physiologists and biologists hoped their work would be eventually reduced to physics and chemistry, psychologists felt more secure and impressive the more their work was in laboratories and approximating to physics and chemistry, the less it dealt with people as people.[10]

The idea of evolution sounds like a re-birth of the sciences of life, but it was in fact another great triumph of the sciences of non-life. Darwinism was hailed as the first great breakthrough in applying the principles of the physical sciences to man. At last, here was a theory which could explain Man as Newton had explained the heavens, showing the whole process of evolution to be caused by chance variations and natural selection. No more need for purpose, God, or mysterious life forces. It was all as purposeless and inevitable as gravity; it all fitted in with Newton's universe.

Freud's discoveries about the subconscious seemed to fit in too, showing that man was moved by forces he could neither understand nor control; that his ideals, hopes and fears were unreal. "This alone I know with certainty," Freud wrote, "namely that men's value judgements are guided absolutely by their desire for happiness, and are therefore merely an attempt to bolster up their illusions by argument."[11]

Marxism too claimed the prestige of science for the explaining of men's aspirations and ideals in terms of economic determinism and historical necessity, and Marx praised Darwin for doing the same sort of thing in his theory of evolution. Pavlov claimed to show that the mechanical process of conditioning reflexes can account for men's thoughts and beliefs. In so many areas the success of science in its dealings with the non-living has provided a distorting model for knowledge of life and mind.

Not that the sciences of life don't need some of the rigour and astringency of the sciences of non-life; they clearly do. But to apply this rigour with such blind idolatry that they destroy their own subject matter is a misuse of rigour.

Wordsworth wrote –

Sweet is the lore which Nature brings;
Our meddling intellect
Misshapes the beauteous forms of things:–
We murder to dissect.[12]

But we had to dissect; we can't go back on that. Only we need not come to think that the living body is nothing more than the bits of the dead dissected corpse; that a chemical analysis of the paint leaves nothing unsaid about the Mona Lisa; that Everyman who is indeed made of atoms in motion is therefore nothing but atoms in motion.[13]

The plight in which Everyman finds himself when his old friend Knowledge denies his humanity, and will only deal in physics and chemistry, has been described in many ways. It is the Absurd of which Camus wrote, it is the nausea of Sartre's hero, it is meaninglessness. The Italian writer Ignazio Silone indicated it when he wrote that "Any portrait of modern man . . . cannot but be deformed, split, fragmented; in a word, tragic," – and when he says about the suicides among writers of his generation that whatever external causes were postulated – "The last writings of these men are invariably a confession of anguish and despair at the effort and the futility of living".[14]

This is Everyman's anguish and despair and, remembering what the philosophers did to his friend Knowledge, we can see where his loss of meaning, of relation to reality comes from. Pushed out of his world by the thinkers trying to clear the way for science, then taken to pieces as part of the physical world, whether he was disembodied Mind or mindless Matter he was no longer himself in natural relation with his world, and all the strange theories about how we know are attempts to get round this dislocation.

The anguish and despair of Everyman is one effect that comes when Knowledge, dressed up as Science, denies or disintegrates his humanity. Other results can be seen. If Everyman takes this murderous dissection seriously he may commit suicide as the only honesty, or turn to nihilistic violence, destruction or terrorism. As Silone says – "Nihilism is the identification of goodness, justice and truth with self-interest. Nihilism is the conviction that beliefs and ideas are ultimately a mere facade with nothing real behind them, and that consequently only one thing counts, success. Nihilism exalts courage and heroism independently of the cause they serve, equating the martyr with the hired assassin".

Everyman may turn to the irrational, to astrology or oriental mysticism or witchcraft, shutting his eyes to the assault of science, choosing instead something that does not claim to be rational, but can give him back at least some of the sense of human value, the sense of being someone, that rationality seems to destroy.[16]

"Great God! I'd rather be
A pagan suckled in a creed outworn –"[17]

cried Wordsworth, and this rebellion against inhuman rationality drives many people into curious pagan refuges.

Another refuge for Everyman is an ideology such as Marxism, which is very ready to help, and seems to have it both ways. It claims the prestige of science, but unlike the physical sciences it claims to answer Everyman's big questions, to show him the meaning of life, and to endorse his passion for ideals. And it binds him once more into a close community of believers. The appeal is tremendous, but the price is high.

The other thing that may happen is that Everyman, particularly if he is British, may not take all this disintegration so seriously, but may indeed enjoy it like a horror film. He does not feel it too deeply;

'custom and inattention' carry him along comfortably enough, and he can indulge in the frisson of seeing himself as a meaningless speck in a vast uncaring universe, or as an automaton, the accidental product of a totally unmeaning evolution, or of economic laws. He doesn't wholly believe it, and in normal times the comforting framework of ordinary life holds him up, but he finds it exciting and relaxing. It lifts the weight of responsibility off him. This state of mind has been described as "cosy despair"[18] and is very profitably ministered to by semi-scientific writers who tell Everyman in the name of Science that his humanity and civilisation are but a thin veneer; that basically he is nothing but a savage or a naked ape or an accidental collocation of atoms.

There is a powerful attraction in this sort of scientific de-humanising, for if that is all we are, of course we can't be expected to be responsible human beings. And human responsibility lies heavy on Everyman, especially since religion, which used to validate and help him to bear the responsibility, is so widely discredited. He doesn't totally accept the irresponsibility either, for again the demands of daily life carry him along. But the responsibility is eased; a naked ape can surely take a day off moral behaviour now and then, he's only being himself! So when the crunch comes the structure of morality is weakened, and the barbarisms of civilisation break through, more horrible than the barbarisms of primitive life.

Michael Polanyi, when he turned to philosophy, set out to rescue Everyman from the scepticisms, numbing or cosily disintegrating, in which he is entangled. He is not without allies in this attempt. But he forged some particularly useful mental tools for the liberation of Everyman. Of his book, *Personal Knowledge*, he wrote[19] – "Its aim is to re-equip men with the faculties which centuries of critical thought have taught them to distrust. The reader has been invited to use these faculties and to contemplate thus a picture of things restored to their fairly obvious nature . . . For once men have been made to realise the crippling mutilations imposed by an objectivist framework . . . many fresh minds will turn to the task of re-interpreting the world as it is, and as it then once more will be seen to be".

It is not science, Polanyi insists, that has imposed the crippling mutilations on our thoughts; not science but a modern myth created from a profound misunderstanding of what science is and what knowledge is. This myth still entangles us in a false idea of 'Objectivity' and tells us that science shows the world to be meaningless and pointless, thus making our hopes and ideals illusory. But, believing that science does not show the world to be meaningless, Polanyi finds a galaxy of clues in science and other domains of thought from which a more liberating world picture emerges.

The purveyors of 'cosy despair' are cheating when they urge us to be 'objective', and to see ourselves as insignificant specks in an uncaring universe. If they were really objective in the sense they mean, in the whole history of the universe not more than a second could be given to the story of man. Looking at the whole of space, their objectivity would mean a lifetime spent in the study of interstellar dust with occasional glimpses of incandescent hydrogen. "Not in a thousand million lifetimes would the turn come to give man even a second's notice."[20] No one really looks at the universe like that, whatever lip-service they pay to objectivity. A view of man's knowledge that obliterates man is not objective but nonsensical.

But how can Polanyi set about building a truer picture of how Everyman knows his world, how can he justify his claim for the validity of 'personal knowledge' and what difference can that make in bringing hope, reality and responsibility back to Everyman?

Notes to Chapter II

1. *Meaning,* p.142
2. See *The Sleepwalkers* by Arthur Koestler
3. *Meaning,* p.142
4. *Meaning,* p.142
5. Prosch, H. *The Genesis of Twentieth Century Philosophy* p.83 (Anchor Books 1966)
6. *Personal Knowledge* p.142 (compare *Zen and the Art of Motorcycle Maintenance* p.71)
7. Karl Pearson *The Grammar of Science,* 1896, p.77
8. *Ibid,* p.86
9. Alan Munn – *From Nought to Relativity* p.24
10. See Liam Hudson *The Cult of the Fact*
11. S. Freud, *Das Unbehagen in der Kultur* Section VIII quoted in *Personal Knowledge* p.233
12. 'The Tables Turned' 1798
13. *cf Zen and the Art of Motorcycle Maintenance* p.77
14. *The Choice of Comrades,* Encounter, December 1954
15. Ignazio Silone, *op cit.*
16. *cf Zen and the Art of Motorcycle Maintenance* p.53
17. Sonnet "The world is too much with us" 1807
18. Michael Wood, 'The Four Gospels', *New Society,* 18.12.69
19. *Personal Knowledge* p.381
20. *Personal Knowledge* p.3

CHAPTER III
DISCOVERY

We are to use the Everyman story, briefly told in the last chapter, as our guide line through Polanyi's argument.

One of Everyman's friends in that story was Beauty. Poor Beauty, the priests disapproved of her then, and nowadays Science murders and dissects her.

But Polanyi, trying to understand the processes of scientific discovery, found the passionate pursuit of intellectual beauty to be a vital part of them.

Beauty is reinstated as a friend to Everyman, leading him to discovery.

REMEMBER how Bukharin had told Polanyi that the current Five Year Plan would set all the problems for Soviet scientists, who would spend their lives discovering whatever the Plan required to be discovered. Science pursued for its own sake, he said, was nothing but bourgeois self-indulgence. This Polanyi could not accept. There must be freedom, he knew, for scientists to follow a hunch, to sense a problem and pursue wherever it led.

What is truly creative discovery that it cannot work to rule but must have freedom? In pondering this, Polanyi found the first clue to unravelling the whole fiction of strictly impersonal scientific knowledge.

Discovery, he believed, is the most illuminating, significant part of science. If we can understand how scientists discover new truths, we shall understand better what science really is. But writers about science have not paid much attention to discovery, at least not to the aspects of it that Polanyi found important. It does not fit their view of science, so they either ignore or misrepresent it. He quotes two of their statements of their aversion – "The philosopher of science is not much interested in the thought processes which lead to discovery" – "The gist of the scientific method is . . . verification and proof, not discovery". "Actually," Polanyi comments, "philosophers deal extensively with induction as a method of scientific discovery, but when they occasionally realise that this is not how discoveries are made, they dispose of the facts to which their theory fails to apply by relegating them to psychology."[1]

Take these two ways of disposing of the facts of discovery – (1) misrepresent and (2) relegate to psychology.

(1) Induction and deduction make the tidy logical formula into which philosophers have fitted discovery. Let Bertrand Russell explain it. "The pioneers of modern science," he wrote,[2] "proceeded from observation of particular facts to the establishment of exact quantitative laws, by means of which future facts could be predicted." "In arriving at a scientific law there are three main stages: the first consists of observing the significant facts, the second in arriving at a hypothesis which if it is true would account for those facts, the third in deducing from this hypothesis consequences which can be tested by observation." To make up an instance – you see from your office window many umbrellas in the street below (fact). You suppose it is raining (induction to hypothesis). If so, the street will be wet and shiny (deduction). You stand up and look (test). It is. Your hypothesis is confirmed. There is a place for this

sort of reasoning. But Polanyi had made his own scientific discoveries and he knew that this is not what discovery is like.

The beginning is not like Russell's first stage, it is a vague sense of a problem, which draws the scientist into a personal obsession in searching for the solution. This carries him through the patient meticulous work, the setbacks and disappointments, till a sudden flash of illumination, an imaginative leap, may show the answer. And the answer is an understanding of an aspect of reality, which may not be experimentally testable for years, and may have unpredictable consequences. It does not fit the rules at all.

(2) Sir Karl Popper recognised that there is something special and creative about discovery, so he took the other way – relegating it to psychology. He wrote a whole book called 'The Logic of Scientific Discovery' and expressly excluded the creative part.

"The work of the scientist consists," he wrote[3] "in putting forward and testing theories. The initial stage, the act of conceiving or inventing a theory, seems to me neither to call for logical analysis nor to be susceptible of it. The question how it happens that a new idea occurs to a man – whether it is a musical theme or a dramatic conflict or a scientific theory – may be of great interest to the empirical psychologist but it is irrelevant to the logical analysis of scientific knowledge. This latter is concerned with questions of validity . . . Can a statement be justified? . . . In order that a statement may be logically examined in this way, it must already have been presented to us."

These two dealing with discovery sound like two Victorian ladies talking about sex. Miss Russell is giving a brisk, dry lecture of sternly scientific interest on how baby theories get born. Dear Miss Popper knows there is more to it than that, but when someone suggests that not many would get born unless sex was really rather fun, she purses her lips and says 'None of that talk in our drawing room please'. The rules of what is proper in science have become so important to the schools of thought which these two represent, that if the reality does not fit the rules, it is the reality that has to be bowdlerised or shut out. Are there rules for seeing a problem? Yes, Russell would say, the rules of induction. No, Popper would argue, there are no rules so I see no point in talking about it, it just happens. But Polanyi's answer is a yes and no. There are rules, but they are like the rules of an art, they can help but they cannot enable you to do it, since it is an art or a skill. Are there rules for painting a good picture or playing a good game of golf or living a good life? Yes and no, in just the same way. The art comes first; the rules are worked out from watching how the best people do it. The book of rules will be a help, but it will not make you a good painter or golfer or person. The art is personal and creative and goes beyond rules; but it is not arbitrary. "The capacity for making discoveries is not a kind of gambler's luck. It depends on natural ability, fostered by training and guided by intellectual effort. It is akin to artistic achievement, and like it is unspecifiable but far from accidental or arbitrary."[4]

Polanyi spoke from experience; he had worked for years at the frontiers of science among the men who were pioneering radically new understanding of the universe. Among these, Einstein recognised the special character of discovery. "The supreme task of the physicist," he wrote,[5] "is the search for those highly universal laws from which a picture of the world can be obtained by pure deduction. There is no logical path leading to these laws. They are only to be reached by intuition, based upon something like an intellectual love."

But though Einstein recognised intuition and intellectual love in discovery he did not follow up this insight. Not actually relegating these qualities to psychology like Popper, he left them hanging like a sign – "Here be mystery". Polanyi took up the challenge; he made this mysterious intellectual love his starting point. It led him toward his answer to Bukharin.

For to stand up to the Soviet view with a consistent theory which would be true to his own experience, he could not have taken either the Russell way or the Popper way. If discovery is a manageable logical process, induction, it can go on just as well under State direction for the Five Year Plan as anywhere else. While if on the other hand it is the sort of chancy unaccountable inspiration that Popper talked of, why should not that be just as likely to strike a Five Year Plan researcher as any other? Either way, there would be no justification for claiming freedom. Bukharin would be right.

Polanyi examined his own experience of scientific discovery and the experience of other scientists, and studied what some thinkers had said about it. What emerged was something that blew the accepted view of science apart.

There is a word in Russell's account which lets the cat out of the bag. The first stage, he says, consists in observing the significant facts. But which are the significant facts? *This* is where discovery starts, by noticing that facts are significant which had not seemed so.

And one does not notice that unless one is liable to be puzzled, intrigued, obsessed. "To select good questions for investigation is the mark of scientific talent, and any theory of inductive inference in which this talent plays no part is a *Hamlet* without the prince . . . Things are not labelled 'evidence' in nature, but are evidence only to the extent to which they are accepted as such by us as observers. This is true even for the most exact sciences."[6]

Here is Polanyi starting from his own conclusions, just as he said was his way. He knew that the personal skill of seeing which facts are significant is an integral part of discovery. The first tentative sense of a problem, the obsession, the daring leap of imagination, are essential; science would never get anywhere by examining any and every hypothesis that happened to come up. A theory which simply dismisses the question of how new ideas arise is a mutilation of science, for "the whole of science as it is known to us has come into existence by virtue of good problems which have led to a discovery of their solutions. The capacity to choose a line of thought the end of which is vastly indeterminate, is as much a part of the scientific method as the power of assuring the exactitude of the conclusions eventually arrived at".[7]

Robert Pirsig's motorcycle book has a good passage about problems and discoveries.[8] There is a torn screw in the motorcycle and you see no way of dealing with it, you're stuck. "The book's no good to you now. Neither is scientific reason . . . You need some ideas, some hypotheses. Traditional scientific method, unfortunately, has never quite gotten around to saying exactly where to pick up more of these hypotheses . . . It's good for testing the truth of what you think you know, but it can't tell you where you *ought* to go . . . Creativity, originality, inventiveness, intuition, imagination – 'unstuckness' in other words – are completely outside its domain – What we have to do is to examine traditional scientific method in the light of that stuck screw . . . According to the doctrine of 'objectivity' . . . what we like or don't like about that screw has nothing to do with out correct thinking . . . We should keep our minds a blank tablet which nature fills for us, and then reason disinterestedly from the facts we observe.

"But . . . this whole idea of disinterested observation is silly. Where *are* those facts? . . . The right facts are not only passive, they're damned *elusive* . . . The difference between a good mechanic and a bad one, like the difference between a good mathematician and a bad one, is precisely this ability to select the good facts from the bad ones on the basis of quality. He has to *care*! This is an ability about which formal traditional scientific method has nothing to say. It's long past time to take a look at this qualitative pre-selection of facts which has been so scrupulously ignored by those who make so much of the facts after they are 'observed'. I think it will be found that a formal acknowledgement of the role of Quality in the scientific process doesn't destroy the empirical vision at all."

Originality must be passionate, Polanyi wrote, in the same vein. "Theories of the scientific method which try to explain the establishment of scientific truth by any purely objective formal procedure are doomed to failure. Any process of enquiry unguided by intellectual passions would inevitably spread out into a desert of trivialities. Our vision of reality, to which our sense of scientific beauty responds, must suggest to us the kind of questions that it should be reasonable and interesting to explore." [9]

So here is Beauty – Quality is her other name – coming back as the indispensable partner of Knowledge when Knowledge looks at the unknown. Neither Russell's 'look at the facts', nor Popper's testing of whatever hypotheses happen to come to mind, can adequately represent the truth of discovery. The personal response to intimations of reality, indicated by scientific beauty, must guide the discoverer in his first dim sense of direction. There are many writers who have confirmed this, though none of them has taken it so seriously or made it so central as Polanyi.

One example is the mathematician Henri Poincaré, whose conclusions about his own mathematical discoveries are quoted both by Pirsig and by Polanyi. Poincaré knew the prolonged obsessional work on a problem followed by a sudden leap of imagination, and pondering how this could happen he attributed it to the 'subliminal self' which with a "true aesthetic feeling which all mathematicians know" selects the right solution demanded by the true harmony of the cosmos; a selection which no amount of work according to rules could make.

Polanyi knew also the work of the biologist Agnes Arber, who wrote, "No one can reach a creative solution of a problem which he does not approach *con amore*". She gave this account of biological discovery.[10]

"New hypotheses come into the mind most freely when discursive reasoning . . . has been raised by intense effort to a level at which it finds itself united indissolubly with feeling and emotion. When reason and intuition attain to this collaboration, the unity into which they merge appears to possess a creative power which was denied to either singly. It is not possible to offer strictly scientific evidence for the idea that not only reason but emotion has a function in biological discovery, as it admittedly has in creative work in the arts; we can only point to slight indications which are at least compatible with its truth. It is recognised, for instance, that the moment at which a fruitful combination of ideas enters the awareness is often charged with a peculiar feeling of joy . . . which precedes and seems independent of the rational satisfaction of goal attainment."

The physicist Sir Arthur Vick has compared the insight of a great scientist to poetic imagination. He cites Newton's First Law – "Every body continues in its state of rest or uniform motion in a straight line unless it is caused by an external force to change that state". "The statement," he says, "ended a long period of groping and stumbling, and illuminated the path ahead so clearly that it has been converted into a broad highway by Newton's followers. Newton's statement represents a leap forward in insight and imagination, a great generalisation, not at all obvious from observation of moving objects. The simplicity and universality of such statements carry with them a certain beauty like the shape of a Greek vase . . . Remember that these statements, these laws formulated by Newton, are not just collections of facts, they are not immediately made evident by observation or experiment; they are achievements of the human imagination and insight hardly equalled by any poet."[11]

Polanyi quoted others from whom he had learnt or who had confirmed his ideas, among them G. Polya and Thomas Kuhn. And he spoke of the "wonderful surprise of finding my basic assumptions anticipated by the nineteenth century philosopher William Whewell".[12] Whewell had seen what Polanyi saw, that 'the facts' look different when you have seen a new pattern in them, and that catching the new pattern is not done by rule but by a special skill and interest.

Think of the sort of picture puzzle where you know there is a face hidden somewhere. You look at the drawing, which shows perhaps three bad boys stealing apples, and you are to find the face of the angry farmer. You look at the corner where the drawing shows a tangle of branches and leaves; that seems a likely area for a piece of trickery. Soon some slight oddity in the drawing catches your eye and you stare at it and suddenly see the face. Once you have seen it you can hardly lose it again, and the lines that seemed before like branches now look quite different as features of the face.

Anyone who has solved problems knows the feeling of the stage when you know and yet don't know; you have a hunch, you sense a connection among the medley of facts before you, but can't quite grasp it. You may know all the facts quite well, but the pattern which they have begun to reveal eludes you, yet you know it is there. Perhaps you go to sleep on the problem and wake up knowing the answer; many discoveries have been made like this. Poincaré had a flash of illumination while stepping into a bus. It happened to Archimedes, we know, in the bath; suddenly he saw the answer and leapt out to rush into the street shouting 'Heureka! I've found it!' Thus the ideas connected with discovery are called heuristic, and it is a heuristic passion that you feel when you are hot on the trail of a discovery.

Discovery can start from noticing an anomaly, some little thing that does not fit with our general interpretation of the facts, like a misprint in a page of print. The 'skill of choosing a problem' then consists of deciding if it *is* a misprint, simply to be corrected to conform with the meaning we expect, or if it is an unusual word which points to another possible interpretation of the whole sentence. My favourite misprint comes from a church paper which reported – "As the Bishop's train drew out of the station, a large crow stood on the platform singing Rock of Ages". We laugh and confidently correct the word to "crowd". But suppose this was an isolated sentence discovered on a scrap of paper, "crow" *might* not be a misprint but the one clue to what the whole thing was about. Suppose it turned out to come from a piece of fantasy in which the Bishop was a modern St Francis who had been preaching to the birds, and this crow had been particularly moved by the sermon and was expressing its religious fervour? An absurd supposition, yes, but it may show how such an anomaly presents a problem to a scientist on which he must make a judgment for which there can be no rules, which can't be conclusively proved or disproved perhaps for a long time.

The same sort of decision faces a scientist when he finds a discrepancy between observed results and his theory. Should he hold on to the theory and dismiss the results as some sort of error, or should he give up the theory? There is no rule to tell which is the right course. There is always a personal judgment to be made at some point. Discretion (Judgment) and Beauty are needed as allies of Knowledge.

If this account of discovery is right, how could others get it so wrong? First because they *wanted* to see discovery their way, so that the rules of science could be kept strict. Second, they were *able* to see it this way because they looked at discoveries backwards, from a point after they have happened. Problems look quite different according to whether you look at them before they are solved or from after. Looked at from after the solution is found, Polanyi says, "the growth of new ideas appears altogether pre-determined . . . Yet looking *forward* before the event, the act of discovery appears personal and indeterminate. It starts with the solitary intimation of a problem, of bits and pieces here and there which seem to offer clues to something hidden. They look like fragments of a yet unknown coherent whole. This tentative vision must turn into a personal obsession, for a problem that does not worry us is no problem; there is no drive in it, it does not exist. This obsession, which spurs and guides us, is about something that no one can tell; its content is indefinable, indeterminate, strictly personal. Indeed the process by which it will be brought to light will be acknowledged as a discovery precisely because it could not have been achieved by any persistence in applying explicit rules to given facts. The true discoverer will be acclaimed for the daring feat of his imagination, which crossed uncharted seas of possible thought".[13] Russell and Popper were not looking at the process of discovery but at the results when they have been tidied up and put in the textbook, and this process changes them. It flattens out the dynamics of discovery. Polanyi gives some interesting examples of how this happens. The discovery of Relativity, according to the textbooks, was started by Einstein in 1905 trying to account for the results of the Michelson Morley experiment in 1887 on the speed of light. Polanyi doubted this, and he asked Einstein, who confirmed that the experiment had nothing to do with it. Einstein as a boy of sixteen had thought of the perplexity about the speed of light which led him to the theory of Relativity.[14] He had imagined what would happen if he could send out a beam of light and chase after it at the same speed as it was moving. No new facts led him on but a new way of thinking about the facts. But the other explanation is tidier for science, and so it got into the textbooks.

The same falsification shows up in Russell's story. He tells how Galileo proved that Aristotle was wrong about falling bodies, by dropping weights from the top of the leaning tower of Pisa. This fits nicely with Russell's thesis that "looking at the facts" was the start of the new scientific outlook. But Professor Butterfield in *The Origins of Modern Science* tells us that there is no evidence for this story, which was a later invention. Galileo did not experiment much; he *thought*, like the young Einstein. He arrived by reasoning at his theory of motion, and was not disturbed by the fact that some experiments which he *had* done in his youth tended to support the opposite conclusion.

The difference made by looking at a discovery from before or from after it is made shows up in two stories of a famous discovery, that of radium by Marie Curie.

Attracted by the title, while my head was full of these ideas about discovery, I picked up a book in the public library called *The Flash of Genius*.[15] The whole purpose of the book is to show how exciting and miraculous scientific discovery is; to highlight the mystery and human interest of the birth of a new idea. But this is how the author sums up Marie's story in his introduction:–

"Madame Curie, a young Polish girl, had just come to Professor Becquerel's laboratory in the middle nineties to do her work for her doctoral thesis. Becquerel had just discovered radioactivity. He called this young lady into his office and asked her if she would take as her thesis problem the analysis of the uranium ore. She was to try to find what element was in it that emitted the deeply penetrating radiations affecting his photographic plates. She took the problem, followed a carefully planned method of separation and analysis, and discovered the new elements polonium and radium." What a banal story! It sounds just about as exciting as if he had asked her to type out his accounts and she had found an error in the addition. In a book which sets out to be about the amazing, thrilling human interest of discovery, it is surely inadequate. The reason is, it looks from after the event. It is largely taken from Marie's own reports, but these of course would be intentionally impersonal and systematic, as routine reports of laboratory work. On the other hand, Eve Curie's story of her mother's work gives us the view from before, or from within. It is written with careful restraint because, says Eve, "it would have been a crime to add the slightest ornament to this story . . . the facts are as stated, the quoted words were actually pronounced".[16]

Eve describes her mother looking for a subject for her thesis for the doctor's degree. "At this moment she was like a traveller musing on a long voyage. Bent over the globe and pointing out in some far country a strange name that excites his imagination, the traveller suddenly decides to go there and nowhere else: so Marie, going through the reports of the latest experimental studies, was attracted by the publication of the French scientist Henri Becquerel of the preceding year . . . He discovered that uranium salts spontaneously emitted . . . some rays of an unknown nature . . . For the first time, a physicist had observed the phenomenon to which Marie Curie was later to give the name of radioactivity. But the nature of the radiation and its origin remained an enigma."

"Turning this mystery over and over in her head, and pointing toward the truth, Marie felt, and could soon affirm, that the incomprehensible radiation was an *atomic* property. She questioned: Even though the phenomenon had only been observed with uranium, nothing proved that uranium was the only chemical element capable of emitting such radiation . . .

"Becquerel's discovery fascinated the Curies. They asked themselves whence came this radiation . . . and what was its nature? . . . It was a leap into a great adventure, into an unknown realm."

Already a big difference appears between this account and the other. Marie was not given the subject, she chose it, because it drew her with the fascination that Polanyi describes. The radiations had not even a name when she started work on them.

Marie Curie was, as her daughter's book shows, a person of intense single-minded devotion to science, and of extraordinary determination and endurance. In other times she might have been a saint or martyr, but being of her time and place, what she hungered and thirsted after was scientific truth.

Marie started, then, on her investigation, and here indeed the textbook scientific method came into its own as she examined systematically all known chemical substances. When she found, in compounds containing uranium and thorium, much more radioactivity than the quantities could account for, she thought she had made a mistake and checked her results again and again, but came at last to the conclusion that there must be a new element, much more powerfully radioactive than either thorium or uranium. Two new elements, as it turned out; radium and polonium.

The reaction of scientists was cold. "The special properties of radium and polonium upset fundamental theories in which scientists had believed for centuries . . . the discovery . . . contradicted the most firmly established ideas on the composition of matter." Chemists therefore would not believe in the new elements until they had seen and weighed them. Marie had to go on and isolate the radium in pure form.

For four years she worked with her husband Pierre's help in appalling conditions and with incredible physical labour, since there was practically no money for the work, no help, no proper laboratory, only a leaking, cold shed. "And yet it was in this miserable old shed that the best and happiest years of our lives were spent, entirely consecrated to work. I sometimes passed the whole day stirring a boiling mass, with an iron rod nearly as big as myself. In the evening I was broken with fatigue." "Entirely absorbed by the new realm that was opening before us . . . we lived in our single preoccupation as if in a dream." So Marie wrote.

"In 1902, forty-five months after the day on which the Curies announced the probable existence of radium, Marie finally carried off the victory . . . she succeeded in preparing a decigramme of pure radium, and made a first calculation of the atomic weight . . . The incredulous chemists . . . could only bow before the facts, before the superhuman obstinacy of a woman."

That evening Marie sat as usual with their little girl while the child went to sleep. Then she said to Pierre, "Suppose we go down there for a moment". They stole into the shed and stood looking at the radium, glowing blue in the dark. "Look! Look!" whispered Marie Curie like a child.

This story as Eve tells it certainly has the human interest and the excitement that the other book promised but did not produce. But is all this relevant to the question of what science is? Or is it of merely psychological interest as Popper thinks? Polanyi, remember, argues just the opposite, that this personal process of original discovery, with the emotions involved in it, is the central core of science, the place where we should seek the essence of the scientific method.

This is the question. There is plenty of evidence for the exciting, creative element in discovery; it is too well attested to be ignored. But how should we deal with it? Is it part of science, revealing something about how science works, or is it to be shut out or to have its wings clipped to make it conform to the rules? Polanyi's stand is that it is the heart of science, this personal intuitive 'intellectual love'; it belongs in the house of science in all its wayward splendour, and if the rules don't allow for it they will have to change.

Some scientists and philosophers are dubious. They fear that if they open the door to Beauty and Discretion they will be letting in all the wild things that were shut out when science began. By what standard then will whims, prejudices, superstitions and all sorts of nonsense be kept out? It is a very important function of the scientific community to keep the standard, to say what theories are scientific and what are not. So scientists react as one did in a letter to *The Times* lately about psychic phenomena, voicing his distaste for "mawkish pseudo-science and faddish mumbo-jumbo". There is a necessary limit to open-mindedness. But to shut out of science the very process by which all scientific knowledge is gained could only be done by men who were afraid.

"The prevailing conception of science," said Polanyi, "based on the disjunction of subjectivity and objectivity, seeks – and must seek at all costs – to eliminate from science such passionate, personal, human appraisals . . . For modern man has set up as the ideal of knowledge the conception of natural science as a set of statements which is 'objective' in the sense that its substance is entirely determined by observation . . . This conception, stemming from a craving rooted in the very depth of our culture, would be shattered if the intuition of rationality in nature had to be acknowledged as a justifiable and indeed essential part of scientific theory." [17] So why should the strict keepers of the house of science let in this intuition of rationality, this unprovable faith?

Basically because all is not so well as it looks in their well ordered house. Polanyi speaks of his persistence in "rattling all the skeletons in the cupboard of the current scientific outlook". [18] Insist as they may on the rigid framework of testable evidence, philosophers admit it breaks down. They can keep their rigid rules only at the cost of losing contact with reality, as the Karl Pearson story showed. Even Russell admitted that there was no solid basis for induction. Laws of nature cannot be proved by any such procedure, since however many times something happens you can never be sure it will always happen – not without the faith, the intuition of rationality. So you can only live in your house of rules and pretend the faith is not there.

"From a psychological point of view," Popper wrote, [19] "I am inclined to think that scientific discovery is impossible without faith in ideas which are of a purely speculative kind and sometimes quite hazy; a faith which is quite unwarranted from the scientific point of view."

So the faith, the passionate personal appraisal, the obsession with a problem, the imaginative leap, are not to be allowed inside Popper's house of science, although we know they exist. Yet he too knows that induction is no sure road to truth. So how is he to keep the house of science clean and secure? There is no proof of the laws of nature but there is disproof. "So deep is the need for the explicit, the formulable, that he grasps at the converse of truth, at explicit error, as the straw that will save the traditional ideal," says Marjorie Grene. You can never prove, however many white swans you see, that all swans are white, for a black one might always turn up and prove you wrong. But you can *disprove* it, quite finally and certainly, if you find just one black swan. So you can still have a rule, a clear impersonal test, to show what is knowledge and what is not. The only knowledge that is certain and testable is the knowledge that you are wrong. Popper put 'falsification' into the rules of the house of science to fill up the gap left by induction. So his picture of scientific discovery is that the scientist has these unaccountable new ideas coming into his mind; his business is to try as hard as he can to prove them false. Those that cannot be proved false are our nearest approach to knowledge.

Certainly he applies this in a critical, not a naive way,[21] admitting that judgment is needed to decide whether a particular fact falsifies a theory or not. But by the time the straw he has clutched is modified and qualified, it has lost its one virtue; it is no longer an impersonal sure test, even of error. It only works if you bring in the unformalisable elements it was designed to keep out.

According to a strict falsification theory, if any fact is found which contradicts a theory, the theory has to be abandoned. But this is not what happens. The theory is only abandoned if a fact is *accepted* as evidence against it, but it may not be. There is no rule. It is a matter of judgment, a matter for Discretion, whether a particular fact falsifies a theory. Polanyi quoted the quantum theory of light, and even the theory of Relativity, as instances of theories which for a time seemed to be contradicted by experiments, yet both were so convincing that scientists simply assumed the contrary evidence would be somehow explained.[22]

"Faith in quite hazy ideas," Popper admitted, is necessary for discovery. Polanyi went on from there – how can we have quite hazy ideas which are nevertheless pointers towards the right solution of a problem? If knowledge were all clear and articulate, discovery would be impossible. How to explain the 'dim fore-knowledge' of a solution which guides us – the gradual sensing of a pattern in the facts; the sense of 'getting warm' in our search, and the 'intuitive recognition of reality' by which the right solution is recognised? These are faculties not amenable to rules of strict logic and this is why Popper threw them out. Polanyi was quite sure that they belonged *in*.

"Science is regarded as objectively established in spite of its passionate origins. It should be clear by this time that I dissent from that belief; and I have now come to the point at which I want to deal explicitly with passions *in* science. I want to show that scientific passions are no mere psychological by-products but have a logical function which contributes an indispensible element to science. They respond to an essential quality in a scientific statement and may accordingly be said to be right or wrong, depending on whether we acknowledge or deny the presence of that quality in it . . . The excitement of the scientist making a discovery is an *intellectual* passion, telling that something is *intellectually* precious, and more particularly that it is *precious to science*. And this affirmation forms part of science."[(23)]

But Popper made an admission which was sad after all his houseproud exclusiveness – "Science does not rest upon rock bottom. The bold structure of its theories rises as it were above a swamp". Into this swamp we can drive piles down, not to the rock but enough "to carry the structure at least for the time being".[(24)]

So when Everyman in his desire to keep on terms with the new Knowledge and accept only truth guaranteed by strict impersonal tests, has thrown out Beauty (Quality) and Discretion, and drilled himself to conform to the rules of the house – after all it is no good; it is a house built on the swamp!

Notes to Chapter III

1. *Personal Knowledge* p.14 note
2. *The Scientific Outlook* p.58
3. *The Logic of Scientific Discovery* p.31
4. *Personal Knowledge* p.106
5. *The World As I See It* – (1935) p.125
6. *Personal Knowledge* p.30
7. Genius in Science. 1972. *Boston Studies in the Philosophy of Science XIV.*
8. *Zen and the Art of Motorcycle Maintenance* p.273–
9. *Personal Knowledge* p.135
10. Agnes Arber *The Mind and the Eye.* C.U.P. 1954. pp.20, 21
11. 'The Making of Scientists'. *The Listener*, Jan 29 1959
12. *Meaning* p.57
13. *The Tacit Dimension* p.75. *cf* Thomas Kuhn, *The Structure of Scientific Revolutions.* 2nd edition p.137
14. See *Personal Knowledge* p.10
15. Alfred Garrett *The Flash of Genius* (Van Norstrand NY 1963)
16. Eve Curie *Madame Curie.* (Heinemann 1938) pp.161, 163, 177
17. *Personal Knowledge* p.15
18. *Personal Knowledge* p.18
19. *The Logic of Scientific Discovery* p.38
20. *The Knower and the Known* p.32. See the whole of Marjorie Grene's chapter 'The Legacy of the Meno' for a comparison of Popper and Polanyi on discovery.
21. See Brian Magee – *Popper* pp.23, 24
22. *cf* T. Kuhn, *The Structure of Scientific Revolutions* p.146–7
23. *Personal Knowledge* p.134
24. *The Logic of Scientific Discovery* p.11

CHAPTER IV

TACIT KNOWING

Everyman, in the old play, had a friend called Five Wits. This name indicated the five senses of Everyman, but it might also include all the inarticulate powers inherited from our evolutionary history. It seems agreeable to think of Five Wits as Everyman's dog.

In the Everyman play, Five Wits was disparaged as a useless unreliable creature, while Knowledge was commended by the priests as Everyman's true friend. And now Five Wits is getting disparaged again, for Science mistrusts these unregulated powers.

This chapter is about the rehabilitation of Five Wits. Polanyi shows how if we are to account for new creative discoveries, knowledge needs Five Wits. Without his powers of tacit knowing no discoveries would be possible.

POLANYI had found the true nature of scientific discovery denied or distorted by governments and by philosophers – by governments because they wanted to set it to useful work, by philosophers because they wanted to keep the house of science clean and respectable even if it was built over a swamp.

But he held on to his two convictions, that he knew what discovery was really like, and that it was the vital core of science. What sort of thing then must knowledge be, if discovery is its most significant form?

To account for discovery as it actually happens, we have to allow there is another kind of knowledge besides the explicit, exact and testable kind; a sense by which we can be dimly aware of the direction in which we must seek for a solution, before we can formulate it. Popper calls this 'faith in quite hazy ideas' and shuts it out of science; Polanyi calls it 'tacit knowing' and finds in it an essential element of his theory of knowledge. Instead of trying to ignore the swamp, he accepts it as if saying, "all right, here is this swamp, it's no use building your glass and steel palace above it and pretending it's not there. Let us see how our knowledge grows out of the swamp. Its roots are down in the water but its stem and branches have emerged into the light, and can become a pursuit of universal standards, a knowledge of reality, a valid basis for science and other kinds of knowledge". Traditional skills, intuitions, scientific systems, poetic and religious insights and the understanding of moral values are all fed from the same root. No longer is science isolated and exaggerated as the one valid form of knowledge.

Most philosophers hate this swampy root[1] and prefer the glass and steel structure; they know it is measurable and there is no mystery about it, except how it stays up. They don't like the way the root eludes measurement, and brings into the house a swampy vagueness – what one modern philosopher has called 'disreputable notions – muddy savagery'.[2] This destroys their persistent dream of a house of science built of standard, guaranteed genuine blocks of hard fact.

> Oh what a dusty answer gets the soul
> When hot for certainty in this our life –

wrote Meredith. A swampy answer may not sound much better, but swamp plants can reach for the light and, Polanyi claims, man can transcend his own subjectivity by striving passionately to fulfill his personal obligations to universal truth.

Polanyi's idea of tacit knowledge is expounded in his writings in so many forms starting from so many different points, that it is hard to know where to begin telling about it without emphasising one aspect more than another. But since we find ourselves now in Popper's swamp, let us start there and see how Polanyi draws out of it the beginnings of human knowledge in the tacit inarticulate powers of earlier forms of life. In a passage of *Personal Knowledge*[3] he traces our powers of knowing back to the first small and yet decisive step towards man's destiny in the emergence of virus-like specks of living matter, centres of self-interest against the worldwide drift of meaningless happenings. Then protozoa, moving purposefully about, then multicellular organisms and the development of higher and lower functions within organisms, the higher prefiguring the brain.

Some creatures are by now exploring their world, and soon the development of sense organs brings perception, and so the need for judgment and the capacity to learn from experience. "Some observers have traced this faculty back to unicellular organisms, and it can certainly be found as far down as the level of worms."

Then come the rudiments of generalising, contriving, understanding; the first faint thrills of intellectual joy, and the liability to puzzlement and frustration.

Five hundred million years of this slow growth of individuality still only led to the threshold of true mental life with the rise of man. Polanyi quotes Teilhard de Chardin's phrase 'the noosphere' for the universe of mind in which man alone of animals can dwell. Man, it seems, is the only creature in the universe which *reasons* with universal intent, that is to say – makes statements that claim to be accepted by anyone who understands the problem for which they offer an answer.

So the story that Polanyi tells of change, emergence and development is worlds away from the accounts of a blind fortuitous evolution which could never produce anything different in kind from the chance physical happenings which started it. All through this long story of life, Polanyi sees energetic initiatives at work in creatures striving, reaching forward to get hold of their world, explore it, make sense of it. "From a seed of sub-microscopic living particles we see emerging a race of sentient, responsible and creative beings." A responsible creative being could not be produced by any number of aeons of blind chance, so either man is *not* a sentient responsible creative being, or he has truly emerged by some more active process. And why not? We have seen how discovery, looked at from afterwards, appears determined, but looked at from the discoverer's point of view is seen as indeterminate, active, powered by passionate personal commitment. The same could be true of evolution.[4]

Man has emerged, but he still has his history in him, in his slowly evolved powers of understanding as in his physical body. Our own urge to know is traceable right back to the urge to get about and grasp and deal with their world that was shown by the earliest forms of life. Our quest, certainly, is pursued with immeasurably more powerful and accurate instruments. The vast spread of explicit organised knowledge that man has, and can preserve and pass on and communicate across the world by speech and writing, and all the technical devices and procedures he has created – all this is a tremendous achievement. But, at the same time, it is only a tool-kit. It cannot work on its own, men have to use the tools, and they still rely basically on the powers that grew in the swamp.

"Everywhere, at all mental levels, it is not the functions of the articulate logical operations but the tacit powers of the mind that are decisive."[5]

So this is one way Polanyi looked; to the roots of tacit knowledge in our evolution.

Then he looked, starting again at another point, at our most everyday kinds of knowledge, kinds that are familiar to us all, not scientific but valid.

"We know more than we can tell." This is the phrase with which Polanyi sometimes introduced tacit knowledge. For instance, you know your child's face, you could recognise it among a thousand with instant certainty. Yet you cannot tell how you know it; you could not specify exactly its shape, size, colouring, the measurement of the features.

You do know these, for you rely on your knowledge of them in recognising the face, but you can't tell them. You know them tacitly. What you have is the power to recognise a whole (the face) of which you can't specify the parts.

I once wrote to Michael Polanyi from the Western Sudan where we had seen the way of life of the nomads who travel continually with their camels and cattle in search of pasture. The Sudan government wanted to arrange schooling for the nomad children, but the parents protested. Their whole way of life depended on the tacit knowledge by which the children could recognise each one of a herd of two hundred camels, and if one disappeared, know at once which it was, recognise its track and find it. The parents feared that if the children went to school and learned arithmetic and algebra and other formal subjects, they would lose their practical powers, and the way of life would be destroyed. Polanyi liked this story as an illustration of tacit knowledge and how explicit knowledge may destroy it.

Another sort of example Polanyi often gave is a skill. Your child rides a bicycle; he knows how to ride yet he could not tell how he does it. It is possible to write out the rule for keeping your balance on a bicycle, but the child knows how to do it without knowing the rule. The rule is – that in order to compensate for a given angle of imbalance (a), we must take a curve on the side of the imbalance, of which the radius (r) should be proportionate to the square of the velocity (v) over the imbalance: $r \sim \frac{v^2}{a}$. That is explicit knowledge, but is not a lot of use if you need to ride a bicycle. The child knows that by a skilful adaptation to all sorts of bodily clues; it's a tacit bodily skill.

Another example of a skill would be cooking; here is an example from '*Goodbye for the Present*' – Eleanor Acland's memories of her childhood. She tells about Anne, the cook in her parents' house. "Her sponge cakes were renowned, so feathery inside and so crisp outside. Visitors would exclaim with admiration and ask if they might as a great favour have Anne's recipe. "Sponge cakes?" Anne would say. "Why they're easy, is a sponge cake. You take yer eggs" – "How many?" "Oh, a fair few: and when you've got yer whites nicely whipped and yer yawkes, you put one to t'other and sugar along with them –" "How much sugar?" "Well, maybe a cupful or two. And then sift in 't flour and keep stirring till all's ready for t'oven. Ye'll have to mind yer oven, you want it just the right heat, that's the main thing." "And how long ought one to leave the cake in the oven?" "Why, till it's done, ma'am."

It wasn't that Anne didn't want to pass on her secret; she just could not see any problem. She knew these details tacitly as part of the process, but could not tell them. Of course, specific instructions for making a sponge cake can be written down, but it is likely that not all the details of Anne's cooking could be specified, since she unconsciously varied them according to factors that she sensed, such as the temperature of the oven on a day when the wind was in the east, or the size and freshness of the eggs. Anyway she was not able to specify the particulars, because she only knew them tacitly in terms of the whole process. And anyone using a written recipe would have to use the same sort of tacit knowledge as Anne's in matching the written instructions to the look and feel of the materials. "Beat till firm" the book might say – but how firm is firm? The book can't tell you everything, or why do people go to cookery classes? They have to learn from skilled cooks like Anne the tacit knowledge with which to interpret the book's instructions.

In such everyday examples of knowing Polanyi found some important facts for his quest. First, there is nothing second-rate about this kind of knowledge. It may be limited but it is knowledge, not guesswork or approximation. You *know* your child's face. He *knows* how to ride a bicycle. Anne *knows* how to make a sponge cake. These knowings are perfectly valid though their particulars are not specifiable, and no scientific procedure would make them more valid. This seems obvious, but we have got ourselves into such a twist that we aren't sure. I once met a woman who had been attending a course of lectures on philosophy. With a stricken face she said, "It's terribly depressing; I've learnt that we can't really *know* anything." Yet she would not have felt any doubt about knowing her own child, nor have fallen off her bicycle because she could not explain how she stayed on.

So here is a real kind of knowledge in which we rely on awareness of details we can't specify or check in any scientific way. Sometimes they *can* be specified, like the rules for keeping your balance on a bicycle, but success in the art does not involve knowing the rules, and in using the details success depends on not concentrating on the rules. If a scientific minded cook stood by Anne and got her attention focussed on the weight of the eggs and the exact temperature of the oven she would almost certainly make a mess of the cake, and the child would fall off his bicycle if he tried to ride according to the rules of balance. As Belloc wrote –

The Water Beetle here shall teach
A sermon far beyond your reach.
He flabbergasts the human race
By gliding on the water's face
With ease, celerity and grace,
But if he ever stopped to think
Of how he did it, he would sink.[6]

So we can see that we are attending to some sort of complex whole thing or skill, the face, the riding of the bicycle, the making of the cake, and that if we attend to the parts separately we may lose the sense of the whole. We focus on the whole by not attending to the parts, or as Polanyi says by attending *from* them *to* something else which is their joint meaning. We integrate the parts into the whole, not by a reasoning process but by a sort of bodily skill, a skill which is so much part of our make-up that we are usually not aware of it – you don't think of it as a skilled performance when you recognise your child among a crowd! Only in learning, discovering, acquiring a new skill, we feel it as a skill and recognise its difficulty.

We have to add, too, the element of *caring* which was mentioned in the motorcycle book.[7] Since tacit knowing depends on where your attention is focussed, it won't work without caring. It's impossible really to attend without caring. You care about your child, he cares about riding his bicycle. Anne cares about her sponge cake and the scientist cares passionately about finding the truth. There is no discovery without a desire to know and *a belief that there is something to know.*

Now we can see how this approach might link up with the first one. We find knowledge in our daily lives which doesn't depend on any purely intellectual reasoning from evidence but on a sort of skill of integrating particulars into a whole. Is it not likely that this skill is an inheritance from our evolutionary past, the flower of that long long urge to grasp and deal with the world that started with the beginning of life?

Think of other skills, the use of language for instance. Here the whole that we attend to is the meaning. In learning a new language we have to attend to the separate words, even the letters of the alphabet if it is an unfamiliar one, but when we have attained fluency we no longer do that, we attend to the meaning. Polanyi has a good example of this transparency of a well-known language. Letters used to come to him in various languages, and there was one he wanted his son to read; remembering his son did not read German he had to glance again at the letter to see whether it was in German or English. He had completely absorbed the meaning without being aware of the language in which it was written. He knew that tacitly.

Think of the skill of using tools. At first a novice will be very conscious of the feel of the tool handle in his hand, but a skilled carpenter won't be aware of that; his focus is on the contact of the tool with the wood and the job he is doing with it. So too when you learn to drive a car, at first you have to attend carefully to gears, steering, accelerator and brake, but as you gain competence you cease to be conscious of these, and focus on the road and the traffic. You have learnt to attend *from* the bits of the car *to* what you are doing with it. So the tool, the car, the language, have become in some way an extension of yourself. You feel at home in them as you do in your own body, and use them to know with or to act skilfully with.

In all these kinds of knowing and know-how there are two levels of objects; the parts, details, particulars *from* which you attend, and the whole or meaning *to* which you attend. This is the characteristic structure of tacit knowing. Polanyi puts the difference in various ways; sometimes he speaks of *subsidiary* and *focal* objects of attention, the subsidiary being the particulars we are attending from, and the focal the whole on which our attention is focussed. Because in this process the meaning tends to be placed away outside ourselves, as when we interpret clues in our own bodies as revealing an object outside us, he also calls the two kinds of objects *'proximal'* and *'distal'*.

Remember, the way we get from one to the other is not formal reasoning, it is a skilled imaginative integration.

We have this sort of power built into us, and to realise this was exciting to Polanyi because it does provide a clue to the way that discoveries are made. The intuition by which a great scientist sees a new pattern in the facts is only a development of an everyday skill. The leap of imagination in a great discovery is the leap from a lot of known particulars to their joint meaning, the coherence to which they are clues.

But all this, you may say, is not science! Surely science gained its successes and prestige precisely by getting rid of this dependence on unspecified details, by testing every step, clarifying and formalising so that the whole process can be repeated? Polanyi claims on the contrary that tacit knowledge, the same kind as we use every day, is in fact the dominant principle of all knowledge, and that its rejection would involve the rejection of any kind of knowledge whatsoever. At the heart of all knowledge, he insists, however exact, however much it uses formal procedure, there is this element of personal judgment depending on an unformalisable intuition, a skilled integration of unspecifiable particulars.

In the sciences where classifying is involved, this is easily seen. Botanists and geologists have to spend a long time learning the skill of recognising plants or rocks as belonging to a certain class or species; medical students have to toil for months to acquire the skill of seeing the meaningful shapes in a lung X-ray. Written descriptions cannot tell all; if they could there would be no need for live teaching or laboratory work. The student has to learn how to recognise the plant or the disease by watching how the expert does it, and trying himself, till he catches the meaning of what the expert is doing – just the way one would have to learn to make Anne's sponge cake. He uses the rules set out in the book, but has to learn the skill of applying them to what is before him. Living micro-organisms never look exactly like the diagram in the book; spots on baby's face aren't identifiable as measles just from reading their medical description. There is always an element of skilled recognition, integrating clues which cannot be exactly specified.

This whole business of classifying things into kinds, classes, species and genera is a puzzle and a bother to philosophers because it can't be explained if you don't recognise the tacit skill we have been considering. Kant called the ability to put things into classes "a skill so deeply hidden in the human soul that we shall hardly guess the secret that Nature here employs".[8] But Polanyi declares that is only *so* mysterious if one is looking for an *explicit* procedure for how the classifying is done. Instead he suggests that the same tacit power by which we see two slightly different stereoscopic pictures as one image in depth, or recognise a face, is the same everyday skill by which you identify the creature you see in the street as a dog. How do you know it's a dog? Dogs differ in colour, size, shape, texture and disposition and in many other ways. There *is* a scientific classification in which a dog would be described as a mammal, quadruped, carnivorous etc. animal, but this is skeleton knowledge, an 'after the event' view; it's not how you *recognise* a dog. It can't be, for cats and children can recognise dogs. It's a summary of the most explicitly identifiable features of doggishness, abstracted from a lot of instances we already know are dogs, whereas the identifying of a dog by tacit knowledge is like the recognition of a face, like the identification by a connoisseur of a painting or a wine – a skill of dwelling in unspecified particulars so that by an imaginative integration we catch their joint meaning.[9]

Here is a story about dog identification from Leila Berg's book – 'Look at kids'.

"At the time I ran a nursery group we had an Old English sheepdog. The first time I let him into the garden, the children were amazed. 'What is it?' 'It's a bear!' 'It's a pussy.' 'It's a bunny.' 'It's a lion' – (at this last, everyone ran away into a small flurry and came back half a minute later) 'What is it?'

"It's a dog," I said. All hell broke loose. Tom hurled himself at me as if he were fighting for his life. 'It's not a dog! It's not a dog!' he screamed, feet and fists pulverising me.

"In the middle of saving myself and comforting him, I wondered how any two-year-old comes to learn that alsatians, pekinese, collies, Great Danes, chihuahuas, are all dogs? Once accepted as a dog and no longer threatening chaos, encouraged to take his verbal place calmly – a tiger sitting on a stool – in their growing classification, the bobtail was painted with vermilion splashes on one side and was ridden on."

The children wanted to classify, they felt strongly about their classification and didn't want to stretch it, but were able to do so through their trust in an expert, followed by realisation of true doggishness in this unfamiliar specimen. There is no explicit procedure for distinguishing the correct stretching of our classification from a wrong one, and this sort of trouble applies to all classifying. "Science is rotten to the core!" exclaimed Quine, though he went on to accept that the rot is useful. But he thought it would eventually be eliminated by devising formal criteria for classification. Polanyi is sure it never will. At the heart of science, as of all knowledge, there remains the element of tacit personal judgment based on our skills. "The facts of biology and medicine, for example, can be recognised as a rule only by experts possessing both special skill for examining the objects in question and a special connoisseurship for identifying particular specimens. The exercise of such an art is a tacit feat of intelligence which cannot ever be fully specified in terms of explicit rules."[11]

You see what has happened; the wild thing, Discovery, allowed into the house of science, has upset the place and infected everything with its wildness just as the correct philosophers feared it would. Not only discovery but classification turned out to have a wild taint, and nothing is free of it. All the articulate framework, all the formal rules of reasoning, all the maps, graphs, formulae, exact procedures and instruments which make our scientific civilisation possible, have to be used by *people*, who have their inherited, but trained and disciplined skills of understanding with which to judge and apply the formal procedures. And this is not a lingering imperfection to be eliminated but the living core of knowledge. That is Polanyi's claim.

But there is a similar unformalisable skill which has always been accepted in the house of science without any fuss, and that is the skill of seeing. Polanyi found in perception a most useful comparison for justifying his account of discovery and of tacit knowing. Seeing is a skill we take so much for granted that we don't realise what an active and astonishing process it is. A small girl was asked jokingly – "Where did you buy those big dark eyes?" "I didn't buy them," she said, indignant at the absurd idea, "They're for shutting and going to sleep with."

Why didn't she say – "for seeing with"? Evidently because seeing had never occurred to her as a thing she did. Probably she had been told – "Shut your eyes and go to sleep" – and that was the only thing she consciously *did* with her eyes. Yet she had learnt as a baby, as we all do, by months of practice, to see the world around her. Not indeed in the absurdly intellectual way described in the Alan Munn book[12] constructing concepts from percepts and making the 'unwarranted assumption' that there are real *things*. She had learnt by being, emotionally, in a real world and setting to work actively and eagerly to see and know the things and people in it.

This three-year-old child lived in a world of real people and things which were just *there*, around her, no question about it could possibly arise. Hume hadn't got at her. Yet at birth she had seen just coloured patches, vaguely moving, light or dark. How did she get from that to the world of real things and people in which she found herself so much at home as soon as she was conscious?

Thinking about the powers of mental integration that he found so important in knowledge; looking for ways of showing them valid, Polanyi turned to perception, to the way we see things, for an understanding of these powers. In perception we discover how centrally important these powers are, and how easy to miss.

In particular he turned to the work of the Gestalt psychologists, who experimented with animals and birds as well as human beings, and showed that the way they see cannot be explained by the sort of mechanical model other schools of psychology had used. Animals respond, they found, to shapes and patterns in their visual field which depend on being seen as a whole. Patterns disappear if the viewer attends to separate bits of them. (Think of the dots which make a face in some printed illustrations, and imagine viewing them separately through a magnifying glass: there is then no face.) Animals can organise what they see so as to read it as a meaningful pattern; birds can relate shades of colour and can 'read' a pattern of arranged objects; apes can organise the whole visual field in terms of a problem and its solution, as when they see a stick as a tool for reaching food.

The Gestalt people concluded that it is a function of our nervous system to organise our visual experience so that we see a coherent world of stable things.

"The study of perception by Gestalt psychologists has demonstrated the tacit operations that establish such coherence. When I move my hand before my eyes, it would keep changing its colour, its shape and its size, but for the fact that I take into account a host of rapidly changing clues, some in the field of vision, some in my eye muscles and some deeper still in my body, as in the labyrinth of the inner ear. My powers of perceiving coherence makes me see these thousand varied and changing clues jointly as one unchanging object, as an object moving about at different distances, seen from different angles, under variable illuminations. A successful integration of a thousand changing particulars into a single consistent sight makes me recognise a real object in front of me."[13]

So the seeing that we do so effortlessly, once we have learnt it, is an integration of many clues to a focal perception of one object. It is not done intellectually but by the exercise of our inherited and practised biological powers for organising and grasping our world. It can be mistaken, it can be cheated by arranged optical illusions, but these in fact help to show how it works, for the illusion often succeeds by cutting out surrounding clues in the visual field on which we rely tacitly. The presence of this integrative power is confirmed too by the experience of people who have been blind from birth and have received sight through an operation. They at first can only see like a baby; they have to learn, through sometimes intensely hard practice, to integrate their visual sensations and read them as real things. But once we have learnt the art of seeing, it is so unconscious, and its tendency to interpret what we see as real things behaving in reasonable ways is so strong, that we can hardly escape it; that fact is the basis of some optical illusions too! We can, however, sort out the illusions from the sensing of real objects in various ways, and this is partly what science does.

A recognition that the art of scientific intuition is like the art of seeing is revealed in this remark by Keynes about Newton – "His peculiar gift is the power of holding continuously in his mind a purely mental problem until he has seen right through it. I fancy his pre-eminence is due to his *muscles of intuition* being the strongest and most enduring with which a man has ever been gifted."[14]

The findings of Gestalt psychology, then, gave one reinforcement for Polanyi's view of knowledge. Ah, you may say, then this theory of knowledge and discovery is psychology, just as Popper said, and therefore not a part of a theory of knowledge in the philosophic sense. Is this a real objection? I take it that a psychological explanation explains why animals see as they do by their structure and physiological make-up, whereas a philosophical explanation has to show whether they see truly, see what is really there. If so, Polanyi transformed the Gestalt theory from psychology to philosophy. The Gestalt people were unable to say how we distinguish an optical illusion from reality, since they thought of seeing as a process of passive equilibration, so that all visual experience is equal.

"Psychologists," Polanyi said, "have described our perception of Gestalt as a passive experience, without envisaging that it represents a method – and indeed the most general method for acquiring knowledge. They were probably unwilling to recognise that knowledge was shaped by the knower's personal action. But having realised that personal participation predominates both in the area of tacit and explicit knowledge, we are ready to transpose the findings of Gestalt psychology into a theory of knowledge."[15]

All our knowing, says this theory, is like seeing in this respect, that it goes on from being aware of a lot of particular bits to grasping how they hang together, what is their joint meaning, the real whole of which they are parts or to which they are clues. Sometimes when we have got used to this operation it is so easy that it is not noticed; sometimes when we are applying it to something new it is very difficult and constitutes discovery. It is done by shifting our attention from the particulars to the whole, the joint meaning, and when we do this it changes the way we are aware of the particulars – (as we saw in the picture puzzle when the lines that we first thought were branches look quite different once we have seen them as features of a face).

The theories of Gestalt psychology as Polanyi used them showed not just that there *is* tacit knowledge – such as your recognition of your child's face – and explicit knowledge – such as the school record of his height and weight – but that there is throughout the whole range of knowledge, tacit and explicit, this same structure – scattered meaningless particulars being converted into parts of a meaningful whole by a change of focus. You stop attending *to* them and start attending *from* them to a whole or a joint meaning which at first you only vaguely sense. But when the whole, the joint meaning, takes over, the particular bits have sunk into a subsidiary place in your attention and don't appear the same.

In trying, therefore, to make any kind of knowledge totally explicit and testable so as to make it reliably 'scientific' we are pursuing a will-o'-the-wisp, because however explicit it may be on its own, it has got to sink into subsidiary status before it can be meaningful as part of a whole, and this will change it. In attending from it we must let it lose its explicit character and so its testability.

This theory of knowledge, which gives a central place to a sort of biological skill developed from animal capacities, brings us right up against the central problem. How could such a capacity develop into a faculty that can reach general *truths?* How can man reason 'with universal intent', which worms clearly can't? Without claiming to show just how this happened, Polanyi thought one could see that it *could* happen, from studying how it happens in an individual, and here he learnt much from Piaget's great studies of child development. Piaget has watched babies and young children as no one has ever done before. He has set problems to them from their earliest days of life, and worked out the logical operations that can be detected in their behaviour at each stage of development.

Piaget showed how babies start to create their framework of space and time by their own activities of moving, looking and grasping. The baby shows at first no sign of realising that the objects around him go on being there when he can't see them; he has no sense of time or space relations, but over the first months he acquires patterns of dealing with his world which Piaget calls *schemata*. Each schema is a rudimentary organisation of experience which becomes the baby's means of absorbing new experience. For instance the very first schema that may grow is a schema of sucking; sucking starts as a reflex action, but quickly picks up the different action needed for sucking a thumb and sucking a nipple, and so grows. A schema absorbs the new into what is already there, modifies what is already there to accommodate the new, and so keeps the baby's knowledge growing as a whole. Soon he shows signs of selecting from his body of knowledge the schema that seems likely to cope with a new experience.

In this sort of way the child advances from a chaotic experience to an understanding of the steady laws that his world runs by; a stable framework of time and space in which things persist even when not seen, in which numbers and sizes don't change capriciously. In fact he recognizes new logical levels which at first he could not grasp, and will come in time to recognise such concepts as truth, fairness or justice as real features of the world. "The appetitive, motoric, perceptive child is transformed into an intelligent person, reasoning with universal intent."[16]

Thus Piaget gives an account of how an individual human being arrives through a process of maturation at a grasp of new logical levels, and an objective understanding of his world, and this helps, Polanyi thought, our understanding of how the human race could do so. We tend to get puzzled about the emergence of the human race towards a capacity for logical, responsible and ethical reasoning, because we tend to ask how did the new powers get there? Were they somehow there from the start or did they appear by the intervention of some outside power – or are they illusory? But looking at children we can see how those new powers can develop by maturation, through the child's activity and urge to understand.

With his theory of tacit knowledge Polanyi firmly sets man's 'indefinable powers of thought' at the centre of science and all knowledge. Scientific knowledge would get nowhere without the dim foreknowledge and the capacity to know more than we can tell. And this means we do believe there is an external reality of which we can thus be aware.

"We can account for this capacity of ours to know more than we can tell if we believe in the presence of an external reality with which we can make contact. This I do. I declare myself committed to the belief in an external reality gradually accessible to knowing, and I regard all true understanding as an intimation of such a reality which, being real, may yet reveal itself to our deepened understanding in an indefinite range of unexpected manifestations. I accept the obligation to search for the truth through my own intimations of reality, knowing that there is and can be no strict rule by which my conclusions can be justified."[17]

So there is a faith involved in our knowledge – a faith in a reality we can gradually understand. Isn't it open to the same criticism as Popper's saying that the foundations of science rest on piles driven down into the swamp, or Quine's reluctant admission of the place of 'disreputable notions, muddy savagery', in our knowledge? The difference is that Polanyi is not trying to build a complete unswampy structure, shutting out all the untamed elements although reluctantly admitting they exist. He is more like Brer Rabbit 'born and bred in a briar patch' and unafraid of being thrown back into one. His profoundly life-orientated philosophy accepts man's history and native powers, and his achievement of a personal perspective towards reality. There is then no finished certainty to our knowledge, but there is no sceptical despair either. Through all our different kinds of knowledge there is a reasonable faith, personal responsibility and continuing hope.

There seem to be two ways in which people tend to regard the briar-bush or the swamp – that is, our prehuman origins. One is to say 'Aha! Now we know what were the origins of the human race – that is what man came from and that is what he still *really* is; all his fine knowledge and morality and the rest is self-delusion!' This is the line taken by the popular purveyors of 'cosy despair'.

The other line is that man's prehistory has nothing to do with knowledge, which must be judged and certified purely by formal rules. Ernest Gellner for example in his discussion in *Men of Ideas*[18] disagrees with philosophies which trace valid ways of knowing back into biological history. "This is the view that cognitive growth has been one continuous story from the amoeba to Einstein, with the same basic plot throughout. One could call this the Continuity Thesis. I think it is mistaken. What is important about our cognitive manners is not what they have *in common* with the amoeba or with the Dark Ages, but what is *distinctive* about them. The important secrets lie in the differences."

Both these ways of looking at our evolution are essentially static. One says 'Once an amoeba, always an amoeba: the changes are superficial'. The other says, 'Now we are on this platform of human reason, what does it matter how we got here?' Polanyi says neither. He sees our history as a true emergence, so that our human powers of reason are real and valid and importantly different from the powers of any other animal: yet it does matter how we got here, for without the powers we have in common with other animals our reason would be impotent. The structure of tacit knowing opens a way between these two dead-end views.

Tacit Knowledge is Polanyi's most profoundly revolutionary idea. We shall not lose sight of it in the following pages; it is the key to so many doors which without it have proved very hard to open. It allows us to give a truer picture of the process of scientific discovery, for the scientist's power of sensing the direction in which a solution of his problem will be found lies in the reservoir of tacit, perhaps inarticulate, skills, aptitudes and awareness which underly all his conscious search. It was this reservoir which enabled Polanyi to sense conclusions before he could articulate the logical steps leading to them;[19] it is this that gives validity to the judgment of many unlettered and inarticulate men. And the same reservoir of tacit knowledge, reliable but not necessarily exact or complete, allows for the role of a traditional respect for truth and other values in a free society: the lack or disregard of it for the 'moral inversion' and nihilism produced by the scientific world view. When we come to the idea of a 'many level world' (ch.8) we find that the structure of tacit knowing works on each level of reality by integrating the particulars of that level into their meaning on the next higher level. The old puzzles of the relation of mind and body dissolve in the light of tacit knowing, and persons take their true place as the most real of realities, known by, and knowing by, indwelling and tacit knowledge.

Finally when we come to the consideration of other than scientific kinds of knowledge, reached through art, poetry, myth and religion, the structure of tacit knowing supplies the link which allows all these kinds of knowledge to be part of one great range of understanding of reality. No longer scorned and devalued because not experimentally verifiable, non-scientific knowledge shares with science the need for faith, imagination and daring.

Notes to Chapter IV

1. *Men of Ideas* p.294
2. W. V. Quine, *Ontological Relativity and Other Essays* Columbia University Press 1969 p.134
3. *Personal Knowledge* p.387
4. see *Meaning* p.163, and Alistair Hardy *The Living Stream*
5. *The Study of Man* p.19
6. Hilaire Belloc *Cautionary Verses:* Collected Album edition Duckworth 1940 p.352
7. see p.34 above
8. quoted in *Knowing and Being* p.105–6
9. see *Personal Knowledge* p.348 (identification of the human shape)
10. W. V. Quine, *Ontological Relativity and Other Essays* Columbia University Press 1969 p.352
11. *The Study of Man* p.23
12. see p.22 above
13. *Knowing and Being* p.138–9 (see also p.173)
14. Quoted by Freeman Dyson in *The New Yorker* 3.8.79
15. *The Study of Man* p.28
16. *Personal Knowledge* p.395
17. *Knowing and Being* p.133
18. *Men of Ideas* p.37
19. see p.2 above

CHAPTER V
REALITY

Is there a reality out there? How can Everyman tell? The priests had told him that only their story of Heaven and Hell was real, and that he needed faith, no other personal qualities, to know it. Now Science tells him that only the world of scientific facts is real and she is rather doubtful if he has any personal qualities, and if he has they are no use. But here comes a message that Everyman can know reality by daring to go and explore what he dimly discerns, risking himself in commitment to the quest, needing all his powers and qualities.

In the last chapter we found Polanyi declaring his belief in a real world external to us. This might seem such banal common sense as to need no declaring, had not the philosophers done such curious things to our ideas of how we know. Polanyi once illustrated the meaning of a real world for the scientific discoverer by a brief and commonplace story of a burglar. Suppose, he said, that we wake up in the night and hear a sound like rummaging in the next room. "Is it the wind? a burglar? a rat? We try to guess. Was that a footfall? That means a burglar. Convinced, we pluck up courage, rise, and proceed to verify our assumptions."[1] The point of the story is that the burglar theory does not enable us to predict exactly what we shall find, because what we expect is a *real* burglar. The theory may be confirmed, when we get into the next room, but any of some quite varied observations – a man with all the silver in a sack, an open window, drawers pulled out, clothes scattered on the floor or even a gun pointed at us. Although we cannot predict, we shall know when we see what is there whether we were right or not; being real, the burglar will behave in unpredictable ways which we shall recognise when we see them as being characteristic of burglars. The burglar story illustrates how discovery implies a real world whose coherences we can recognise. When the path of a planet is predicted it is assumed to be a real planet, and this means that the prediction could be confirmed in many different ways which the astronomer may not foresee or imagine. This often happens with scientific discoveries, as one would expect in a real world, but not in the Karl Pearson world of mere sense impressions (page 21).

Ernst Mach, like Karl Pearson, maintained we can only have knowledge of our own sense impressions; we cannot legitimately go beyond describing these, to claim any understanding of a real world. Thus he said that atoms and molecules were just convenient mental concepts. But scientists who believed they were real things followed up the consequences and deduced the weights of individual atoms, their arrangement in crystals, and started to investigate their internal structure. Thus science progresses by guessing at aspects of reality indicated by clues in what is seen and heard, just as we guess that certain sounds indicate the presence of a real burglar and go to look. But there is this powerful school of thought which follows Pearson and Mach in denying that we can find out anything about a real world. If sufficiently scared by the burglar noises one might join that school of thought, get under the bedclothes and recite Karl Pearson's admonition – "It is idle to postulate shadowy unknowables behind that real world of sense impressions in which we live".[2] This could be followed, if the noises continue, by Alan Munn's incantation – "Nothing is logically or practically gained by adding to our postulates that of a primary world of *real* things". And why get up and go looking for more sense impressions? It wasn't real silver anyway, only concepts.

Polanyi was a realist, he had no truck with such theories. But let us look again at his declaration of belief, because there are unusual things about it which show that his idea of reality, like his idea of knowing, was original. We may find it has avoided the pitfalls of the established ways of thinking on these two subjects, which have led to the curious solution of abolishing reality altogether.

"I declare myself committed to the belief in an external reality gradually accessible to knowing, and I regard all true understanding as an intimation of such a reality, which, being real, may yet reveal itself to our deepened understanding in an indefinite range of unexpected manifestations. I accept the obligation to search for the truth through my own intimations of reality, knowing that there is and can be no strict rule by which my conclusions can be justified."[3]

There are three striking statements in that declaration; the first is "I declare myself committed . . . I accept the obligation" and the next, related to it, is "there can be no strict rule by which my conclusions can be justified". These two are about the way we know, the third is about the kind of reality we know – a reality "which being real, may yet reveal itself . . . in an indefinite range of unexpected manifestations".

What did he mean by commitment (I declare myself committed)? He sometimes cited Christopher Columbus as an example of the faith in reality, the commitment, that is a necessary element in discovery. Columbus sailed away westwards to discover the East, staking his life and reputation on a belief. "His genius," says Polanyi, "lay in taking it literally and as a guide to action that the earth was round, which his contemporaries held vaguely and as a mere matter for speculation."[4] With hindsight we can see that his belief was a small distorted fragment of the truth, but it impelled him to set out in the right direction. Unlike his contemporaries he must have actually felt himself to be treading a round world, and although he got it considerably wrong and never found what he set out to find, he did find the reality of an unknown continent. Columbus embodied for Polanyi the risk and daring involved in discovery, when we commit ourselves to a glimpse of reality which may be mistaken and is certainly incomplete. And if like Columbus we have got hold of a profound aspect of reality, what we discover may not be exactly what we expected but may open up worlds we never dreamed of. Our commitment is a vital part of our discovery.

It is rather hard to think of commitment in this way, it is not how we are accustomed to think of scientists working or truth being found. As we ordinarily use the word, commitment to a particular view is the opposite of open-mindedness. It shuts people up in positions that cannot be reached by argument. Terrorists are committed people; totalitarian regimes are committed to their impervious beliefs. Bukharin denied the independent reality of science because of his commitment to Marxist doctrine. Committed people are responsible for some of the most horrendous aspects of our world, from the Nazi tyranny to Pol Pot's Kampuchea or the ghastly 'People's Temple' of Jim Jones. People committed to a belief do not progress or learn; they remain stuck in primitive irrationality or the bigotry of peculiar sects.

So is not commitment a great danger? Certainly it seemed so to the pioneers of modern science. To them, the obstinate blindness of men committed to traditional beliefs was the enemy of truth. When they thought about the new scientific knowledge, its certainty, rationality and power, so different from the old ways of knowing, one significant characteristic of it seemed to be its impersonal, uncommitted stance, its strict procedures for arriving at the truth without personal feelings or traditional loyalties.

But with Polanyi we have repudiated this impersonal, rule-bound method; it cannot account for discovery. "No rules can account for the way a good idea is found for starting an enquiry, and there are no firm rules either for the verification or the refutation of the proposed solution of a problem."[5] Instead, the scientist is passionately committed; he is committed as a *person* to *reality*, a commitment as daring as Columbus' commitment in sailing round the world. "To accept commitment as the only relation in which we can believe something to be true is to abandon all efforts to find strict criteria of truth and strict procedures for arriving at the truth. A result obtained by applying strict rules mechanically without committing anyone personally can mean nothing to anybody. Desisting henceforth from the vain pursuit of a formalised scientific method, commitment accepts in its place the person of the scientist as the agent responsible for conducting and accrediting scientific discoveries. The scientist's procedure is of course methodical, but his methods are but the maxims of an art which he applies in his own original way to the problem of his choice. Every factual statement embodies some measure of responsible judgment as the personal pole of the commitment in which it is affirmed."[6]

So the sense in which we ordinarily use commitment turns out almost opposite to Polanyi's sense. We may think of those fanatically dedicated to an ideology as committed, but in his sense they are not committed, they are chickening out. What they are all doing is to stay uncommitted by passing the buck, avoiding responsibility, setting up some rigid structure which can be left holding the baby. As Dostoievski's Grand Inquisitor said, man has "no more pressing need than the one to find somebody to whom he can surrender as quickly as possible that gift of freedom with which he, unfortunate creature, was born".[7] In all of us there is in some degree this craving to be able to say, "I followed the correct procedure – it was not my fault".

Thus the Newtonian world view, accepted at first as a liberation from stifling authority into the freedom of reason and truth, has now itself become a formula by which to escape from personal responsibility. And *doubt* has gone the same way. It is deeply ingrained in the modern mind that it is more honest to doubt than to believe. But Polanyi shows that the way of radical scepticism, that of doubting everything that can be doubted, is impossible, and is not practised by those who advocate it. When they claim that they hold no belief that could be doubted, they simply mean that they have decided not to accept the arguments against the beliefs they do hold. There are unprovable assumptions built into our very language and perception, and it is impossible to doubt any belief except from a commitment to a different belief. To doubt everything that could be doubted leads not to truth but to imbecility.

What has happened is that doubting too has become a formula, a refuge from responsibility. "I doubted everything that could be doubted, so what is left is the best we can do for truth." This is like Popper's argument (p42). But in fact, in the practice of science, to doubt an accepted belief *may* be the way to new discovery, but so may holding on to the accepted belief. There is no rule which tells us which is appropriate, only the skilled and daring judgment can choose.

"Some discoveries are prompted by the conviction that something is fundamentally lacking in the existing framework of science, others by the opposite feeling that there is far more implied in it than has yet been realised . . . Vesalius is praised as a hero of scientific scepticism for boldly rejecting the traditional doctrine that the dividing wall of the heart was pierced by invisible passages, but Harvey is acclaimed for the very opposite reason, namely for assuming the presence of invisible passages connecting the arteries with the veins."[8]

True commitment does not allow us to hand over our choice of beliefs to an authority or a rule or a formula, though these are useful tools; the commitment is of *ourselves* to *reality*, and as it is a characteristic of reality that we can never know it completely, such a commitment is always risky. Like Columbus' voyage, it is backing a hunch, venturing out from our known world to find the unknown.

The other part of Polanyi's declaration was about what kind of reality we are committing ourselves to – an infinite, inexhaustible reality that draws us on by its beauty and profundity. We cannot be truly committed to what we think we know all about but only to something of which we are not certain and which we will never know completely, because it is real.

"We make sense of our experience by relying on clues of which we are aware only as pointers to their hidden meaning, this meaning is an aspect of reality, which as such can yet reveal itself in an indeterminate range of future discoveries. *This is in fact my definition of external reality;* reality is something that attracts our attention by clues which harass and beguile our minds into getting ever closer to it, and that, since it owes this attractive power to its independent existence, can always manifest itself in still unexpected ways . . . If we have grasped a true and deep-seated aspect of reality, then its future manifestations will be unexpected confirmations of our present knowledge of it."[9]

Here is a striking definition of reality; according to this we recognise something as real because it draws us on, makes us feel an obligation to search and discover, rewards us by revealing more and unexpected but recognisable meaning. This definition of reality leads on to a very important conclusion, that whatever has more depth of meaning and thus more attractive power to our minds, is more real.

"Is that a dagger that I see before me?" asked Macbeth. The answer must be no, it was a hallucination, because it could only be seen. If it had been a real dagger it could have been grasped, turned over, weighed, used to cut with, handed to someone else, and so on.

"The sight of a solid object indicates to everyone that it has both another side and a hidden interior which we could explore; the sight of another person indicates to us a set of unlimited workings of his mind and body. Perception has this inexhaustible profundity because what we perceive is tacitly understood by us to be an aspect of reality."[10]

A person or a theory is more real than a cobblestone, Polanyi asserts. The mind boggles a bit at this assertion, it seems to fly in the face of common sense, and were we not promised a vindication of common sense? Do we not think of tangible facts like stones as more real than intangible theories, or even persons? It is a challenge, this assertion about theories and cobblestones.[11] It is meant to challenge, for Polanyi never promised us a rose garden, his common sense is not a complacent acceptance of all our common ideas. These *common* ideas got us into trouble in the first place by not making *sense*; if only cobblestones are real then minds are not real and cannot even know about cobblestones. It is the outdated assumptions of the Newtonian world view that have saddled us with this belief in cobblestone reality. "What is most tangible has the least meaning, and it is perverse then to identify the tangible with the real. For to regard a meaningless substratum as the ultimate reality of all things must lead to the conclusion that all things are meaningless. We can avoid this conclusion only if we acknowledge instead that the deepest reality is possessed by higher things that are least tangible."[12]

This is a sort of Copernican revolution that Polanyi has made, and like the Copernican theory it is at first disorientating. Yet common sense now happily accepts that the earth goes round the sun, as Copernicus said it did, and we have a firmer hold on reality through this theory than we had through centuries of observation. The Polanyi view of reality too is surely acceptable to common sense once one has adjusted to it. Take a book for example; would anyone maintain that the printed letters on the page are more real than the meaning, because they are visible and tangible? Clearly the contrary is the case, the reality of the letters depends on the meaning they express. The reality of the meaning does not depend upon the printed words, for it can be expressed in many other visible or audible forms. The excitement of an archaeologist finding an inscription in an unknown script lies in his hope of discovering its meaning; if it were found to be meaningless it would be nothing. And the discovery or knowledge of a person uses the physical tangible reality of the person as a set of clues to the deeper reality of his mind and character.

I once read a science fiction story in which some sinister and mysterious power was removing people and replacing them with exact replicas, like androids, programmed to act and speak in the removed persons' manner. I don't remember why this was being done, but I remember, because it was so vividly conveyed, the creeping horror of the gradual realisation by a wife or a friend that these were not the real people. All the clues were correct, but as they did not flow from the reality of a person they were bound gradually to reveal themselves as false. The special thing, as this story illustrated, about knowing a person is that you know and yet do not know what he will do or say, how he will look, in new circumstances. If you know someone very well you may say, "That's just the sort of thing he would do!" – or you say, "He would never do such a cruel or dishonourable thing". Because he is a person you can never know precisely what he will do, but when he has done it you can say – "Yes, that is in character; that's just like him". His action both confirms and modifies or deepens your knowledge of him. It's like hearing a Mozart sonata you have never heard before; it's Mozart, it couldn't be anything else. Had you known before you heard it that it was Mozart you could not have predicted exactly what it would be, but you recognise it without doubt, and having heard it you know Mozart better.

Reality is like that, Polanyi says. Even the cobblestones reality of the physical world has a real coherence, so that a theory such as Copernicus' gets a hold on reality which will reveal more, unpredictably yet recognisably. A scientific theory is called *objective* or true because it grasps a coherence in reality; its implications have an unknown range and scope.

And the reality of a mind or a person is more real because it has much more internal coherence and greater richness of consequences, we know it more deeply because more personally. This Polanyi revolution goes against some of our habits of thought, but makes sense once we feel able to accept it, since we really always have basically believed in the reality of persons, until science taught us that we could not respectably do so. We can only go along with the revolution and fully believe again if we can accept that there are valid ways of knowing the reality of persons and intangible things, and so Polanyi has been leading us towards such acceptance with his account of tacit knowing and commitment. He has shown these ways of knowing to be essential to science itself. He used another word for the kind of knowing that science has tended to discredit; the word is *indwelling*. It expresses the relation of the knower to the tacit particulars which are clues to the reality he is seeking to know. Its meaning could be illustrated by this story, which appeared in a history of the Oxford University Press compiled to celebrate the Press's 500 years of publishing. An experienced compositor at the Press was setting up a text of the Rig Veda; he knew no Sanskrit, but he pointed out where he thought there must be a mistake in the text. How could he know? He had got used to the regular patterns of the arm movements that he made as his hand moved from one compartment to another to pick up the type, and he was alerted by a movement that was different. He realised that this particular movement must indicate a combination of letters so unusual that it was most unlikely to be anything but an error, and he was right.

There was explicit reasoning in his conclusion, but what led him to notice the mistake was his bodily awareness of a complex and varied rhythm, and of a sudden change in this rhythm. An inexperienced compositor concentrating on each letter would not have noticed, for he would not have felt the pattern to which this movement was an exception. This man could be said to have been *indwelling* in his arm movements and attending *from* them to something outside which he believed to have meaning. He did not know the meaning, but he sensed when the pattern of movements lost contact with it.

Our own body, says Polanyi, is "the only assembly of things known almost exclusively by relying on our awareness of them for attending to something else".[13] We do not normally experience our body as an object, but as making sense of the outside world. "To be aware of our body in terms of the things we know and do is to feel alive. This awareness is an essential part of our existence as sensuous active persons."[14]

The compositor story is simply a striking instance of this faculty that we all have of dwelling in our body, its feelings, movements and capacities, and using all these as clues to an outside reality. The 'body' that we dwell in is not just the body that a dissecting student would see if he were cutting us up after death; it is the whole complex of habits, aptitudes, skills and awareness that we have built up – as Piaget showed – ever since our first days of life, by interacting interestedly and purposefully with our environment. This 'body' is in fact myself, my individual personal self, nurtured by my environment and grown by my activity. Dwelling in it is my only means of knowing the world. The boundaries of this self are not fixed, but changing. Consider Piaget's account of how the child incorporates his growing skills and experience into his body of inarticulate knowledge of how things work. All the mastery and understanding that he is building into his schemata become part of himself; part of his body of knowledge and his tool for grasping more. When he begins to speak and understand language, this too becomes part of himself. He is at the same time entering into the common inheritance of his parents and community, by acquiring their language, and giving it his own individual stamp as he uses it, for nobody speaks or understands words in quite the same way. There is some individuality, some personal specialness, in the language incorporated into his body of knowledge.

As the child grows he learns to adjust his own sense of words to the general sense, but there is always some contribution of his own in his use of the language. We treasure a child's exploring use of words because, in trying to find a word for a new thing he may make a vivid analogy. "Daddy is going to climb that tree and pick the pears," says his mother, "But how will Daddy get up the handle?" asks the three-year-old, conveying perfectly the problem of the straight unbranched trunk which separates Daddy on the ground from the round bower of branches at the top. In his body of language the saucepan with its long handle offers itself as a bridge from the known to the unknown but similar. Language incorporated in him, in which he dwells, enlarges his self as he uses it as his tool for grasping the world. He is acting just like the scientist who describes light as waves or particles, reaching out from known to unknown but somehow similar conceptions. In this reaching a person changes and extends himself into external reality.

We learn to extend ourselves in many ways by the use of hammers, screwdrivers, paintbrushes, microscopes, telescopes, theories, books, maps, diagrams. When a man first handles any of these he has to concentrate on it and be aware of it as an object, but as soon as he has acquired the skill of using it he no longer concentrates on it, but on what he is seeing or doing with it. The use of it has become 'second nature', he has extended himself into it and dwells in it.

"Read, mark, learn and inwardly digest" says the Prayer Book, and the Polanyi idea of indwelling gives a firmer outline to the meaning of 'inwardly digest'. Knowledge that has not been digested and made a part of the self is inert knowledge. Inwardly digested it is in organic relationship with the rest of the person's body of knowledge and becomes an extension of the self, a tool for further exploration of reality.

Our whole cultural heritage in which we grow up, the language, the moral values, the artistic standards, the ways of behaving and dressing and looking at the world – all this is gradually taken into ourselves, or we come to dwell in it, and to use it as our means of handling and understanding the world. It is futile to think we could get to any understanding of the world except by starting from the particular inheritance in which we happen to have been brought up, any more than we could learn language without learning a particular language, or than a child can get a religious sense except through being nurtured in a particular religion.

Does this not impose limitations on our power of knowing the real world? Yes, being a particular person or belonging to a particular culture does limit our vision, but without these limitations there is no vision. Only by using the senses that we have, only by dwelling in the culture in which we are, can we come to transcend these limitations.

Another sort of extension of ourselves is found in imaginative sympathy. Starting from the self-centred world of childhood, we can learn to indwell in other people's minds and feelings and thus to know them as real people. This is what Simone Weil called 'creative attention' given by one person to another. Polanyi took the idea of indwelling from theories of history which maintain that we come to understand history by dwelling in the actions of historical figures, 'getting inside their skin' feeling their situation as they felt it and reliving the workings of their minds.[15]

But the studies of history in which Polanyi found the idea of 'indwelling' sharply distinguished this kind of knowledge, needed for the understanding of history, from the impersonal factual knowledge which they believed to be the sole method of science. Polanyi, however, saw 'indwelling' in all kinds of knowledge. He believed the whole range, from physics up to the study of man, to involve personal indwelling in tacit particulars. The part played by personal involvement increases as we ascend the scale, but there is no sharp division, rather a gradual intensification of the personal element.

The idea of *indwelling* gives a firmer outline to the idea of *commitment*. If we must indwell in the clues we perceive, using them as an extension of ourselves and a tool for discovering more, we have to commit ourselves to them. In using any kind of tool or apparatus, you cannot at the same time concentrate on it to test it, and use it as an extension of yourself to deal with other things. To use it as a tool you must not attend to it but attend *from* it to the things you are dealing with, so that in using it you have to commit yourself to it. Such commitment involves the risk of being wrong. One very matter of fact way in which scientists have to commit themselves is in their choice of a problem. At some point the decision must be made to commit scarce resources of time and money to this piece of research rather than that, as Columbus had to decide in which direction to sail. If the hunch is mistaken, the time and resources will be wasted. A scientist with a general commitment to truth will accept this, but he cannot *wish* to be proved wrong. He is committed emotionally as well as financially and must suffer if his hunch proves an illusion, just as he will rejoice if it proves right.

To state as Polanyi does that one is committed and under obligation to search for the truth, is to state an ultimate belief which is not provable. Is it any different then from Popper's admission that science rests on 'faith in quite hazy ideas'? Yes it is different because Popper then tries to construct science on rules as if it were not resting on this faith, while to Polanyi the faith, which is not just an intellectual acceptance but a risky commitment of the whole person, is an integral part of knowledge. This commitment is the link between the personal aspect of knowledge in which it is my knowledge, and the universal aspect in which it is knowledge of reality, valid for anyone. My commitment is from where I am, what I am, to a reality beyond myself. It is the difference between personal and subjective.

Commitment, conscience, responsibility are words that Polanyi uses which seem to belong more to morals than to science. This is indeed part of his theme, that man's moral nature is involved in knowing as much as in doing. If this is so, the gap between science and other kinds of knowing disappears. The English critic F. R. Leavis has written of the role of personal responsibility in literature, relating it specifically to what Polanyi says about responsibility in science. "Without creativity, there is no apprehension of the real, but (that) if experience is necessarily creative, the creativity, as every great artist testifies, is not arbitrary, it is self dedication to a reality that we have to discover, knowing that discovery will at best be qualified by misapprehension and certainly incomplete." "All through, to be creative is to assert responsibility."[16] Polanyi makes the same point when writing about originality.

Originality is personal but not subjective, it seeks by personal choice a truth which is impersonally given. He found Luther's declaration "Here I stand, I can do no other" an example of the framework of commitment in which the personal and the universal are related. "A person asserts his rational independence by obeying the dictates of his own conscience."[17]

A judge is acting in this spirit when he has to decide a case not covered by the existing rules. In his decision he has to *find* the law. It is his personal decision, yet in it he is responsible to the interests of *justice*, excluding any subjectivity. "The freedom of the subjective person to do as he pleases is overruled by the freedom of the responsible person to do as he must."[18]

There is a paradox about the originality of discovery. If the judge has to *find* the law, this implies it is there already, which of course it isn't in any obvious sense. Robert Pirsig made play with it in his book, asking what it meant to say Newton *discovered* the laws of gravity. Did it mean "the disembodied words of Sir Isaac Newton were sitting in the middle of nowhere billions of years before he was born and that magically he *discovered* them".[19] This of course is absurd, but it's equally absurd to say Newton *invented* the laws of gravity.

Such paradoxes arise, Polanyi says, when we look non-committally at the fragments of a commitment. "If we ask whether Euclid's theorems existed before they were discovered, the answer is obviously No, in the same sense as we would say that Shakespeare's sonnets did not exist before he wrote them. But we cannot therefore say that the truth of geometry or the beauty of poetry came into existence at any particular place and time, for these constitute the universal pole of our appreciation which cannot be observed non-committally like objects in space and time."[20] Truth being a disciplined as well as passionate response to reality by a person, cannot be seen apart from such a response. Bertrand's Russell's 'correspondence theory of truth' makes truth the correspondence of my thought to an existing fact – but who can say what is an existing fact? There is no way of peering round the screen of what I believe true and what you believe true, to see a 'fact' with which to compare our beliefs. So philosophers who cannot accept the sort of account of knowledge that Polanyi gives, by personal commitment and indwelling, are driven to use various devices to avoid any mention of reality; they may describe scientific truths as 'working hypotheses', a convenient shorthand, or they may act on their beliefs while denying that they hold them.

They have to do this while they remain stuck in the assumptions of the Newtonian world view, which do not fit modern science. There is no limited fixed truth about the natural order which can be finally known, there are not two separate substances called mind and matter, and there is no clear and unchanging knowledge. Yet there *is* knowledge, there is truth, science is authoritative. So the sureness of impersonal tests and rules has to be replaced by what Polanyi calls a 'society of Explorers' where the committed person in an organically functioning community learns his skills from its traditions in order to make his own contact with reality. Within this society a person's commitment stretches him between the knowledge already held in tradition and the new shape of reality he discerns. Neither the existential idea of completely free choice, nor the authoritarian idea of standard tests can provide this cutting edge to reality.

Readers of Thomas Kuhn's book – *The Structure of Scientific Revolutions* will notice some kinship between his ideas and some of Polanyi's, and Kuhn acknowledged his debt to Polanyi. But Kuhn's thesis is concerned with only a small part of Polanyi's subject. The Paradigm in Kuhn's theory is like Polanyi's account of the role of authority and tradition in science. They agree about the acceptance of the premises and methods of science, the need of a tradition resistant to change, and the way that a new paradigm is accepted not by proof but by 'conversion' as scientists come to find it more satisfying than the old one. Kuhn even talks about 'faith' being needed for scientific discovery – but faith in what? Since at the end Kuhn disclaims the notion of *truth* or of the progressive discovery of *reality* and sees science evolving as Darwin saw life evolving, from one form to another but not *towards* anything. He has none of Polanyi's vision of life and mind striving towards deeper meaning.

This affects his use of 'tacit knowledge' which he mentions but cannot fully believe in, since he does not consider how we know life or minds, and misses out the whole area of a hierarchy of levels and our recognition of achievement in living beings.

For instance, in the Postscript to his book he deals with the way we recognise members of a class, which to Polanyi was an example of tacit knowing, dwelling in our knowledge of the members of the group and attending from these to their joint focal meaning. Kuhn agrees that such recognition is not done by rules and criteria, but he is scared of the wildness of an unspecifiable *skill* such as Polanyi's tacit knowing, so he insists the process is not less systematic or less analysable than knowledge by rules and criteria – "our seeing a situation as like ones we have encountered before must be the result of neural processing, fully governed by physical and chemical laws".

So with Kuhn we have escaped from rules only to be tied down more firmly by physical and chemical laws. We have no control over our recognition, we cannot choose to see things in a new way. But we can, in Polanyi's understanding, *learn* the skill of seeing in a new way, by straining to see a new pattern, in the faith that there is a reality which can thus be discovered.

Notes to Chapter V

1. *Science, Faith & Society* p.23
2. see p.21 above
3. *Knowing and Being* p.133
4. *Personal Knowledge* p.277
5. *Knowing and Being* p.4
6. *Personal Knowledge* p.311
7. *The Brothers Karamazov* Everyman ed. 1927 p.260
8. *Personal Knowledge* p.277
9. 'The Unaccountable Element in Science'. *Philosophy* vol XXXVIII no 139 p.13
10. *Meaning* p.188
11. see Marjorie Grene, *The Knower and the Known*, chapter on 'The Multiplicity of Forms'.
12. 'On the Modern Mind' *Encounter* 24, 1965, p.4. Compare *The Tacit Dimension* p.33
13. *Knowing and Being* p.147
14. *The Study of Man* p.31
15. W. Dilthey; R. G. Collingwood. See *Knowing and Being* p.166, *The Tacit Dimension* p.16, *The Study of Man* p.100
16. *Nor Shall My Sword* p.12
17. *Personal Knowledge* p.302
18. *Personal Knowledge* p.309
19. *Zen and the Art of Motorcycle Maintenance* p.34
20. *Personal Knowledge* p.396

CHAPTER VI

TRUTH AND THE FREE SOCIETY

Everyman, in the old play, had a friend called Fellowship. The priests taught Everyman that Fellowship was a worthless rascally friend. Science ignores him.

This chapter is about how Everyman needs Fellowship, since truth can only be pursued in a Society of Explorers.

Fellowship comes back to go with Everyman on his quest.

POLANYI has abandoned "all efforts to find strict criteria of truth and strict procedures for arriving at the truth".[1] Instead, the scientist as a person committed to reality, using his responsible judgment, is the criterion of valid knowledge. But how do we know a particular scientist *is* committed and responsible? That his daring is not just ignorant rashness, more like Icarus than Columbus? Because he is a member of the community of science. Thinking about this community and how it works, about the kind of freedom the scientist needs and what are the conditions of this freedom, Polanyi came to very definite conclusions about freedom in political and national terms.

He started from his own experience of scientific work in a small group. He knew what it was like to work closely with a group of scientific collaborators who knew each other well. "Here he was gaining experience of working in a trusting but critical team; experience of what he later called the 'conviviality' of intellectual work – which was to provide an essential element in his subsequent thought about the process of discovery."[2] Also in his subsequent thought about democracy and freedom.

Not only in the small group of scientists working together on a problem, but in the whole worldwide body of scientists, and the way that science as a whole organises itself, he found illumination about freedom and the pursuit of truth.

"In the free co-operation of independent scientists," he wrote,[3] "we shall find a highly simplified model of a free society, which presents in isolation certain basic features which are more difficult to identify within the comprehensive functions of a national body."

Polanyi started from the certainty that science needs freedom, yet when he looked at the way science actually works he came upon an often unrecognised fact, that the freedom of a scientist is by no means unlimited. Scientists are under authority, the authority of the scientific community in its pursuit of truth.

At the beginning of the era of modern science, scientists were everywhere doing battle against authority. The authority of Aristotle, the authority of the church, were age-old barriers that had to be broken through; authority was the enemy of progress, and this tradition has persisted, that authority is the enemy of truth just as it was for Galileo, for Bacon, for Darwin. "The triumphs of science," wrote Bertrand Russell, "are due to the substitution of observation and inference for authority. Every attempt to revive authority in intellectual matters is a retrograde step."[4]

Polanyi knew that science must be free from *external* authority, but he reached the conclusion that both authority and tradition are vital elements of the free community of science, and this is a finding that he applied to his picture of the free society. The early scientists were right in their time, he says, but "when we reject today the interference of political or religious authorities with the pursuit of truth, we must do it in the name of the established scientific authority which safeguards the pursuit of science".[5]

Here then are the main points he brings out about the community of science.[6] The scientific community is a reality. Scientists everywhere, choosing and pursuing their own problems, are co-operating in a close, continuous way. Science would grind to a halt if scientists did not know what other scientists were doing, and take account of it. Polanyi calls their co-operation a co-ordination by mutual adjustment of independent initiatives. It is a form of *spontaneous organisation*, like that among a group of people working on a huge jigsaw puzzle, where each person has a number of pieces to fit in and is watching what all the others are doing so as to use opportunities to the maximum. This is the set-up that works best, and assures the most efficient possible use of resources for scientific progress. Any one central authority trying to direct the process would paralyse the co-operation. In this free setting each scientist finds a problem not too easy and not too hard for him, and one to which his previous experience draws him. Thus he can be fully stretched and working at the height of his capacity.

But he is under authority, for the professional standards of science put limits to the problems he can choose. His contribution will not be allowed if it is considered scientifically unsound. Its scientific value will be judged in terms of its accuracy, its importance and its intrinsic interest. Its originality will also count for a great deal; paradoxically, because this means it has got to conform to scientific orthodoxy but yet will get the highest praise if it considerably departs from the orthodox line. How can this be? "This internal tension is essential in guiding and motivating scientific work. The professional standards of science must impose a framework of discipline and at the same time encourage rebellion against it . . . Thus the authority of scientific opinion enforces the teachings of science in general for the very purpose of fostering their subversion in particular."[7] In Piaget's terms, the scientific 'schema' must be strong as well as open, in order to test and digest new insights.

Having broken through the rigidity of an outside authority,

science cannot give up its own authority and let things in piecemeal, indiscriminately, otherwise its relation to reality dissolves, for piecemeal reality is meaningless. There can be no progressing body of knowledge that is not a real whole of which the parts affect each other; in which a contradiction sets up tension – as in the healthy schema of an individual.

Who exercises this authority? No one scientist knows enough of the vast area of scientific knowledge to do this, but each knows his own patch and enough of the neighbouring patches to have a good judgment about the standard of what is going on in them, and so the whole area can be covered by a network of overlapping expertise, which can ensure that the same sort of standard will be maintained in all the various branches of science, in spite of the great differences in their subject matter and methods.

The power of this network of authority is very great. It controls appointments to university posts, the acceptance or rejection of papers by journals, even science teaching in schools. Money goes to one centre rather than another by its recommendation. No outside body can know, as this does, where the growing points of scientific knowledge are at the moment; which branches are nearing a break-through to an important new insight, who are the high-flyers in each branch.

Scientific opinion represented by this network may be mistaken. It may suppress a valuable new idea. Polanyi gives instances of major discoveries to which this happened. "It took eleven years for the quantum theory, discovered by Planck in 1900, to gain final acceptance. Yet by the time another thirty years had passed, Planck's position in science was approaching that hitherto accorded only to Newton."[8] And a discovery of Polanyi's own, the discovery about the adsorption of gases that was quoted in Chapter I, was rejected for even longer before being vindicated. Yet this authority of the scientific community is absolutely necessary, and the risk of mistakes has to be taken. "Only the discipline imposed by an effective scientific opinion can prevent the adulteration of science by cranks and dabblers. In parts of the world where no sound and authoritative scientific opinion is established, research stagnates for lack of stimulus, while unsound reputations grow up based on commonplace achievements or mere empty boasts. Politics and business play havoc with appointments and the granting of subsidies for research; journals are made unreadable by including much trash."[9]

The existence of this community of science is an amazing fact. There are times and places where it does not show itself, as where governments interfere or the right conditions have not arisen. But in the main it works, better than any possible alternative. Here is a world-wide community open to anyone whose skill and dedication to truth makes him a scientist. It has no elected or appointed rulers, yet it manages its own affairs impartially and efficiently and makes possible the fantastic range of scientific achievements which forms our modern world. In this community the body of science supports and judges the work of individual scientists, imposing conformity and encouraging non-conformity with such general sureness that scientific thought lives and progresses.

Are scientists then superhuman? No, but there are certain conditions which make this kind of functioning possible. The members believe in a common truth, ultimately self-consistent, which they are pursuing. And they know that this truth is inexhaustible and can always be understood more deeply; known more comprehensively. No one of them can think he has the final answer and try to keep others from discovering other possibilities. They are only members because they are bitten with the bug of pursuing the never-ending truth. So the authority of the scientific community over its individual members is not that of a ruler who claims to know best, nor is it that of a majority suppressing a dissident minority. Nor does it rest on the fact that any member of the community could at any time repeat any of the experiments that have been made and satisfy himself of the result. He could not; science is so vast and varied that members of one branch could not possibly undertake the experiments that have been done in another, and if they could, and got a different result, they would assume they had made a mistake. The authority is a product of the way scientists work together.

The community depends on mutual trust, on confidence that other members are as devoted to truth as oneself. Scientists cannot possibly only accept new theories on experimental evidence, as the popular view of science suggests; they accept them by trusting the judgments of those in a position to judge, and of scientific opinion as a whole. Polanyi gives examples of theories that have had a lot of evidence to support them but have been rejected out of hand by the scientific community as being scientifically implausible. The community is continually making delicate value judgments in rejecting, accepting and rewarding the work of scientist. In joining the community each scientist accepts the totality of these judgments and learns in his turn the skill of sharing in their making.

"Thus, the standards of scientific merit are seen to be transmitted from generation to generation . . . in the same way as artistic, moral or legal traditions are transmitted. We may conclude therefore that the appreciation of scientific merit too is based on a tradition which succeeding generations accept and develop as their own scientific opinion. This conclusion gains important support from the fact that the methods of scientific enquiry cannot be explicitly formulated and hence can be transmitted only in the same way as an art, by the affiliation of apprentices to a master. The authority of science is essentially traditional. *But this tradition upholds an authority which cultivates originality.*"[10]

You see how the way we know is the basis of this view. The orthodox teaching about science is that nothing is to be accepted but those facts which rest on clear experimental evidence which could be repeated at will, and that leaves no room for tradition. Tradition is almost a dirty word now, and 'the traditional wisdom' is a sneer at what is thought of as a collection of old saws, while liberty, independence of thought, means complete repudiation of authority. Yet here is Polanyi showing how science itself cannot live except in the traditions of a community united by trust and by love of truth and acceptance of authority. If new insights in science arise by indwelling in our tacit knowledge and sensing new coherence in it, and if this is a skill which cannot be exactly specified but has to be learnt from a master, then without tradition and authority there will be no new discovery.

Polanyi offered this astonishing worldwide community of science as a simplified model of a free society, in which some of the principles of freedom would show up. The relation of freedom to tradition and authority is the feature to which he drew special attention. He recalled the old argument over the French Revolution, when Burke warned that such a complete break with tradition as France had made could only lead to despotism, while Tom Paine was passionately proclaiming the right of each new generation to self-determination. The model of the scientific community that Polanyi has drawn shows a way of transcending the argument between Burke and Paine; for it shows, like Burke, that freedom must be rooted in tradition, but it shows tradition as the only real basis for radical change.

So freedom in political terms, on which freedom in science

depends, has certain conditions. "Science cannot be free," Polanyi had written to John Baker,[11] "in a state formed as a sovereign master of the community's fate, but only under a state pledged to the guardianship of *law, custom and of our social heritage* in general, to the further advancement of which – *on the lines of the universal ideas underlying it* – the community is dedicated."[12] Of course the principles are not so clear on the national scale, for no nation has the same sort of coherence as the community of science. A nation has to include everyone, and that means it must allow for people with very different aims and it must use compulsion to safeguard law and order. But Polanyi's comparison with the Republic of Science is an argument for the least possible central control of objectives. The Soviet state was quite sure of its objectives and so could claim to set the objectives of its members, but a state which recognises to some degree the infinite nature of truth and other values, and the personal and 'convivial' way in which they are gained, will accept that it can never know exactly what its objectives ought to be, for it will never know what new aspect of reality may appear in the future. Its function will be to safeguard the free centres within it – universities, churches, professional and voluntary associations – which nurture the trust and mutual co-operation and dedication to truth without which the free society could not exist. In these, as in the community of science, tradition and authority give an apprenticeship to men who will later learn to challenge the tradition in the name of the universal ideas underlying it.

Polanyi often cited the way that law develops and maintains its standards as a parallel to the way science advances. The tension between tradition and new interpretation is very much part of the legal scene. A leader in *The Times* about Lord Denning began – "Among the many desiderata for a good legal system is that the law should be reasonably certain in its contents and application. The individual coming to the courts should know that his case will be considered according to principles which are ascertainable and constant. At the same time, however, undue rigidity in conformity with precedent leads to ossification of the law and ultimately to the commission of injustice".

Voluntary societies for all sorts of aims, for art and literature and social service, anti-vivisection societies and societies for stamp-collectors and pigeon-fanciers and philosophers, as well as churches and trade unions and Quaker meetings – all these have in some degree the scope for freedom and spontaneous organisation that

Polanyi describes in science, and are thus training grounds for citizens of a free society. Some countries are particularly rich in such voluntary associations for all manner of purposes ranging from the wise and important to the eccentric and trivial. A state that has this rich variety of independent associations has a strength to its freedom, and can to some extent be like the society of science in the way it handles the societies within it. It is significant that the beginning of the Nazi domination of Germany was the destruction of such associations.[13] Society was atomised, social structure destroyed and trust between people broken down. "There was no more social life, you couldn't even have a bowling club." Men had to choose between solitude and the mass relationship of a national organisation. It was a failure of perception that let this happen. No one saw what was coming about, for each little group destroyed was a small thing, but "when it's too late, it's too late". Then one could see what was lost, and how freedom only lived in the traditions of free associations. There is a test, Polanyi says, "which proves that all such groups effectively foster the intrinsic power of thought. For these circles, these professional associations – some perhaps no more than coteries of mutual admiration – are feared and hated by modern totalitarian rulers . . . They are feared more than are scientific associations, because the truth of literature and poetry, of history and political thought, of philosophy, morality and legal principles, is more vital than the truth of science. This is why the independent cultivation of such truth has proved an intolerable menace to modern tyranny".[14]

A recent example: Oxford philosophers visiting the officially disapproved Czech philosopher Tomin to take part in philosophic discussions in his flat, were expelled from the country with no reasons given. A leader in *The Times* commented,[15] "What annoyed the Czechoslovak authorities had nothing to do with visas or regulations or assemblies. Their annoyance derives from their fear that their system cannot survive any unauthorised exercise of the human spirit". These societies are the ground where the practice of democracy may be tacitly absorbed. A democratic style of life in a free society is an art, and we have seen that the principles of an art are more truly embodied in its practice than in its maxims. We can see, therefore, why it is so difficult to export democracy. The maxims can be exported, new independent countries can be given a democratic constitution, a voting system, a parliament building; but the tacit components cannot be exported because no one can specify them; no one can learn them except by tradition.[16]

I saw this vividly demonstrated in the Congo (Zaire) at the time of its independence. We sat in a gallery watching the first meeting of the Congolese parliament. It was a historic occasion and quite moving; we saw the traditional procedures and said to each other that a new democracy was taking its first steps before our eyes. But no previous experience of responsibility had been allowed to the Congolese; at the time of independence there was not a single qualified Congolese engineer, army officer, doctor, or higher civil servant, so the democratic procedure was an empty form; a facade with no real coherence behind it; and fell to pieces at the first blow. There was no tacit knowledge of democratic life on which to build.

At the beginning of this chapter the question was raised – if knowledge rests on no impersonal test but on the skill and responsibility of persons, how can it be reliable? Now we begin to see how scientific knowledge is reliable partly because the persons who seek and achieve this knowledge are supported and disciplined by the scientific community of which they are members. The business of this community, dedicated to the pursuit of scientific truth, is to preserve the structure of science, the rules of valid method and the accepted premises, while at the same time encouraging creative dissent; to preserve, that is, the balance of assimilation and accommodation which, for a society as for Piaget's child, is the means of contact with reality.

The same is true for other kinds of knowledge; justice is maintained within a legal community which builds up and codifies the structure of law, while allowing its modification by new decisions which are allowed to be in the spirit of justice. Historians are in the same sort of way supported and disciplined by the community of historians, moral traditions are similarly built up, preserved and upheld by a moral community while being modified by the new moral insights of persons within the community. Art and music flourish in the same way in communities dedicated to these values, upholding the traditions and styles that have meaning for that community while accepting creative changes initiated by persons within it.

Such communities can only exist within a society which respects their work and allows them freedom to pursue it; conversely there can only be a free society if there are within it these communities dedicating their freedom to the pursuit of the various values men live by. So the principles which can be seen in the community of science apply also in other communities.

Here two examples may provide, one in the political and one in the moral field, analogies with the scientific community as Polanyi has described it. They may thus show how the same sort of lively tension between tradition and innovation can operate in these two fields as in the scientific field.

First the political example, from the Putney Debates.[17] In this remarkable document are preserved the very words in which the men of Cromwell's army argued out what sort of government England should have. It was a unique moment when the ways they thought about government were forced to the surface of men's minds as perhaps never before. They were pressed by the fresh memory of the breakdown of government in the war, and by the responsibility of deciding what should be the way of the future for their country. Like scientists, they had a common faith and purpose, and a common tradition; their religion. They believed in God's purposes and in the individual conscience as the means of knowing God's will. What they were debating was how the purposes of God were to be realised in the organisation of the state, and how individual consciences which gave different views were to be reconciled. For they believed in the infinity of God's will, so that no one's understanding of it was to be dismissed; there was always more to learn about it. "I am verily persuaded," said one, "that the Lord hath more truth yet to break forth out of his holy word."

This Puritan belief in the liberty of conscience, says Professor Woodhouse, the editor of the Debates, went along with belief in the strength of truth. "This experimental spirit, this eager quest of truth, with the attendant confidence in truth's power to guard itself and to prevail if given an open field, is the deepest and most abiding element in the Puritan campaign for liberty of conscience," he says, and the words he uses of it, "An attitude tentative, yet confident and expectant," could well apply to science.

When Colonel Goffe said,[18] "If the Lord hath spoken to us, I pray God keep us from that sin, that we do not hearken to the voice of the Lord," Cromwell's reply would do well, with a few changes of words, in the scientific community. "I shall not be unwilling to hear God speaking in any man . . . But I shall speak a word in that which Lt.-Colonel Goffe said . . . that at such a meeting as this we should wait upon God and hearken to the voice of God speaking in any of us. I confess it is an high duty, but when anything is spoken as from God, I think the rule is, Let the rest judge. It is left to me to judge for my own satisfaction, and the satisfaction of others, whether it be of the Lord or not, and I do no more. I do not judge conclusively, negatively, that it was not of the Lord, but I do desire to submit it to all your judgments whether it be of the Lord or not . . . Truly we have heard many speaking to us, and I cannot but think that in many of those things God hath spoken to us. I cannot but think that in most that have spoke there hath been something of God laid forth to us, and yet there have been several contradictions in what hath been spoken. *But certainly God is not the author of contradictions* . . . when we have no other more particular impressions of the power of God going forth with us, I think that this law and this word speaking within us which truly is in everyman who hath the spirit of God, we are to have regard to. And this to me seems to be very clear, how we are to judge of the apprehension of men as to particular cases, whether it be of God or no. When it doth not carry its evidence with it, of the power of God to convince us clearly, our best way is to judge the conformity or disformity of it with the law written within us, which is the law of the spirit of God, the mind of God, the mind of Christ . . . for my part I do not know any outward evidence of what proceeds from the Spirit of God more clear than this, the appearance of meekness and gentleness and mercy and patience and forbearance and love, and desire to do good to all, and to destroy none that can be saved . . . where I do see this, where I do see men speaking according to this law which I am sure is the law of the Spirit of Life, I am satisfied . . . On the other hand, I think that he that would decline the doing of justice where there is no place for mercy, and the exercise of the way of force for the safety of the kingdom, where there is no other way to save it, and would decline these out of the apprehensions and difficulties in it, doth lead us from that which is the law of the Spirit of Life, the law written in our hearts."

Isn't it remarkable how much in that is comparable to the scientific spirit as set out by Polanyi? There is the recognition of each person's will to find the truth, and each person's access to the truth of God's purpose, but also the referring of this individual insight to the common tradition and judgment. The object of this *not* being to reach a majority decision, but to discover what all believed to be discoverable, by the interaction of their individual insights. There is the general belief in a truth existing independent of men, but also the faith that this has to be interpreted and applied by individual and common judgment, for there is no rule. Because you believe in the law it does not follow that there is a standard way to find the right application. "We ought," said Cromwell, "to consider the consequences, and God hath given us our reason that we may do this." The individual conscience which gave individual insights was comparable to the intuition of the original scientist, and the acceptance of his insight as valid was not automatic but subject to the authority of the religious community – "Let the rest judge".

It is interesting to contrast this spirit, which balanced individual insight against the reason and tradition of the community, with the extreme individualism that emerged about the same time in sects like the Ranters.[19] The Ranters were like Dostoievski's hero in *Crime and Punishment*, believing themselves not bound by law. They aimed at the dissolution of all human society and denied "the necessity of Civil and Moral righteousness". "Sin is a name without substance." "Be not so horridly, hellishly, impudently wicked," said one, "as to judge what is sinne, what not, what evil, what not, what blasphemy and what not . . . Sin and transgression is finished." For them, freedom meant doing just what you choose and they became a great nuisance, but the Quakers seem to have argued with them and sometimes converted them. "This principle of truth overthrows their principle," said Justice Hotham to George Fox, and their principle was uncontrolled individualism, as the Quaker doctrine of the "Inner Light", which gives divine guidance to each individual, might be without the Society of Friends.

To turn to the moral example – this again is a simpler example than can easily be found in modern society for it is taken from a small close-knit moral community, but it shows basic features which can be traced in more complex settings.

A Swedish farmer is ploughing his fields and thinking. He has a serious problem. His young betrothed is about to be released from prison and he has to decide what to do about her.

This is the opening of Selma Lagerlof's book *Jerusalem*, which is about real historical events but is cast in a fictional form. It is a work of art and cannot be abridged, but I want briefly to tell this first incident because it embodies so beautifully the meaning of a moral community, its traditions and authority and its response to a new view of moral truth.

The story is set in the last century, and according to the old custom then prevailing the families had arranged the marriage, and the girl, unloving, had come to live in the dour, silent household of the man she was to marry. The wedding would be held later, when they could afford it. But it was a bad year on the farm, and the wedding was still to come when their baby was born; the girl in desperate bitterness killed it. Both families, and the whole community, condemned her, and the man was expected to have nothing more to do with such a wicked woman. As he ploughs, the young farmer wishes he could consult his dead father, a man of high moral authority known to all as Great Ingmar. The young man imagines himself arriving in heaven and finding his father and all the old Ingmars sitting round; they listen while he lays his problem before them. They seem to condemn the girl, but they have really no answer; such a thing has never happened to an Ingmar before. Though young Ingmar gets no answer, he begins to be sure what he must do, though he still does not know if he will be strong enough to do it; it seems so hard.

He goes to meet the girl on the day of her release, still not knowing. They drive homewards in miserable doubt and misunderstanding, and encounter at once the bitter hostility of the old mother, and the disapproval of the community. Angry and desperate he takes her away again. It will never do, they both see; it is impossible. But suddenly, accidentally, the truth emerges that now they do care about each other, suddenly they understand each other and find that nothing else matters at all. He drives her home again happy and confident, to find that there has been a change there too; they are met with acceptance and rejoicing. Young Ingmar has made a true creative moral decision, and from then on the neighbours begin to call him "Great Ingmar" like his father.

This story of a moral discovery is strikingly similar to Polanyi's account of how scientific discoveries are made, and how they relate to the tradition and authority of the scientific community.

First there is the problem. Part of the scientific genius is the choice of a good problem. Here the problem did not have to be found, it was pressing on the man; yet he still had to recognise it as a problem. No one else did; to them, there was a perfectly satisfactory traditional solution. But he felt it as a problem and was absorbed in it, labouring with it, passionately involved, just as the scientist is with his problem.

Then the tradition; the man is set in his tradition so firmly that he cannot think outside it. So is the scientist, Polanyi says, set in the tradition of the scientific community, thinking in its terms and upholding its values. He can only criticise it from within, by seeing where its spirit is not truly expressed in its current beliefs; appealing from these beliefs to their deeper meaning. In this he is upheld by the faith that the beliefs of his tradition are aiming at a truth which is discoverable; that they are partial expressions of a rationality sensed in the universe.

Just so young Ingmar in the story, set in the tradition of his community, is upheld by sensing a universal intent in the tradition. He has the faith, passed on in the tradition, that there is a right course of action and that he ought to find it. "The Ingmars have always walked in the ways of God." His father's prestige in the community had been based on the creative interpretation of the traditional morality; on knowing the right thing to do in circumstances where there was no precedent. Ingmar is searching for the same wisdom. His arguments with himself show that he is aware that although he has walked in the ways of tradition he has not walked in the ways of God; he feels partly to blame for what has happened.

He explores the tradition and finds no definite answer, but a sort of direction. He feels the obligation to search on, believing that the right answer is not just what the tradition says, not just what he wants, but has to be discovered. He gropes his way towards the solution, guided by a hunch, not fully aware of the most important clue which is that he loves the girl. But his actions in getting the farm buildings painted, setting up birch trees at the door for her homecoming, show that it is so. Coincidences such as the house-painter turning up looking for work seem to him to be some sort of guidance; his mother's schemes to dissuade him only serve to strengthen his hunch that this is what he has to do. But there is so much against it; his doubts and fears and the disapproval of all round.

The scientist too has this period of groping and vague intuitions of a new solution. "Science is constantly revolutionised and perfected by its pioneers, while remaining firmly rooted in its traditions," as Polanyi says, –[20] and the movement of growing up from the roots towards change is always painful and doubtful at first. But then in science, as in Ingmar's dilemma, comes the leap of imagination to the right solution, grasped with an intuition of its rightness. Ingmar had to shape his choice with active painful labour, but when he made it, it was not just his choice but a discovery, an apprehension of wider moral realities, and the tradition which had opposed it now accepted it through the voices of his family and community, saying by their acceptance, 'Yes, you were right, this is in the true line of our tradition'.

"Mother is not so terrible when she sees that one has made up one's mind," says Ingmar to his bride at the end. There is so much meaning in that remark. It is mother's business to be terrible up to that point, for she has to hold together the tradition which her son has to reinterpret, and if she did not hold it together he could not change it. Mother is the strength of the community's schema, which will not lightly let in new ideas, but having accepted will make them an integral part of the tradition and a growing point. Mother belongs with Cromwell's "Let the rest judge", and with the authority of the community of science.[21]

There can only be a moral community if there is a moral reality, comparable to the physical reality the scientific community pursues. Then communities are moral in so far as their moral traditions and rules are, though imperfect, aiming at the embodiment of moral reality. Otherwise there are only different communities with their own social rules, convenient for their common life but having no wider significance. But if there is a moral reality, different communities can be seen as tending towards it by the rectification and purification of their moral rules and ideals.

The moral community cannot be the same sort of community as the scientific, because moral truth is dealing with a different aspect of reality from scientific truth. This makes moral communities less closely knit, more varied. But, as in the community of science, the moral community must impose its traditions and at the same time encourage dissent from them. "Such processes of creative renewal always imply an appeal from a tradition as it is to a tradition as it ought to be. That is a spiritual reality embodied in tradition and transcending it."[22]

The free society, which will allow the independent pursuit of values, is thus not the open society. "A *wholly* open society would be a wholly vacuous one – one which could never actually exist since it could never have any reason for existing."[23] It would be like an untrained perception, a blank mind – or like scientists without the scientific community. But the authority and tradition of free societies rest on the co-operation, mutual trust and belief in their values of the members of the society. It cannot be imposed by a central authority. The state cannot set objectives for its members because it cannot know what these should be; they are only gradually discovered in the fellowship of independent groups.

Long ago Thomas Hobbes used his understanding of science to interpret how society works, but his was a disastrous misunderstanding of science which led to the gloomy picture in his 'Leviathan'. He held that, like the atoms of science, men are held together by force and fear. Polanyi, applying his very different understanding of science, gains a more hopeful vision of society. It is in a common life inspired and disciplined by the pursuit of freely accepted values that freedom can survive. Bukharin was logical, according to the Hobbes understanding of science, to claim that the state can set the objectives and demand conformity, the only alternative to conformity being individual self-indulgence. That is the extreme form of the totalitarian claim to democracy; the rulers can claim to be democratic because they can know what is best for all and enforce it. The other extreme, sometimes held in the West, is that democracy is simply one man one vote, or what the majority wants. The missing ingredient in both is the reality of values never wholly discoverable but growing in the fellowship of free men pursuing them. Then the function of the state is to safeguard the free associations in which this pursuit of values can go on. No Utopia is possible, and we have an allegiance to an imperfect society, because only from its traditions can progress be made. This is not Hobbes' static society held together by fear, but a society engaged in a continual adventure, a 'Society of Explorers'.

Notes to Chapter VI

1. See p.66 above
2. Wigner. Biographical memoirs of members of the Royal Society vol 23, p.415
3. *Knowing and Being* p.49
4. *The Impact of Science on Society* p.110, 111. (Quoted in *Knowing and Being* p.94)
5. *Knowing and Being* p.65
6. See *Science, Faith and Society* chapter 2
7. *Knowing and Being* p.54
8. *Ibid*. p.66, 67
9. *Ibid*. p.57
10. (my italics) *Ibid* p.66. (See the whole chapter, 'The Republic of Science')
11. see page 5 above
12. my italics
13. W. S. Allen – *The Nazi Seizure of Power*, London 1966, p.215
14. *The Tacit Dimension* p.84
15. *The Times* 16.4.1980
16. *Science, Faith and Society* p.76
17. A. S. F. Woodhouse *Puritanism and Liberty*
18. A. S. F. Woodhouse *op. cit.* p.101–
19. Norman Cohn, *The Pursuit of the Millenium*, p.319
20. *Science, Faith and Society* p.64
21. Compare T. S. Kuhn, *The Structure of Scientific Revolutions* p.65 – "Resistance to change has a use . . . By ensuring that the paradigm will not be too easily surrendered, resistance guarantees that the anomalies that lead to paradigm change will penetrate existing knowledge to the core." *cf* Peter Marris, *Loss and Change*, p.6
22. *Science, Faith and Society* p.56
23. *Meaning* p.184

CHAPTER VII

MORAL INVERSION AND
THE UNFREE SOCIETY

*Good Deeds and Knowledge were Everyman's
best friends, in the play. But now Knowledge
in her scientific dress shows Everyman how to
stand Good Deeds on her head and observe
her feet of clay.*

*Everyman is furious with his old friend Good
Deeds; his fury is fuelled by his former belief
in her. Hate and Despair will come up soon
and offer themselves as the only honest friends.*

Is hypocrisy the one deadly sin in our society? It sometimes seems so. A society so permissive in many ways is curiously terrified of any imputation of hypocrisy. For instance, a few years ago when Lord Longford led a group of investigators to Denmark to study the effects of unrestricted pornography, one member of the party remarked afterwards that it would have been much less embarrassing to tell his friends that he was going to enjoy some porn, than that he was going as a member of this investigating group. Because the announced motives of the group were moral, he expected to be automatically labelled a hypocrite; received with knowing smiles. It is now in many circles much more acceptable to be avowedly acting from low motives than from high ones. 'Unholier than thou' is a more comfortable stance than the old-fashioned hypocrite's 'holier than thou'. The only virtue that may safely be claimed is a certain kind of honesty, sometimes called courageous or unflinching realism. It is not only that people who want to defend a traditional virtue or protest at something they think wrong, are afraid of being *accused* of hypocrisy: they are often afraid that they *are* being hypocritical, and so they are silenced.[1]

This fear of hypocrisy is one minor ripple from a great wave which Polanyi called 'moral inversion' and traced back to the same disastrous error that he had found at the root of modern violence and oppression – *a wrong understanding of how we know things*.

To put the connection in the simplest terms; if we believe that nothing is reliable knowledge unless it is clear and explicit and testable by experiment, then we cannot know anything about intangible things like justice, love, purity, compassion or beauty. There are no experiments nor ever will be, to prove that it is wrong to bear false witness. Anyone then who pretends to be acting on such principles must be a hypocrite; he is professing to be motivated by something that has no reality. He must really be motivated by whatever really produces these so-called principles – here you can take your choice – the class structure, the survival strategy of the genes, or the Freudian unconscious. If we are not worried by the first two explanations we may be by the third. Freud has made us all uneasily aware that our motives are a good deal less respectable than we like to think, and that in uttering any overtly moral sentiment we are probably revealing something we would prefer to conceal. Better boldly to claim an amoral motive, even a disreputable one, and at least get some credit for honesty.

It is healthy to be aware of the risk of hypocrisy in high moral sentiments, but it is dangerously wrong to equate all moral sentiment with hypocrisy. Most people do actually have in them what Polanyi called 'moral passions'; strong currents of belief in some kind of moral good, hatred of some kind of evil, which is more than just a personal preference or a cover-up device. Where is this tide of moral feeling to go when its normal outlet is blocked?

Facing this question as he had seen it in Europe on an infinitely larger and more tragic scale, Polanyi wrote about 'moral inversion'.

In the Eddington Lecture of 1960[2] Polanyi began his diagnosis of moral inversion with a paradox. According to the statutes of these Lectures, the lecturer was required to attempt an explanation of why science has advanced so rapidly while moral progress has been so slow.

They have got the question wrong, said Polanyi. Man's moral sense has not lagged behind. "I believe that never in the history of mankind has the hunger for brotherhood and righteousness exercised such power over the minds of men as today." What we are faced with is not a sluggish rate of moral progress, but "the outbreak of a moral fervour which has achieved numberless humanitarian reforms and has improved modern society beyond the boldest thoughts of earlier centuries. And I believe that it is this fervour which in our own lifetime has outreached itself by its inordinate aspirations and thus heaped on mankind the disasters that have befallen us".

Too *much* moral fervour? This is an unusual diagnosis. The simple analysis, that moral ideals are made suspect by a theory of knowledge which cannot allow them to be knowable, is not enough, although the discrediting of moral judgment has often been attributed to the rise of modern science with its sceptical questioning. But Polanyi maintained that this scepticism by itself would not necessarily have done much damage. The eighteenth century scientific rationalists did not think it would; they looked forward to a calm, harmonious advance of mankind, freed from the passions and bigotries of religion, towards ever higher levels of moral and social improvement. For instance, in 1784 a memorial was hidden in a building, to be found by future generations. – "Our days," it said, "comprise the happiest period of the eighteenth century . . . Hatred born of dogma and the compulsion of conscience sink away, love of man and freedom of thought gain the upper hand. The arts and sciences blossom and our vision into the workshop of nature goes deep . . ."[3]

What this hopeful outlook did not reckon with was the giant wave of man's unlimited moral aspirations which, turned from its Christian channel, poured like a destructive torrent through the channels of rationalism.

This state of affairs, Polanyi thought, has not been recognised because it is unprecedented. We have no words or categories to deal with the idea of morality in flood and out of control.

The same diagnosis was hinted at in my first chapter, where I said that what seemed to Polanyi to be new in the modern disasters of Europe was "the combination of a ruthless *contempt* for moral values such as truth, compassion and justice, with an unbounded *moral passion* for Utopian perfection".[4] Or in another phrase – "the disastrous dissonance of an extreme critical lucidity and an intense moral conscience".

Again and again Polanyi came back to this diagnosis and worked it out in various forms.[5] Here is the gist of what he said about it, starting with his simplest account of moral inversion in the individual.[6]

"A man looking at the world with complete scepticism can see no grounds for moral authority or transcendent moral obligation; there may then seem to be no scope for his moral perfectionism. Yet he can satisfy it by turning his scepticism against existing society, denouncing its morality as shoddy, artificial, hypocritical, and a mere mask for lust and exploitation. Though such a combination of his moral scepticism with his moral indignation is inconsistent, the two are in fact fused together by their joint attack on the same target. The result is a moral hatred of existing society and the alienation of the modern intellectual . . . Having condemned the distinction between good and evil as dishonest, he can still find pride in the honesty of such condemnation. Since ordinary decent behaviour can never be safe against the suspicion of sheer conformity or downright hypocrisy, only an absolutely amoral meaningless act can assure man of his complete authenticity. All the moral fervour which scientific scepticism has released from religious control and then rendered homeless by discrediting its ideals, returns then to imbue an amoral authenticity with intense moral approval. This is how absolute self-assertion, fantasies of gratuitous crime and perversity, self-hatred and despair, are aroused as defences against a nagging suspicion of one's own honesty."

This theme can be traced in literature and art. "Today we have a whole literature, much of it of high quality, in which absurdity and a sombre fantastic obscenity are presented as tokens of unflinching honesty," Polanyi wrote. (Punk is a lower-grade manifestation of the same trend!) Historically Polanyi outlines the phenomenon like this.

At first the new scientific scepticism was able to work harmoniously with the secularised moral aspirations and to produce great benefits. This was possible as long as the traditional framework persisted, unconsciously relied on by those who were busy sawing it through. The benefits of this co-operation were great, not only for science but for social and moral ideas too long cocooned in traditional form. Authority and tradition were indeed stifling, were often corrupt and dishonest, needed the pruning knife of bold criticism. But after a time the inherent contradictions of total scepticism and high moral aspirations became sharper. The scientific outlook not only demonstrated that much of what tradition had taught was not true, but began to probe to destruction the foundations of authority and tradition themselves. From the other side, moral aspirations stirred up by change, then inflamed and corrupted by a clearer view of the hypocrisies of society, found no outlet in traditional forms of action. No society can live up to Christian ideals, so there is always some hypocrisy to be found in a society which professes such ideals, once a clear sceptical gaze is turned on it.

These two forces, scepticism and moral passion, then fused together in various ways, without losing their dangerous incompatibility. The first kind of fusion produced the individual nihilist, burning with moral fervour and hatred of existing society. Polanyi traces this figure in European literature, from Rousseau through Dostoievski and Turgenev; from Nietzsche to Hegel. An angry individualism repudiated all traditional ideas of good and evil; the romantic figure of the completely free self-determining superman took hold of men's imagination. Existentialism has followed this line of total individualism, allowing Simone de Beauvoir to admire the morality of the Marquis de Sade as a passionate exposure of the bourgeois hoax of erecting class interests into universal principles.[7]

The second kind of fusion of moral passion with scientific scepticism appears when the individual nihilist turns to political action and chooses political violence; this occurred in Europe with the rise of the 'armed bohemians' who were the agents of the European revolution. "The popular idea of the Russian enlightened youth from about 1860 onward was the hard, impersonal, scientific nihilist first embodied in Turgenev's hero, the medical student Bazarov."[8] In real life these men were strict materialists combining total denial of genuinely moral ideals with a frenzied hatred of society for its immorality. The same inversion accounted for the hold that National Socialist doctrine had on the minds of German youth. The Nazis denounced all humanitarian ideals as dishonest, morality as hypocritical. Moral passions were thus diverted into a cult of naked power, the only channel left open to them.

When such scepticism demanded total individual freedom, the logical outcome was total state control, since there could be no other way for totally free and sceptical individuals to combine. Thus repudiation of all authority led to total control by authority, nihilism to tyranny, romantic individualism to contempt for individuals.

Of course the conditions had to be present, but it was the power of ideas that brought this about. It was this philosophy, Polanyi said, which defeated the hopes aroused by President Wilson's appeal at the end of the first war. I have a vivid personal feeling of those hopes, as I saw many years later the letter which my father wrote to my mother from his post with the army in France, after he had read Wilson's speech. It expressed his excitement, elation and hope for the end of militarism and the prospect of real peace. Such a hope could still be expressed in America and in England, but the 'morally inverted' intelligentsia of Central and Eastern Europe found it naïve and ridiculous; their *philosophy* defeated it. Within twenty years there was a comprehensive system of totalitarian governments all over Europe. Polanyi argues that these could not have been established by force, had not the way been prepared by this philosophy, which denied reality to thought and to moral motives.

We have to remember here Polanyi's deep emotional involvement with the fate of Europe. "Why did we destroy Europe?" he still asked, tragically, near the end of his life. Writing on 'The Foolishness of History' in *Encounter*[9] on the fortieth anniversary of the Russian Revolution, he complained that our scientific approach to history debars us from realising the folly, the mistaken thinking, that shaped it. As with discovery, the view from after it has happened flattens out the dynamics; only an understanding by dwelling in the minds of those who made the events can give a true picture. The volumes of scholarship accumulating about the revolution are burying it under a 'mountain of monographs'.

"Yet I know that it was something quite different. Not only when it actually happened, but all along, up to this day – for it still lives in our own blood. It was boundless; it was infinitely potent; it was an act of madness. A great number of men – led by one man possessing genius – set themselves limitless aims that had no bearing at all on reality. They detested everything in existence and were convinced therefore that the total destruction of existing society and the establishment of their own unlimited power on its ruins would bring total happiness to humanity. That was – unbelievable as it may seem – *literally* the whole substance of their projects for a new economic, political and social system of mankind."[10]

When he writes about England, Polanyi's tone always changes. He saw England and America as countries which had escaped the destruction of Europe, partly because we were never so apt to put our faith in theories. We were more inclined to find out what worked in practice and to pay little attention to theories that obviously would not work. Then, Christian ideals were never so completely detached from their religious matrix here, and Christian inspired individuals worked along with others to improve and humanise society without violent disruption of traditional ways. So our 'Age of Reform' vastly improved nearly all aspects of life, and we tamed and domesticated for home consumption the theories which we exported to other countries, who turned them raw and burning into ideologies. Thus, having been regarded in the eighteenth century as dangerous pioneers of scepticism, we came to be looked on as backward in the nineteenth, as we learnt to relax the tension between scepticism and moral fervour by not paying too much attention to either, and by the gradual humanising of society. Bentham's utilitarian philosophy, for example, though produced in England, was only imbibed here in small doses which gave a stimulus to reform; across the channel it became an ideology fuelling moral inversion.

So it is, Polanyi thought, that "after a hundred and fifty years that have transformed every particle of her life, Britain's institutions still form a single harmonious system, upheld without serious dissent by the entire nation". . . . "Thus Britain avoided the self-destructive implications of the Enlightenment of which she was one chief author."[11] Too kind, too optimistic a picture perhaps; but so it seemed to this distinguished refugee from a Europe in flames.

For Europe had put into practice what we only discussed. The French Revolution marked the transition in Europe from an age-long past in which human societies had always accepted custom and tradition. The Revolution worked on the new logic that if society has no divine sanction but is made by man, men can and must make a perfect society *now*, and for that purpose must take complete power, while all opposition must be crushed. And later revolutions have followed that same path.

In fact in England and America we have mostly practised what Polanyi called 'spurious, moral inversion'. This means that the inversion is limited to vocabulary and logic but not put into practice; men talk a language of materialism, behaviourism, value-free sociology or utilitarianism, and yet continue in practice to respect the principles of truth, justice or morality which their vocabularies anxiously deny.[12] They may even justify moral aims in this vocabulary, and then "the public, taught by the sociologist to distrust its traditional morality, is grateful to receive it back from him in a scientifically branded wrapping. Indeed a writer who has proved his hard-headed perspicacity by denying the existence of morality will always be listened to with especial respect when he does moralise in spite of this."[13]

This scientific disguise of moral aspirations may sometimes protect them from destruction, but it is a dangerous refuge, which only holds when moral aspirations are moderate. A great upsurge of moral demands, when injected into a utilitarian framework, may lead to true moral inversion, turning into the fanatical force of a machinery of violence.

So the stage was set for the Russian experiment. Marxism, says Polanyi, was the perfect system for channelling the boundless moral fervour released by the secularisation of Christian hopes, in men who could only believe in material forces. Since all bourgeois societies are unmasked as hypocritical for professing a morality which is not scientifically real and which in any case they do not fully practice, men need a faith expressed in material terms, and this Marxism provided. Its contradictions became its strength, as it allowed the modern mind to satisfy both its passion for ruthless objectivity and its intense moral fervour. Its circularity and its all-embracing power came from this contradiction. While bourgeois ideals were shown to be simply a covering for material interests, the moral motives of Marxism were safe from attack because they did not profess to be moral but scientific and material.[14] The passion for objectivity and the passion for ideals, which have often led to mental conflict and confusion, are here fused together into a powerful engine for action. "The more inordinate our moral aspirations and the more completely amoral our objectivist outlook, the more powerful is the combination in which these contradictory principles mutually reinforce each other." "Thus originated a world-embracing idea, in which moral doubt is frenzied by moral fury and moral fury is armed by scientific nihilism."[15]

For a comparison with Polanyi's analysis, if we look at the discussion with Charles Taylor in 'Men of Ideas',[16] we find that discussion also stressing the two incompatible strands in Marxism and the way that the strength of its appeal springs from their combination. Its claim to be a science expounding inexorable laws, as the laws of physics and of evolution were supposed to be, gave it the immense appeal of modern enlightenment; but at the same time there was the messianic element offering a utopian future of human fulfilment. The elements are incompatible but the political punch depends on holding on to both.

"The claim to be a science . . . and yet at the same time to answer that deep hunger for a new age, a new era of freedom and fulfilment . . . has appealed across a tremendous gamut, all the way from semi-disabused intellectuals in Western societies . . . to third world populations among whom there has been a rapid breakdown of an established tradition . . ."[17]

In the same sort of way Polanyi explains how intellectuals are attracted to Marxism in spite of its denial of the freedom on which their pursuit of truth depends. Uneasy about bourgeois society and its hypocrisies, without religion and with inordinate moral demands, they may feel alienated from society and lacking meaning in their lives. Marxism offers them a status as anti-bourgeois, a close-knit fellowship of believers and a safe refuge from doubt in the security of a scientifically inevitable progress. Polanyi's account seems to explain more deeply the dynamics of the combination of incompatibles, while Charles Taylor brings out more clearly the paradox of a system which in the name of liberty imposes such total control. For the idea of human liberation demands that men not only obey, but enjoy and believe in, the society brought about by historical necessity. It *must* be perfect, anyone who does not enjoy it must be mad and should be put in an asylum. It is intolerable that artists should not celebrate it, they *must*.

Thinking about the extraordinary power of Marxism, which gives it so strong a hold on its adherents, Polanyi returned to an anthropologist's account of a primitive society which fascinated him.[18] In Azande society the whole system of thought is based on magic, and the witch doctor's lore has an explanation in terms of magic interference by some person the witch doctor can identify, as the cause of every disaster. The system is so complete and the reasoning so circular that any European trying to argue against it finds it impossible to break into the circle. "They reason excellently in the idiom of their beliefs, but they cannot reason outside or against their beliefs because they have no other idiom in which to express their thoughts," says Evans Pritchard. Any evidence brought from outside against the system is automatically transformed by the idiom of thought into supporting evidence. No *one* argument makes any impact because the system already has an explanation for any possible anomaly; and because *each* argument is rejected in this way it is never possible for enough arguments to build up and make a persuasive case apparent to a member of the tribe.

Polanyi remarks on the similarity of this highly stable but mistaken system of thought, this very tightly closed and rigid schema, to some modern systems such as Marxism. Those who have left the Communist Party have described how when they were in it, all contrary evidence became transformed into supporting evidence by the same sort of circular reasoning as in Azande society. For instance Arthur Koestler wrote in *The God That Failed* – "My party education had equipped my mind with such elaborate shock absorbing buffers and elastic defences that everything seen and heard became automatically transformed to fit a pre-conceived pattern".

Similarly prisoners in faked trials in the USSR under Stalin were so completely gripped in the system of thought that they could doubt their own selves and the evidence of their own eyes and memories, sooner than doubt the system. This happened to Bukharin a few years after he had blandly told Polanyi that truth pursued for its own sake was a bourgeois self-indulgence. Prisoners confessed to the crimes they were charged with, just as a primitive tribesman confronted by the whole system of tribal thought may confess to having turned into a lion and eaten his neighbour.

Among the Azande this system just grew, but in modern societies it has to be cultivated and maintained. For example, Frank Meyer who worked for years in the American and British Communist organisations had much experience of the training of communist cadres – he wrote[19] about the aims of this training. "The ideal type of communist is a man in whom all individual, emotional and unconscious elements have been reduced to a minimum and subjected to the control of an iron will, informed by a supple intellect. That intellect is totally at the service of a single and compelling idea, made incarnate in the Communist Party, namely the concept of History as an inexorable god whose ways are revealed 'scientifically' through the doctrine and method of Marxism-Leninism." He tells of the sureness that this faith brought him, "the vision of a correlation of all aspects of experience, each with each, the certainty that an answer could be found to every meaningful question and that everything which did not fit could be dismissed as meaningless vapourings without weakening the architecture of one's view of life. That this was achieved through denying the existence of the richest areas of human experience, the ideal and the spiritual, seemed unimportant at the time in comparison with the lifting of doubt and anxiety that accompanied it."

Such a system can transform any fact. "That is why," Meyer wrote, "the known realities of the Soviet Union – oppression, slave labour camps, purge after purge, murder in the millions, brutal and unprovoked aggression, even Kruschev's exposure of Stalin and the Hungarian Revolution of 1956 – slide off the cadre Communist's conscience like water off a duck's back. They make no live impact on him. Intellectually he explains them as necessary casualties of the historic process, unfortunate but unavoidable. Emotionally they are simply not real, even when he has actually seen horrors with his own eyes. Facts that do not fit the theoretical outlook of Marxism-Leninism have only a shadowy existence. Reality rests only in the doctrines of Communism and the institutions of the Party."

Although all-embracing in its circularity, the faith of Marxism has proved unstable, since to doubt at any point endangers the whole edifice. Some have been able to break away, although the experience is deeply traumatic since so much of a man's life is bound up in the system, and to leave it seems at first like the abandonment of all meaning in life. But some, unlike the Azande, remain capable of reasoning outside the system and of recognising the impact of reality. It is an interesting note in Frank Meyer's account that *individual emotional and unconscious elements* had to be reduced in the cadre communists. These are the very aesthetic elements which, for Polanyi, play an essential part in the sensing of a new reality.

Yet Polanyi recognised that the mind formed and disciplined by one particular tradition is also necessary for the sensing of new truth. In a challenging passage he explained that the Azande-type attitude is found in science too, when scientists simply will not examine a theory that goes against current scientific belief. "We shrug our shoulders and refuse to waste our time on such an obviously fruitless enquiry."[20] What is more, this attitude is absolutely essential, for scientists could not possibly examine every new theory. But in science it lives in lively tension with the opposite impulse, the urge to break out of the dominant pattern, whereas in Marxist systems the denial of an external standard and the suppression of criticism is much more complete.

The rise of such closed systems of thought protecting themselves from criticism and dissent shows once again how the insistence on certainty, the denial of reality to anything but 'scientific facts' ends by cutting off the possibility of any contact with reality, just as in the Karl Pearson model of knowledge.[21] In the free society, belief in an objective reality, able to be known but never fully known, able to be sensed and explored, can be maintained. And only a society in which tradition and authority support such belief can be free. This is how the way we know things affects the life of society. But a mistaken theory of knowledge makes this role of authority and tradition appear unjustifiable.

The Hungarian Revolution of 1956, which Frank Meyer said could run off the conscience of a cadre communist like water off a duck's back, was for Polanyi of immense significance as a revolt *against* moral inversion and *for* the reality of truth and justice. Since then we have seen other movements, as in Czechoslovakia and Poland, besides the individual heroism of many dissidents within the Soviet Union. But still to a large extent we in the West are dominated by the philosophies which led to the moral inversion, and so cannot give moral or intellectual support to these heroes and these movements. All our 'value free' sociology, our belief in detached impersonal knowledge, disables us from a true judgment of these movements.

We might look as an example at an Address given in 1978 by our then Foreign Secretary Dr David Owen.[22] I believe that Dr Owen's moral inversion was of the spurious kind and his practice better than his theory; I only quote the Address as a typical example of the confusion which undermines our policies. The title of the Address was 'The Morality of Compromise'. These are some of its statements – "The search for a unified solution, absolute values, is not something new. Philosophers, historians, writers, theologians, have searched for ultimate truth all through our existence. I question whether there are absolute values, ultimately compatible with one another . . . I am very doubtful that there is one objective and universal human ideal. I don't believe there is a fundamental unity underlying all phenomena, a single universal purpose . . . I suspect the advocacy of a unitary truth. I do not believe that contradiction is always wrong . . . A single central vision is a characteristic of what I will call the pseudo-religions, fascism, Marxism, fundamentalism . . ."

This is an indiscriminate mixture of true and false statements. It makes no distinction of levels, as if it were the same thing to say "There is one truth and I know it, it is A B C D —" and to say "truth cannot be ultimately self-contradictory".

That truth cannot be ultimately self-contradictory we learnt from the Greeks; this is the proper sense of 'truth is one'. That good is not ultimately self-contradictory, or 'God is one' we learnt from the Jews. Without these faiths, science could not progress and morality would be nothing but social convenience. If scientists thought that contradictions were nothing to worry about, why should they seek for deeper coherences in which to resolve them? And unless there is a coherence in moral truth, how can moral standards be compared? Mine is as good as yours, Hitler's as good as Christ's. The 'single central vision' of the pseudo-religions is in fact the opposite of a belief in one transcendent truth, which we can all know in some degree but none of us can know completely.[23] It is when the ultimate oneness of a transcendent truth is denied that the pseudo-religions can claim that their particular truth is final and try to impose it on everyone. Bukharin in his words to Polanyi was denying validity to the pursuit of truth in science, claiming the central vision of the Party to be the only truth, a truth clear, final and complete, ready for the cadre communist to embrace.

Dr Owen praised the man who is ready to compromise, to modify his principles, to bend to the collective view and follow expedience, as against the man of rigid consistency and unbending views. But this is a muddle again, for there are two quite different ways of changing one's view. If two people believe in a reality which is ultimately consistent, they can talk together and one or other may come to see that he was wrong; or they may both come to see that there is a deeper truth of which both their views are partial expressions. This is democracy by discussion, or the Quaker 'sense of the meeting'; it is what Polanyi called the 'conviviality' of intellectual work. It is the way of progress and discovery, and when that is going on the man of unbending views, concerned only to be consistent, is indeed out of place.

But if there is no belief in a unitary truth, which is ultimately consistent, then there is no appeal between the two views, and the only possible attitudes are either obstinate consistency in my view, or accepting that your view shall prevail in the spirit of 'Have it your own way – anything for a quiet life'.

"I believe in moral values," Dr Owen wrote. But if there is no objective truth, justice, rationality towards which we strive, it makes no sense to talk of moral values. "When we claim that an action of ours is prompted by moral motives," Polanyi wrote,[24] "or else when we make moral judgments of others – as in recognising the impartiality of a court of law – we invariably refer to moral standards *which we hold to be valid*. We do not prefer a court of law to be unbiased in the same way as we prefer a steak to be rare rather than well done; our appeal to moral standards necessarily claims to be *right*, that is, binding on all men." "God is not the author of contradictions," as Cromwell said.[25]

The change that happened in the Hungarian Revolution was the re-awakening of this sense of a transcendent reality of intangible things such as truth, justice, morality, which the morality of compromise would deny. Polanyi quotes Miklos Gimes, who was hanged by Kadar for his part in the revolution. Gimes asked how it could have happened that he himself had become unable to see the difference between truth and falsehood. "Slowly we had come to believe," he wrote, "at least with the greater, the dominant part of our consciousness, that there are two kinds of truth, that the truth of the Party and the people can be different and can be more important than the objective truth, and that truth and political expediency are in fact identical. This is a terrible thought, yet its significance must be faced squarely. If there is a truth of a higher order than objective truth, if the criterion of truth is political expediency, then even a lie can be 'true', for even a lie can be momentarily expedient, even a trumped up political trial can be 'true' in this sense, for even such a trial can yield important political advantage. And so we arrive at the outlook which infected not only those who thought up the faked political trials, but often affected even the victims; the outlook which poisoned our whole public life, penetrated the remotest corners of our thinking, obscured our vision, paralysed our critical faculties, and finally rendered many of us incapable of simply sensing or apprehending truth. This is how it was, it is no use denying it."[26]

To profess support for dissidents in the Soviet empire, while denying the reality of truth, is to write off and betray what they are doing, the meaning of their courage and sacrifice. But hold on, someone may say – was it not for our spirit of compromise that Polanyi admired England? – for not carrying theories to their logical conclusion but going by experience and common sense? Does not that mean compromise? Is it not compromise to say that we owe allegiance to an imperfect society?

But Polanyi's admiration for England was based on his belief in our institutions and traditions as the ground in which a basic respect for truth and justice could grow and be transmitted. Without this respect for truth, real toleration and freedom cannot flourish, he believed; and the lack of it opens the way for totalitarian rule.[27]

"In order that a society may be properly constituted there must be competent forces in existence to decide with ultimate power every controversial issue between two citizens. But if the citizens are dedicated to certain transcendent obligations and particularly to such general ideals as truth, justice, charity, and these are embodied in the tradition of the community to which allegiance is maintained, a great many issues between citizens, and all to some extent, can be left – and are necessarily left – for the individual consciences to decide. The moment, however, a community ceases to be dedicated, through its members, to transcendent ideals, it can continue to exist undisrupted only by submission to a single centre of unlimited secular power. Nor can citizens who have radically abandoned belief in spiritual realities – on the obligations to which their conscience would have been entitled and in duty bound to take a stand – raise any valid objection to being totally directed by the state. In fact their love of truth and justice turn then automatically . . . into love of state power."[28]

To come back for a moment to the theme with which this chapter started, our modern fear of hypocrisy. This fear, which we saw as a small ripple from the great upheavals of 'moral inversion', has brought about a curious inversion of hypocrisy itself. The dictionary definition of hypocrisy is 'simulation of virtue', and people who hate this or fear to be accused of this may honestly turn to an admiration of honest amorality, as intellectuals have turned to Marxism for its exposure of the hypocrisy of traditional virtues. Sceptical doubt may truly undermine belief in traditional moral values. Men may abandon their moral beliefs with pride in their fearless objectivity. But they may also do it hypocritically, and this is the inversion of hypocrisy which might be called 'simulation of vice'.

Moral beliefs make moral demands on us, and to abandon them

can be relaxing and convenient. Two benefits can be obtained, the reputation for an honest progressive outlook, and the freedom from the moral restraints we condemn as hypocritical. Camus once wrote, expounding the great destructive idea of 'the Absurd', that 'the great adventurers of the Absurd have wanted its hardships, not its conveniences'. But some want its conveniences.

This inverted hypocrisy is often unnoticed because our stereotypes of hypocrisy are for instance the respected establishment figure in a brothel or the temperance campaigner dead drunk. Those are people paying lip service to morality while secretly indulging their lower tastes. The modern inverted hypocrite is not ashamed of what he is doing, he holds up proudly the banner of freedom and progress over his pornshop, extols the most degraded tastes as healthy and liberating, though what he really admires about them is their profitability.

This hypocrisy of honesty also covers a great area of laziness and insensitivity. People read or see the 'sombre fantastic obscenities' of art and literature without more reaction than is enjoyable. How clever, they say, how honest; how fearlessly we see ourselves as we are. Then there is the hypocrisy of protest. It is so much more satisfying to seething moral fervour to march in protest against wrongs across the world, of which we cannot see the complexities and about which we cannot do anything. Wrongs at a distance are clear cut, black and white, and we can give our moral fervour a good run without getting our scepticism dirty by actually doing something. If you do something you are bound to get involved in the complexities of real life and might be labelled a hypocritical do-gooder. This sort of feeling can be at the roots of, for instance, student support for the IRA.

Of course, doubt, dissent and protest are not always hypocritical – but neither are conformity, faith and commitment. Either may be honest, either may be dishonest. It is a matter of judgment, as it is in science to choose between the established theory and the new one. But at present the confidence in their judgment of those who want to defend a traditional value is undermined by an automatic suspicion of hypocrisy, just because they are on the side of an acknowledged virtue. It has been said about Michael Polanyi that just because his language was sometimes noble, he was suspect. We see accusations of hypocrisy flung indiscriminately at those who criticise as immoral the behaviour of a public figure. The criticisms may be hypocritical, but they may not: the only reason for such a wholesale accusation of hypocrisy is the assumption that *any* moral stance *must* be hypocritical.

We need to learn to hold our beliefs though they might be mistaken, Polanyi tells us. We are not going to go back on science nor give up our moral ideals, and we have to find an understanding in which both ways of seeing the world can live.

Such understanding depends on believing there is a valid way of knowing the truth of the values we believe in, although they cannot be 'scientifically' proved. If the faith, skill and judgment we need in order to believe in them can be learnt only by apprenticeship, within a tradition, to those who have this faith and skill, the same is true of science, Polanyi has shown.

"We need a theory of knowledge which shows up the fallacy of a positivist scepticism and authorises our knowledge of entities governed by higher principles. Any higher principle can be known only by dwelling in the particulars governed by it. Any attempt to observe a higher level of existence by a scrutiny of its several particulars must fail. We shall remain blind in theory to all that truly matters in the world so long as we do not accept indwelling as a legitimate form of knowledge.

"Indwelling involves a tacit reliance on our awareness of particulars not under observation, many of them unspecifiable. We have to interiorise these, and, in doing so, must change our mental existence. There is nothing definite to which we can hold fast in such an act. It is a free commitment.

"But there is something imponderable for us to rely on. We have around us great truths embodied in works born of the very freedom which we are hestitating to enter. And recent history has taught us that we can breathe only in the ambience of these truths and of this creative freedom. I, for one, am prepared to rely on this assurance for acquiring and upholding knowledge by embracing the world and dwelling in it."[29]

So Polanyi at the end of his essay on 'the Modern Mind' states the faith without which he believed the life of a free society was impossible.

In the next chapter we shall look at the validity of 'higher principles' and at Polanyi's idea of levels of reality which can admit higher and lower principles.

Notes to Chapter VII

1. see *Meaning* p.23
2. *Knowing and Being* chapter 1
3. Quoted by J. Robert Oppenheimer in *Science and the Common Understanding* OUP London 1954
4. Ch. 1, p.6, above
5. *Personal Knowledge* pp.231–5. *Science, Faith and Society* p.78–. *The Tacit Dimension* p.57–60. *Meaning* p.16–21
6. 'On the Modern Mind', *Encounter* XXIV, 1965, pp.7, 8
7. Quoted in *Knowing and Being* p.12
8. *Knowing and Being* p.15
9. *Encounter* IX, Nov. 57
10. Quoted in *Knowing and Being*, p.38
11. *Knowing and Being* p.12
12. *Personal Knowledge* p.233
13. *Ibid* p.234
14. *Ibid* p.227 – The Magic of Marxism
15. *The Tacit Dimension* p.59
16. *Men of Ideas* p.42 –
17. *Ibid* p.55
18. Evans Pritchard – *Witchcraft, Oracles and Magic among the Azande*, quoted in PK p.288
19. F. S. Meyer – The Moulding of Communists – 1961 New York Harcourt Brace, p.16, p.53
20. *Personal Knowledge* p.294
21. see Chapter 2 p.21 above
22. Reported in *The Times* of 29.4.78
23. compare *Science, Faith and Society* p.78
24. *Knowing and Being* p.33
25. See chapter 6, p.89 above
26. *Knowing and Being* p.20
27. *Science, Faith and Society* p.70
28. *Ibid* p.78
29. 'On the Modern Mind', *Encounter* XXIV May 1965 p.9

CHAPTER VIII

A MANY-LEVEL WORLD

Another of Everyman's friends was his Goods.
The priests told him his Goods were a snare
and a delusion.

Science tells him 'you are *Goods'.*

But in this chapter Everyman finds that his
Goods can make a ladder by which he can
climb to find his true reality.

OUR minds are still largely dominated by the feeling that everything ought to be explained on one level; that life and mind, like anything else, can be defined in terms of the physical chemical structure of matter. As I said at the beginning of this book, we have this deeply ingrained idea that what is really *true* is the universe of atoms in motion. So we have biologists and psychologists, archaeologists and economists, who are happier the more closely their sciences approach chemistry and physics.[1] To admit any other sort of explanation is then regarded as cheating; avoiding the rigours of the game. Once go outside the physical world and its known laws and you could be on the way back to superstition or whimsy, seeing gods and spirits in natural objects or indulging in vague notions that can explain everything and so really explain nothing.

Polanyi does seem thoroughly to demolish this idea of explaining life in terms of physics and chemistry, and to do it without recourse to irrational notions. His argument starts with a typical piece of Polanyi ju-jitsu. Some living organs function like machines (indeed sometimes their functions can be performed by machines, for instance a kidney machine). This has been taken to prove that life can be explained in terms of physics and chemistry. On the contrary, says Polanyi, neatly throwing his opponent over his shoulder, it proves just the opposite, since *machines* cannot be explained in terms of physics and chemistry. If some living organs function like machines, then life transcends the domain of physics and chemistry, as machines do, or even tools.

He illustrates with a simple example:[2] he once found that he had picked up unwittingly and brought back with him from America an object that looked like an instrument of some sort. No one could tell him what it was until he got back to America and learnt that it was designed to make two holes simultaneously in a .can of beer. No physical or chemical investigation could have revealed this fact. Imagine sending it to a laboratory to be analysed. Such analysis would have revealed what it was made of, and if its shape had been due to the nature of the material, that could have been discovered. But its shape was due to the purpose for which it was made, and physics or chemistry can take no account of that. A team of physicists and chemists examining an unknown machine, say a clock, could not discover what it was through their physics and chemistry; they could only understand it if they also knew about the operational principles of machines and the purpose of this machine, i.e. telling the time.

One characteristic clearly separates machines and living organisms from the rest of nature; they can fail, they can go wrong. Other things cannot. It would be nonsense to set up an enquiry into why thunderstorms go wrong or why acids make mistakes. They cannot be judged in these terms. This means that in judging machines and living creatures we necessarily have in mind the idea of achievement, although the achievement of a machine is that of its human maker. All living beings, and the machines and contrivances made by men, have aims, functions or purposes or standards of rightness in which they can succeed or fail. Nothing else has. Only living creatures can make mistakes; machines cannot do that, for the purposes they embody are not their own purposes, and only a being with some intelligence, however rudimentary, can make a mistake. One is sometimes told rather smugly if one complains of the behaviour of a computer – "Computers cannot make mistakes". That is true, but they can go wrong and break down, and so fail in the purpose for which they were designed.

When machines or living organs fail to perform their function, the *failure* may be explained in terms of physics and chemistry, for the machine and the organ are composed of matter like anything else and so are subject to the laws of physics and chemistry. The failure of a plane to fly may be due to metal fatigue; the failure of an ear to hear may be due to physical blockage. But in their successful functioning the plane and the ear are not *determined* by physical and chemical laws, for knowledge of these laws will not enable anyone to recognise or understand a plane or an ear; this can only be done with a knowledge of their purpose or function.

Another piece of Polanyi ju-jitsu supports his argument for the special nature of life. It concerns the famous discovery by Watson and Crick of the 'double helix', the DNA chain which is the code of heredity and transmits the information according to which the offspring's cells construct themselves on the parental model. This discovery was hailed by some as the final proof that living things are physically and chemically determined. No, says Polanyi again, it proves just the opposite. No arrangement of physical units can be a code and convey information unless the order of its units is *not* fixed by its physical chemical make-up.[3] His example this time; a railway station on the Welsh border where an arrangement of pebbles on a bank spelled the message – "Welcome to Wales by British Rail".[4] This information content of the pebbles clearly showed that their arrangement was not due to their physical chemical interaction but to a purpose on the part of the stationmaster, just as the discovery of the function of the beer can opener showed that its shape was due to someone's purpose of opening beer cans.

The letters of an alphabet, the units of a code, can only convey information because of the possibility of arranging their order for the purpose. Watson and Crick recognised that the DNA chain conveys information of an immense richness; that is only possible because the items in a DNA chain do not *have* to be arranged (chemically) in the manner in which they are. "Each item of a DNA series consists of one of four alternative organic bases (actually two positions of two different compound organic bases) . . . If DNA were an ordinary chemical molecule, its structure would be due to the fact that it had achieved maximum stability in that structure, and this chemical orderliness would prevent it from functioning as a code. But it is not an ordinary molecule and so it can function as a code."

Others have compared the function of the DNA chain in guiding the development of the foetus to that of an architectural blueprint in guiding the construction of a building. But the way that DNA works is much more complex and would have to be compared to a blueprint and builder in one. In some cases, if part of the embryo has been prevented from developing normally, other tissues may be diverted from their usual roles to take its place; as though the builder faced with an unexpected shortage of one material had to use something else to complete the building according to plan.

The arrangement of DNA *could* have come about by chance, just as the pebbles on that station *could* have rolled down a hillside and arranged themselves in the words of the message, but it would be bizarre to maintain that this was so, only someone doggedly defending a thesis would attempt it – in this case the thesis that there is nothing different about life.

"We are so used," says Marjorie Grene, "to thinking, or thinking that we think, of the *real* as the physico-chemical real; we are so used to apologising for life and assuring ourselves that Nobel prize-winners are just on the verge of explaining it away . . . that to admit, au fond, to the reality of living nature seems a betrayal of science itself. What is real is by definition the non-living. That is the fundamental untruth we still have to overcome."[6]

But, you may object, living things and man himself *are* part of the natural order; their being *does* obey the laws of physics and chemistry, so how can they not be determined by these laws? This is a common stumbling block. Bertrand Russell, remarking that physics was very nearly complete and therefore uninteresting, went on – "Of this physical world, uninteresting in itself. Man is a part. His body, like other matter, is composed of electrons and protons, which, so far as we know, obey the same laws as those not forming parts of animals or plants. There are some who maintain that physiology can never be reduced to physics, but their arguments are not very convincing and it seems prudent to suppose that they are mistaken. . . . Undoubtedly we are part of nature, which has produced our desires, our hopes and fears, in accordance with laws which the physicists are beginning to discover.

"Dehumanisation as the price of the advance of knowledge," Ernest Gellner calls this sort of view. "The more we can explain the world, the more we are ourselves explained".[8] Russell, with gloomy fortitude, submits to be explained, and explained away as a person, but he takes comfort in thinking our *values* are somehow quite different. We ourselves are the ultimate and irrefutable arbiters of value, there is no outside standard to show us that our values are wrong.[9] He does not ask how creatures entirely determined by the laws of physics and chemistry can *have* values, or what values can be but purely subjective likes and dislikes if there is no way of comparing them or judging them. Values are left hanging in a void, while our bodies and minds, hopes, desires and fears are physically determined. Existentialists accept this sort of suspension in the void, but it is a nausea-producing position for man, and risky for his fragile values.

A much more real freedom, a much more satisfying recognition of the reality of *persons,* would be open to us if we could accept Polanyi's explanation that life operates by principles *made possible* and *limited* by physical and chemical laws but not *determined* by them. Can it be accepted? Can it be scientifically responsible to accept that there is something different, not reducible to the one level, about living beings?

Here Polanyi moves in with a very important original idea; *boundary conditions.* The term is borrowed from physics but he gives it a wider meaning, roughly like this –

Yes of course machines and living beings obey the laws of physics and chemistry, but within the operation of these laws there is an area of possible variation left open. Without transgressing the laws of physics and chemistry, machines and living things are also controlled by another set of laws which deal with the areas left open. Thus they harness the laws of inanimate matter by a principle different from those laws for a purpose outside those laws. They impose *boundary conditions* on the laws of the lower level. "Ah," says the rigorous physical-laws man – we'll call him Rigour for short – "Ah, then you are bringing in another principle to explain life; the principle of this new set of laws. You're a vitalist!" This is a rude word among Rigour and his friends, it means 'you have gone over to magic; you are no longer a scientist!' Polanyi has indeed shown the need of a new organising principle to explain life, but he has cunningly protected his flank against this terrible charge of vitalism by bringing machines over to the other side to join living beings. That makes it harder for Rigour to deny that this new principle is needed and to treat its introduction as irrational or obscurantist.

Rigour has shown himself ready, in defence of his severity, to deny the reality of life and mind, to claim that Shakespeare's sonnets could have been produced by physical chemical processes, but he may find it harder to deny the facts about machines. There is that absurd saying which Rigour supporters sometimes bring out as an illustration of the capabilities of blind chance working in a merely physical world; the saying that if a couple of monkeys sat typing for long enough they would in the end type the whole of *Hamlet* – which is after all only an arrangement of letters on paper. Though prepared to swallow that nonsense, Rigour has not yet, I believe, suggested that if the monkeys sat there long enough the *typewriter* would appear eventually through the random action of physical forces.

A four-year-old child came back from her first Sunday School and told her younger sister – "God makes everything, Rachel". "Even spoons?" asked Rachel, who was eating her dinner. "Well, actually people make spoons," said the grown-ups. "And houses?" Rachel persisted. "Well of course people build houses –". The grown-ups were getting into a *slightly* difficult position, but the Sunday School girl said lightly and profoundly, "God makes children and flowers and easy things like that". Substitute 'physical chemical forces' for 'God', and it seems Rigour can easily accept that these make children and flowers, and Shakespeare sonnets; he can maintain his severity against these, since their individual spontaneous loveliness seems to him a sort of luxury which we must be prepared to sacrifice in the interests of detached strictly scientific explanation. Lines from one Shakespeare sonnet might have been addressed to Rigour –

"How with this rage shall beauty hold a plea,
Whose action is no stronger than a flower?"

But spoons and houses – and microscopes and lasers and nuclear accelerators – these are different, they are real in Rigour's terms, they belong to his world. When Polanyi demonstrates that Rigour cannot account for *machines* in his physical chemical terms; that a different principle must be involved in explaining a machine, Rigour must pay attention and cannot dismiss this as vitalism, i.e. mumbo-jumbo. It is ironic that the full reality and value of man, with his aims and purposes, is not thought worth so much – can be disregarded in the interests of hard scientific explanations; but that he may be saved by the fact that he has embodied some of his purposes in machines, and machines are obviously real. So if they show evidence of purpose, the only creature that can make them must be real too.[10]

How then does the idea of *boundary conditions* and dual control work in all this? A simple example could be a watermill, which harnesses the physical properties of water, the laws of gravity and other physical facts for the purpose of grinding corn. The laws of gravity continue to operate, the water flows downwards, but by choosing a site and contriving a channel the miller makes it flow over and turn his wheel. The area left open for higher control is that as long as the water flows downwards the laws of gravity have nothing to say about which direction it flows in; the new principle of control makes it flow in a certain direction for a purpose, imposing boundary conditions by not letting it flow in any of the other directions it might have flowed in.

This illustrates the pattern of dual control. The laws that are to be harnessed are thought of as a lower level, and the new principle that harnesses them as a higher level of control; this higher level control can never be accounted for on the lower level. For instance if one asked 'Why does the water run in this channel and turn the wheel?' it would not be a sufficient answer to say 'Because water runs downwards', although this (a) is true, (b) sets limits to where the wheel can be placed, (c) is a necessary condition for the operation of the wheel. The working of the wheel turned by the water cannot be explained without speaking of purpose, but if one day it stopped working, the stoppage could be explained without the idea of purpose, for instance it stopped because there had been no rain and the river had dried up. (N.B.: there is a variation in the sense in which Polanyi uses the term 'boundary condition' – it makes no difference to the argument but may be confusing if not grasped. Mostly he called the area left open by the laws of the lower level, its 'boundary conditions', and the higher principle that controls these 'the principle of marginal control'.[11] But later he called the restrictions imposed by the higher level 'boundary conditions' imposed on the laws of the lower level.[12] I shall use this second meaning.)

Two sorts of explanation – the water turns the wheel *because* water flows downwards; the water turns the wheel *because* the miller planned to grind corn. Neither alone is a sufficient explanation. Socrates discussed these two sorts of explanation over two thousand years ago as he sat in prison awaiting execution. He mocked the people who, to explain why he was sitting in prison rather than escaping, would say – "that I sit here because my body is made up of bones and muscles . . . and as the bones move in their sockets by the contraction or relaxation of the muscles, I am able to bend my limbs, and that is why I sit here in a curved posture . . . forgetting to mention the true cause, which is that the Athenians have thought fit to condemn me, and accordingly I have thought it better to remain here and undergo whatever sentence they impose; for I am inclined to think that these bones and muscles of mine would have gone off long ago to Megara or Boeotia – by the Dog they would – if I had not thought it better and nobler, instead of playing truant and running away, to endure any punishment which the State inflicts. There is surely a strange confusion of cause and conditions in all this. It would indeed be true to say that without bones and muscles and the other parts of the body I cannot execute my purpose. But to say that I do as I do because of them, and that this is the way in which minds act, and not from the choice of the best, is a very careless and idle way of speaking".[13]

Socrates' will to obey the law imposed boundary conditions on the functioning of his body, which would otherwise have acted quite differently though working according to the same physical and physiological laws. His bones and muscles were under dual control. They would also have been under dual control if he had run away to Megara; the control of their physical construction and the control of his desire to save his life. But still another higher level imposed control; his belief in the duty of obedience to the law. There are not just two levels of control possible but a whole hierarchy of levels, each made possible, and limited in its action, by the one below, but not determined by it. Polanyi illustrated this hierarchy of levels from the way we express ourselves. Here the lowest level is the sounds the voice can make; above that the vocabulary of words we use sets boundary conditions to the sounds we make. Above that again a grammar regulates the way the words can be put together in sentences, and at the highest level an author or orator marshals the sentences to convey the meaning he intends.

Music shows the same pattern of consecutive levels, the musical scale controlling the sound of each instrument, the laws of harmony the way they can combine, and at the top the composer's idea controlling the musical whole which the performance constitutes.

Town planning is another instance of this pattern; here the lowest level is formed by the essential physical components of the town; the buildings, roads, railways, water supply, sewage etc. These may be sited by independent agencies making purely utilitarian choices. But they need not be. If the notion of a pleasant townscape, a place that looks and feels like a setting for civilised living, is given scope, it can impose boundary conditions. There is a good deal of room for manoeuvre on the lower level, a railway or road can be placed here or there, within limits, without too much extra expense, and so the art of town planning imposes its own principles without contradicting those of the lower level. If the town thinks enough of itself to want dignity and splendour as well as comfort and pleasantness, another level of control could arise.

In living beings the hierarchy of levels includes a level on which, as we have seen, organs function like machines, but in all living organisms there is a higher level setting boundary conditions to the mechanical level.

"All living functions rely on the laws of inanimate nature in controlling the boundary conditions left open by these laws, the vegetative functions sustaining life at its lowest level leave open, both in plants and animals, the possibilities of growth and also leave open in animals the possibilities of muscular action; the principles governing muscular action leave open their integration to innate patterns of behaviour, such patterns are open in their turn to be shaped by intelligence, and the working of intelligence can be made to serve the still higher principle of man's responsible choices."[14]

Hierarchies of levels – this idea makes possible a very different kind of explanation from the kind that means reducing everything to one level of simple elements. All the levels are real; the higher levels built from the lower by using the 'play' that is left free in the operation of the lower level laws. The higher levels, it is true, are at the mercy of the lower, in that the lower levels may break free from the control of the higher. With all living creatures they will do so eventually in death. But the higher levels are no less real, indeed they are more so, by Polanyi's definition of reality, since they are more meaningful, more attractive of our interest because of the potentiality of still undiscovered implications in them. This structure of levels can be seen in everything connected with life, most of all in man, his consciousness, his skills, his powers of reasoning and creating, and his continuing vision of yet higher levels to explore and achieve.

This view of life would transform the whole outlook for man's reality and freedom. We need not feel that dehumanisation is the necessary price of the advance of knowledge, nor say in Bertrand Russellish mood – "How boring, how dull, we are all made of electrons and protons". Instead we can say with Wordsworth –

"Dust as we are, the immortal spirit grows
Like harmony in music."

In this view, the laws of nature only *rule* if nothing harnesses them. Seen from the point of view of the harnesser, they are his horses, steady and reliable in their own habits but willing to serve his needs and purposes as long as he respects their nature. One can see the laws of nature from two directions, as we found discovery can be seen from before or from after, and looks quite determined one way and quite indeterminate the other way.

Now one can see what was the matter with that.

– 'young man who said Damn,
I clearly perceive that I am
A creature that moves
In predestinate grooves
In fact not a bus but a tram'

He was a bus, but *he was looking out of his back window!* The parallel lines he saw were the tracks the bus had made, not grooves in which it had to move. He had only to look forward and drive, within limits wherever he wanted.

But if you look back, it all looks as though it could not have happened any other way but the way it did happen, as if those tracks were grooves. When Newton discerned in the heavens the laws of gravity and planetary motion, it seemed of course that everything happening as it was happening, and governed by those laws, must always behave in the same way. There were no persons up there to put those laws through their tricks. If only Newton could have seen astronauts dancing with his laws and hitching a lift to the moon from them!

The people Socrates was arguing with, the 'bones and muscles men' sounded convincing – 'this is how bones and muscles behave and you are made of bones and muscles therefore you are sitting here, your muscles having drawn your bones into this curved posture you *have* to be sitting here'. Polanyi shows not only that reducing what Socrates is doing to the bones and muscles level has not yet been done in a way that really explains it, but that it *cannot* be done. The higher levels of organisation in living creatures cannot be explained on the lowest level. The higher level organisation imposing the boundary conditions is an integration of particulars of the lower level into a meaningful whole, whose principle of integration is not discoverable on the lower level.

It now appears how similar this pattern is to the pattern of how we *know*. We saw how in tacit knowing an imaginative integration of particulars reveals their joint meaning, which is, we now see, the higher level coherence in which they become parts; and how this power can be seen as a development of the primitive powers of knowing and grasping the world that developed in the simplest forms of life. Now we are seeing the same pattern in the arrangement of the world that we thus know; in the *being* of the world. Evolution is now seen as a progressive intensification of the higher principles of life, advancing from inanimate nature to vegetative life, then to animal and on to human life and to the unlimited possibilities open to man in thought. "A panorama of meaningful achievement of almost breathtaking proportions."[15]

In the last chapter of *Personal Knowledge*, called 'The Rise of Man', Polanyi confronts the question how this hierarchy of levels could have come into being, in the light of what we know about evolution. Darwinism cannot allow for it. As Marjorie Grene wrote,[16] "what was so triumphantly successful in Darwin's theory was precisely its reduction of life to the play of chance and necessity; its elimination of organic categories from the interpretation even of living things". "Darwinism," says Professor Grene, "is teleology decapitated; natural selection selects what is good for something – good for what – for survival, for going on being good for going on being good for, and so on ad infinitum." Although this is still the prevalent faith, a number of biologists she quotes are dealing with concepts which suggest – "not that life's history is a function of two variables, variation and selection, but that it hides a much richer complexity, a spontaneity, an inventiveness, an orderliness which eludes explanation in terms of such simple conceptions".[17] Why then, she asks, has Darwinism such a hold on us? "Because neo-Darwinism is not only a scientific theory, but a theory deeply embedded in a metaphysical faith; in the faith that science can and must explain all the phenomena of nature in terms of one hypothesis, and that a hypothesis of maximum simplicity, of maximum impersonality and objectivity. Relatively speaking, neo-Darwinism is logically simple: there are just two things happening, chance variations, and the elimination of the worst ones among them, and both these happenings are just plain facts, things that do or don't happen, yes or no. Nature is like a vast computing machine."

Darwin himself felt a 'horrid doubt' that this conclusion is self-destructive, since if the mind is wholly the product of natural selection its conclusions are not reliable.

Recent advances in science, say Professor Torrance, 'have gone far to establishing science upon a deeper basis in reality, and to restoring in it the integrity of man's personal and rational inquiry into the meaning of the universe. Here old analytical methods have given way to synthesising ways of thought which are more capable of grasping the many levels of existence and integrating them in such a way that a gradient of meaning rises through them all, in which the higher intangible levels of reality are found to be possessed of the deepest significance, so that man's natural knowledge expands continuously into the knowledge of the supernatural".[18]

Marjorie Grene and Polanyi both explore the lines in modern biological work that seem to lead to a more open theory than Darwinism, one that could allow for the emergence of higher levels of being only to be understood as real wholes. Such a theory would be part of a philosophy of *life*, which Darwinism cannot be.

In modern biology there is a great deal of support for theories involving the idea of a hierarchy of levels. Arthur Koestler's book *The Ghost in the Machine* explores these tendencies.[19] Polanyi said that "the notion of a field in embryology could, if it were not handled too mechanically, provide an opening for an entry into the picture of a notion of a hierarchy of levels of being, in which higher levels emerge into existence in and through the establishment of new boundary conditions which in turn reorganise elements of the lower levels in which they are rooted".[20] He quoted Spemann, who worked on the growth of the embryo and showed in his experiments how the developments of parts is regulated by the needs of the whole. The term 'field' is taken from physics, but an 'embryonic field' is in an area of influence which evokes potentialities in the material, stimulating its development according to the whole plan. Spemann's conclusions were a support to Polanyi, for he found the reaction of a germ fragment in an embryonic field more comparable to mental processes than to a common chemical reaction.[21]

Arthur Peacocke in *Creation and the World of Science*[22] explores a view of evolution which, like Polanyi's, allows for a groping, exploring activity in early forms of life; processes which like discovery are intelligible after they have occurred but could not have been predicted. He shows freedom to be possible only within the law-like nexus of the evolving universe, allowing the emergence of a hierarchy of levels of living beings. While as a biologist Paul Weiss writes that, "in the light of realistic studies of actual phenomena the principle of hierarchic order in living nature reveals itself as a demonstrable descriptive fact".[23]

It seems as though the spell of Darwinism may at last be losing its hold. A number of evolutionary scientists now say the evidence for Darwin's theory is quite insufficient; some say it has never been seriously examined because, once the theory was stated, scientists had a psychological need to believe it in order to rout the fundamentalist religious forces which upheld the literal truth of the biblical account of creation. The present fundamentalist lobby with its uncompromising literalism may again be preventing the scientific acceptance of new insights; it is these insights from within science which look like toppling the Darwin edifice.

A recent book[24] comes to the reluctant conclusion that evolution as a random meaningless process could not begin to account for the complexity of living matter, and that if the beginnings of life were not random they must have been the product of purposeful intelligence. Unlike the psychologists quoted by Polanyi who deny the reality of consciousness because they cannot explain it, these authors can say that the whole process of consciousness probably has profound cosmic significance.

The way forward on these lines will not be without difficulties. But it is clear that Darwinism cannot explain how man's mind has arrived on the scene, and unless minds capable of reasoning *have* arrived, neither Darwinism nor any other theory has any validity. Polanyi takes his 'conclusions first' stand, which is that of common sense. Responsible, sentient, creative beings exist, so a valid theory of evolution must allow for their existence.

"It is obvious, therefore, that the rise of man can be accounted for only by other principles than those known today to physics and chemistry. If this be vitalism, then vitalism is mere common sense, which can be ignored only by a truculently bigoted mechanistic outlook. And so long as we can form no idea of the way a material system may become a conscious responsible person, it is an empty pretence to suggest that we have an explanation for the descent of man. Darwinism has diverted attention for a century from the descent of man by investigating the *conditions* of evolution and over-looking its *action*.[25] Evolution can be understood only as a feat of emergence."

'Vitalism is mere common sense' – why then has it become such a bogey? Reading Waddington's book *The Nature of Life*[25] I began to understand better. What the anti-vitalists can rightly object to is our putting in a 'vital principle' to explain life, just as we put vitamins into white bread to compensate for all the rich elements we have previously taken out of the flour. We are putting in what we never ought to have taken out! In other words, we start from the wrong end. If you begin by thinking that you know all about the mechanistic behaviour of the ultimate particles that make up the inanimate world, then you have no way to get from there to life. There are two wrong things you can do in that situation, and both have been done. You can say that life is just more of the same mechanistic happenings, there is only "pure chance, absolutely free and blind, at the root of the stupendous edifice of evolution,"[27] and any search for meaning is simply "the unwearying heroic effort of mankind denying its own contingency".[28]

That is one way, the other is to open your eyes and look at life in all its spontaneous richly meaningful creativity, and to admit that it could not possibly have come out of the dead world of mere 'chance and necessity'. But here it is, so it must be magic – a vital principle! This is how we arrive at vitalism in its objectionable magic sense.

But if you start by accepting the clear reality of life – Polanyi's common sense – then you can look differently at the inanimate world, as a world that had the potentiality for life to emerge. It was you, the observer, who had taken your own abstraction for reality and made a world from which life and mind could never have come.

Paul Weiss says that when we find other principles than those of physics to be necessary in understanding higher levels of life, we are only putting back principles that we had taken out in our analysing descent to the lower levels.[29]

The origins of life will remain mysterious, but we can choose with Polanyi to believe in life and mind, which we experience and without which we know nothing, rather than believing that we know all about the ultimate constitution of the universe. Remembering Polanyi's experience of discovery, where the view *from after* looks all determinate, while the view from before looks undecided, hesitant, daring – we may realise that as we only see evolution *from after*, we leave out the groping, striving activity of myriads of living beings, achieving emergence to higher levels within the framework of physical laws.

Notes to Chapter VIII

1. see Ch. 2, p.23 above
2. Royal Society of Medicine lecture 'Science and Man'. 1970
3. *Ibid.* (*Knowing and Being* p.228)
4. *Personal Knowledge* p.33
5. *Meaning* p.171. Compare Marjorie Grene, *The Knower and the Known*, p.226 'Time and Teleology'
6. *The Knower and the Known* p.186
7. Russell *'Why I am not a Christian'* p.46, 49
8. *Men of Ideas* p.296
9. Russell *'Why I am not a Christian'* p.50
10. Compare *Knowing and Being* p.232
11. e.g. *The Tacit Dimension* p.40
12. e.g. *Knowing and Being* p.226
13. *Phaedo* – trans. Livingstone
14. *Knowing and Being* p.155
15. *Meaning* p.173
16. *The Knower and the Known* chapter 7 'The Faith of Darwinism'
17. *Ibid.* p.199
18. T. F. Torrance *Belief in Science and in Christian Life* (Introduction)
19. Koestler, Pan Books 1970
20. *Meaning* p.176 *cf Personal Knowledge* p.354–9
21. Hans Spemann – *Embryonic Development and Induction* quoted in *Personal Knowledge* p.339
22. A. R. Peacocke – Clarendon Press 1979
23. Koestler (Ed) *Beyond Reductionism* p.4
24. *Evolution from Space*, Hoyle and Wickramsinghe
25. *Personal Knowledge* p.390
26. E. R. Waddington *The Nature of Life* 1961
27. J. Monod *Chance and Necessity* p.110
28. *Ibid.* p.50
29. Koestler (Ed) *Beyond Reductionism* p.11

CHAPTER IX

MIND AND BODY

Discretion was another of Everyman's friends. She was in fact his Mind. The priests said to him 'Your Mind will let you down, don't trust it, only listen to what we tell you'.

Science tells him 'You have no Mind, only brain processes, they are your Mind'.

In this chapter we see Science examining Everyman's brain and assuring him she has found his Mind, while Everyman's mind is on the cat.

WHEN Descartes divided the universe into Mind and Matter he had his reasons; it helped in the short term to solve some problems about knowledge. But it created other problems, and these are still with us, all the more intractable from having sunk into the unconscious background of thought.

The long-standing puzzle about man's mind and his body that Descartes left us cannot be solved either way; it is a sort of philosophic Catch 22. Once the puzzle has been put in that form we beat to and fro without seeing any way out. We go along first with Descartes, saying 'Mind and Matter: two different things'. So Mind is entirely immaterial, a 'ghost in the machine', no scientific tests could discover its presence or absence because it isn't, in any material sense, there. Matterless mind on one side, mindless matter on the other. Then all value, meaning, purpose must be on the side of Mind. But this Mind has become so ghostly that it is an easy target for scepticism. How do we know it really is anything? It may be an idea like 'Phlogiston' which scientists once passionately believed in but which turned out to be a mistake. All we can measure and weigh and handle and be sure of is Matter. This ghost, 'Mind', cannot be found anywhere, it cannot have any effect on Matter since it has no power. Better to admit that Matter is all we can know about. But then comes the catch. To put it crudely, if your mind is simply your material brain, then its thoughts have no objective validity, because all that is happening when you think is movements of matter which cannot be right or wrong. So, your statement that the mind is just the brain is a meaningless noise produced by an automaton and cannot be taken seriously. All meaning, value, truth has been abolished, with Mind.

Can we turn another kind of light on to this problem of Cartesian dualism as it is called, using Polanyi's ideas of tacit knowing, indwelling, levels and boundary conditions?

We might ask first – Does it matter? or Why should we mind? Is this just one of those philosophic puzzles about what to call something, that common sense can ignore? No, it matters, because it is the source of all that reduction to meaninglessness, that assumption that only the tangible is real, which has boundless destructive effects on our lives.

Polanyi believed he had resolved the dilemma of Cartesian dualism. But the strength and persistence of the problems that brought it into existence are shown by the way people still question whether he was a dualist or not. Professor Marjorie Grene, who has so sensitively interpreted Polanyi's work, has told[1] how she used to argue with him about this, and she says – "Polanyi believed he was reviving dualism when in fact he was helping to refute it". This would be a curious thing to happen, and her saying this illustrates how hard it is to get away from seeing the problem in Descartes' terms – either dualism or not dualism; either mind and matter are two things or they are the same thing.

In one sense dualism does fade away in Polanyi's picture of knowledge, where it is a person who knows, not an immaterial mind in a simply physical body. A person exists on all levels. The boundaries of his 'mind' are not fixed, or limited to the physical brain. Whatever the person dwells in becomes an extension of himself, used for thinking and knowing, and so a part of his mind; whatever he looks at from outside as an object is matter. So in this sense Polanyi was not a dualist.

Yet Polanyi said repeatedly and clearly that "mind and body are profoundly different, they are not two aspects of the same thing".[2] This is surely a kind of *duality* and to this Polanyi held firmly, since without it there is no defence against behaviourist theories. "If mind and body were two aspects of the same thing, the mind conceivably could not do anything but what the bodily mechanism determined."

Polanyi often discussed Cartesian dualism in the light of his own philosophy.[3] He recalled, in doing so, his explanations of the pattern of tacit knowing; how by a change of focus we attend *from* a collection of facts *to* their joint meaning; how this works in our knowledge of various kinds of comprehensive wholes such as skills, the recognition of a face or of the meaning of its expression, and the integration of bodily sensations into objects in the world outside us. In all these and other instances the pattern proved to be the same. Sometimes the subsidiary facts can be known specifically, sometimes they cannot, but the two kinds of awareness are mutually exclusive; to grasp the comprehensive whole you have to leave off attending *to* the subsidiary facts and attend *from* them.

That was the structure of knowing that emerged, and the structure of being, of how things are, proved to be similar. Comprehensive entities not only have to be known by a tacit integration, they exist on different levels, and the principles of organisation of the higher level cannot be discovered from focussing on the lower level facts. The physics and chemistry of the parts of a machine do not tell us what it is or how it works, without a higher level view of its function, and in the higher levels of living things, right up to man and his responsible judgments, ever new principles of organisation have to be recognised.

Now if this pattern is applied to brain and mind, what happens? The brain is, on one level, a very subtle machine, and it can be studied on that level by physiologists; these studies have made great progress, partly because of abstracting those aspects and looking at them alone. But such study will never see the *mind*, which is the experience and activity of the person whose brain it is. The person is dwelling in the bodily processes in a relationship not open to anyone else, and using them as clues to an outside reality, the physiologist is looking at them as objects.

Imagine a man looking at a cat, while a physiologist is studying the brain of the man who is watching the cat. "To see a cat," says Polanyi, "differs sharply from the knowledge of the mechanism of seeing a cat . . . These two experiences have a sharply different content, and the difference represents the viable core of the traditional mind-body dualism."[4]

Marjorie Grene quotes the cat story and agrees with Polanyi's use of it.

"The neurologist does not see my seeing – and that's Polanyi's point. Knowledge of the brain is not identical with knowledge of the mind, nor is the brain identical with the mind, even though the latter depends necessarily upon the former for its operation and its existence."[5] So she seems to agree with Polanyi: she even says just as he does that the mind is the meaning of the brain.[6] Yet she goes on to lament his wrongheaded defence of the separateness of mind and body, as though he was defending the full rigour of Cartesian dualism, when, she says, what he could have done and had found the means to do, was to slip between the horns of its dilemma. "For the theory of mind mediated by the doctrine of tacit knowing is a theory of mind as fundamentally and irrevocably incarnate."[7] Yes, this is true, but incarnation surely requires two things, one to be incarnate in the other?

This sort of argument just shows how difficult it is to step outside the habitual ways of speaking about mind and body. The word 'thing' is a tricky one because to speak of two 'things' seems to imply two material things, and that seems to be the cause of Marjorie Grene's dismay at Polanyi saying "mind and body are two different things, just as our common sense tells us they are".[8]

The mind, then, can be described as the meaning of the brain, as a functioning whole can be seen as the meaning of its parts. Thus it is a different thing from the brain, though not a separately existing thing. Is it better though, to call the mind the *meaning* of the brain, as Polanyi does, rather than calling it another *aspect* of the brain, which he rejected? Well, yes, for the meaning of a sentence is not just another aspect of the printed letters on the page, it is a different thing, as 'the Bible' is a different thing from 'this Bible in my hand'. The meaning of a sentence can be expressed in Chinese or Morse code, perhaps in graphs or pictures, it can cause things to happen, it can have its verbal form changed to express it better. There is quite a lot of sense in calling a meaning a different thing from its material representation.

Polanyi's explanation of tacit knowing allows us to say that brain or body is what you see when you focus on the physiological facts; mind is the integration of these facts from within by the person who is attending from them, using them as clues to meanings outside himself. The brain processes are facts on a lower level, while mind is their control by a higher level principle imposing boundary conditions on the workings of the brain and body.

In this perspective the duality of mind and body becomes just one instance of a duality that occurs at each level, when the facts of the lower level are themselves, and are also elements of the comprehensive whole existing at a higher level. "Each level is subject to dual control, first by the laws that apply to its elements in themselves and second, by the laws that control the comprehensive entity formed by them."[9] "Mental principles and the principles of physiology form a pair of such jointly operating principles. The mind relies for its workings on the continued operation of physiological principles, but it controls the boundary conditions left undetermined by physiology. This lends substance to the conclusion we derived from the structure of tacit knowing, that body and mind are profoundly different; they are not two aspects of the same thing."[9]

Lack of this structure of ideas leaves us with the Cartesian dilemma and the deadening theories which have come from resolving it by saying only the material facts are real. These theories were the justification of Behaviourism, first started by J. B. Watson in a paper in 1913. Arthur Koestler, who gives an account of it in *The Ghost in the Machine,* calls it a pseudo-science "whose doctrines have invaded psychology like a virus which first causes convulsions, then slowly paralyses its victim". In spite of its crudity and restricted outlook the Behaviourist view has continued to influence thinking in

many different fields. Curiously, as Arthur Koestler points out, it
used to be the psychologists and logicians who said that mental
events are different from physical events, while physiologists in
general took the materialist view that all mental events are reducible
to brain processes. But lately it is the other way round. Behaviourist
psychologists and philosophers reduce it all to the material brain,
while "those men whose life work was devoted to the anatomy,
physiology, pathology and surgery of the brain became increasingly
converted to the opposite view". He quotes experiments by the great
neurosurgeon Wilder Penfield, stimulating the mental cortex and
causing the patient's hand to move. Penfield concluded his report –
"There are, as you see, many demonstrable mechanisms in the
brain. They work for the purpose of the mind automatically when
called upon . . . But what agency is it that calls upon these
mechanisms, choosing one rather than another? Is it another
mechanism, or is there in the mind something of a different essence?
. . . To declare that these two things are one does not make them so
but it does block the progress of research".[10] So Professor
Penfield's account allows for levels and for control of brain
mechanisms by a higher principle. But another neuro-physiologist,
Professor J. Z. Young, gave in his Gifford Lectures[11] a different
account which illustrates the behaviourist position; the strange views
of the relation of mind and brain to which one is driven for lack of
Polanyi's structure of ideas. The whole gist of these lectures is to
suggest that study of the brain will enable us to understand the
mind. This is done by the sleight of hand which Polanyi calls
'pseudo-substitution'. Drawing on our ordinary knowledge of how
minds work, Professor Young constantly disparages such
unscientific knowledge in comparison with the superior knowledge
we now should have through our knowledge of how *brains* work.

"The brain works in certain organised ways that may be described
as programs, and the action of these programs constitute the entity
that we call the mind of the person." "The lives of human beings are
governed by sets of programs written in their genes and brains.
Some of these programs may be called practical or physiological and
they ensure that we breathe, eat, drink and sleep . . . perhaps the
most important programs of all are those used for the activities that
we call mental, such as thinking, imagining, dreaming and
worshipping."[11]

So, he says – "the knowledge collected recently by neuroscientists,
clinicians and psychologists has transformed our understanding of

human motivations and actions". But when it comes to giving us any sample of this transformed understanding, we wait in vain; all we get is our ordinary non-transformed descriptions of, say, seeing a cat, together with a promise of how much better it will be when the neuro-scientist has looked long and hard enough at the cat-watcher's brain.[12] We get no new light on the *mind* at all, and of course it is impossible that we should.

For instance, about aesthetic values Young says[13] "Proper study of the organisation of the brain shows that belief and creative art are essential and universal features of all human life". The degree of pleasure we experience from the sights and sounds we enjoy can be expressed in terms of the degree of arousal it causes, which can be measured by electroencephalogram and plotted to show a line called 'Wundt's curve' – "it may result from the operations of the reticular formation of the core brain and the reward systems. In this way we certainly gain the beginnings of a basis for a scientific study of aesthetics, but unfortunately there is still very little precise quantitive information about these activating and rewarding systems in humans".[14]

Too bad! We shall have to wait a while to know scientifically which poet or painter to prefer. "The subject is so complicated and the workings of the brain so little understood, that it is often still necessary to rely on vague opinions and judgments rather than on precise measurements," Young laments, but he plods on undiscouraged through programs for such 'useful activities' as creativity, art and worship. "I am not at all devaluing these experiences," he protests. "To say that religion or art or music are useful seems to me not in the least to devalue them." "I believe that these 'spiritual' and creative activities are even more important in the literal practical sense than the more mundane ones . . . These are the things that together ensure the continuity and survival of human communities, even more than do the provision of food and shelter. The teaching that 'man does not live by bread alone' is perhaps more needed than ever today. I believe that a proper study of the brain will enable us to see more clearly the place that so-called cultural and spiritual activities play in human homeostasis" – (that's his word for staying alive, going on as we are).

How would Young complete his quotation 'man does not live by bread alone'? Presumably – 'but by every stimulation of his reward centres'. Under a show of valuing art and worship he emasculates them. The truth, beauty, or religious understanding to which a man may devote himself, and which may indeed give him some reason for living because of his passionate wish for contact, through the activities of science, art or worship, with reality, is emptied of all content except its value in keeping him alive. The same murderous substitution happens with other concepts. Professor Young can profess belief in such ideas as *purpose* – yes of course there is purpose, it is the aim of every living thing to keep alive – ("Our central concept is that the main goal of organisms is to maintain themselves, in simple words, to remain in good health")[15] – free will – yes of course man has *free will*, it means that he is so complex that we can't discover all the causes of his actions. ("Neither he nor anyone else can foresee what the result of his brain actions will be.")[16]

The old Cartesian puzzle has tied up this modern scientist in philosophic knots. He is caught in the catch, though he does not admit it. Brain processes are real because they can be measured. Mind is not another real thing, so it must be brain processes. Then the intangible unmeasurable things, beauty, worship, compassion, justice and truth are unreal – including of course the truth of his own theories. But he does not see this because he floats over his theories on a balloon of intangibles which he would have just shot down had his theories been true.

In effect he, with his neuro-science, is saying the same thing as Bukharin said to Polanyi; thought, the pursuit of truth, is not an independent reality, it just serves the system. Thought dictated by the five-year plan, or determined by the brain programs, is equally cut off from contact with reality. And Professor Young's explanation of mental and 'spiritual' activities, like thought and worship, as brain programs for keeping the organism alive is a piece of reduction to meaninglessness, of the same sort that made Silone's friends commit suicide for the futility of living – not being able like Young to carry on believing in the values that his theory reduces to nonsense.

Robert Pirsig wrote[17] of "the ghost which calls itself rationalism but whose appearance is that of incoherence and meaninglessness . . . which declares that the ultimate purpose of life, which is to keep alive, is impossible, but that this is the ultimate purpose of life anyway, so that great minds struggle to cure our diseases so that people may live longer but only madmen ask why. One lives longer in order that he may live longer. There is no other purpose. That is what the ghost says".

"We need all the knowledge we can get about our programs in order . . . to learn how best to regulate our actions," says Professor Young.[18] This is surely nonsense. We do not need any such knowledge in order to make our decisions, any more than Socrates needed to know the anatomy of his knees in order to decide whether to stay in prison or to run away. Certainly without knees he would not have had any choice, and without a brain we could not make decisions, but the study of brain programs is as irrelevant to our moral, aesthetic and practical judgment as a course of anatomy would have been to him. It is certainly very interesting in its own right, and may become useful if the mind breaks down in some way – if the cat-watcher started being unable to see the cat or seeing two cats, the neuroscientist might be able to show the reason, since mental operations do use brain processes. But to start concentrating on brain processes to help our mental processes would be as absurd and confusing as if the cat-watcher hoped to see the cat more clearly by listening to the physiologists' description of his brain processes than by watching the cat.

Young wants physiologists and philosophers to get together to study the brain, because the programs for thinking must be there, somewhere, and "study of the brain should be of great help in identifying them".[19] Polanyi's understanding of the mind-brain relationship rules that out as a way of knowing the mind. He sums up the relationship – "No observations of physiology can make us apprehend the operations of the mind".[29] But the workings of the mind will never *interfere with* the principles of physiology, and as the operations of the mind rely on bodily principles, disturbances in the body can affect the mind, and bodily developments may offer the mind new opportunies.

How then do we know a mind? From the person's expressions, gestures, speech and actions – but not by focussing on these as if they *were* the mind, as the behaviourists maintain. Behaviourism can't avoid the Cartesian catch. We know a person's mind by indwelling in the manifestations of it, as clues to their meaning – it is the meaning which is the person's mind.[21]

A very young baby was lying in her carrycot, gravely and alertly regarding her surroundings, as babies sometimes do when not preoccupied with internal troubles. Her older sister exclaimed, "Oh, look at Ann – she's thinking about!" "What's she thinking about?" "I don't know; she's thinking about." The three-year-old recognised in the baby, with surprise, a mind like her own, actively getting hold of the outside world: thinking *about*, that was what was noticeable, not just thinking as she might have been yelling or sleeping or burping. It was what Polanyi would call a convivial recognition, he says indeed that all observations of life or mind are convivial. "The sight of a man's alert eyes and face instantly conveys to us the presence of a conscious, sane and intelligent mind having the same faculties that we ourselves exercise as conscious, sane and intelligent beings."[22] (Our power of recognition of *mind* in the alert face is the reason, it occurs to me, why it is so very disturbing to see a face that is not alert; does not signal mind, but insanity or unreality. "Thou hast no speculation in those eyes!" cried Macbeth, recoiling in terror from the ghost of Banquo.)

After explaining his view of how we know other people's minds, Polanyi 'placed' his work in the philosophic scene.[23] He mentioned the Continental philosophers; Husserl, and Merleau Ponty's *Phenomenologie de la Perception*, which gave a vivid description of the way in which we experience our bodies and the way we understand the gestures of others. But without the logic of tacit knowing and the theory of 'levels of being' he finds Merleau Ponty's insight inadequate – "an abundance of brilliant flashes without a constructive system".[24] Both Merleau Ponty and Gilbert Ryle, agreeing there is no intellectual interpretation in the way we follow the workings of another person's mind, are left without an adequate account of what could take its place, and so Ryle has to say that the intelligent performances we see are not clues to the mind, they *are* the mind. Ryle demonstrates that the mind does not explicitly operate on the body, and so he concludes mind and body are the same thing. "But what actually follows from the fact that mind and body do not interact explicitly is that they interact according to the logic of tacit knowing. And it is this logic that disposes of the Cartesian dilemma by acknowledging two mutually exclusive ways of being aware of our body."[25] Tacit knowledge on the other hand gives a convincing idea of how we know another person's mind. We know a chess player's mind by dwelling in the stratagems of his games, and know another man's pain by dwelling in his face distorted by suffering. But if we looked at the bits of their behaviour as separate objects we would lose sight of their mind, as happens whenever we focus on the particulars of a comprehensive entity.

Tacit knowledge and the idea of levels also enables us to admit the existence of brain programmes and yet to insist that there is a higher level involved, on which some higher principle uses and organises the brain programmes for purposes they do not recognise, as the mind of Socrates carried out *his* purpose – to stay in prison, not the purpose of his brain programmes – to stay alive.

Theories of the relation of mind to body have been explored by Eccles and Popper in their joint book *The Self and Its Brain*,[26] and their views are in some respects close to Polanyi's. Although they differ from each other in some particulars they agree on a duality of mind and body; Eccles sums up their position as a strong dualist hypothesis, saying, "Its central component is that primacy is given to the self-conscious mind . . . the integrating agent building the unity of conscious experience from all the diversity of brain events". Thus they have turned back, against the distortions of materialism, to what Polanyi calls the common sense view; they do not think mind is brain processes; they see conscious mind as active and shaping; they believe that evolution is creatively emergent and that with the emergence of man the creativity of the universe has become clear.

Curiously, although they are thus close to Polanyi, and Eccles has said that Polanyi influenced him, the book does not mention Polanyi except in one footnote, and the ideas of tacit knowing, indwelling and the hierarchy of levels are not used or discussed. Some of these ideas appear in other forms in the book, for instance the theory of 'downward causation' meaning the influence that a whole organism can have upon its parts, as opposed to the atomic components determining the whole, is like Polanyi's theory of a higher level organisation imposing boundary conditions on the lower level particulars.

Notes to Chapter IX

1. Journal of the British Society for Phenomenology, Oct 1977
2. e.g. *Meaning* p.51
3. e.g. *Meaning* pp.48–51, *Knowing and Being* pp.147–8, 222–3
4. *Meaning* p.49
5. Journal of the British Society for Phenomenology Oct 1977 p.169
6. *Ibid* p.170
7. *Ibid* p.169
8. 'Logic and Psychology', American Psychologist XII Jan 1968
9. *Meaning* pp.50, 51
10. Penfield; paper delivered at the Control of Mind Symposium at the University of California Medical Centre 1961. Quoted by Koestler – *The Ghost in the Machine* p.236
11. *Programs of the Brain* – 1978 p.7
12. This is what Eccles and Popper call 'promissory materialism' (*The Self and its Brain* p.97)
13. *Programs of the Brain* p.231
14. *Ibid* p.38
15. *Ibid* p.143
16. *Ibid* p.23
17. *Zen and the Art of Motorcycle Maintenance* p.78
18. *Programs of the Brain* p.145
19. *Ibid* p.192
20. *Knowing and Being* p.221
21. *Meaning* p.139, *KB* p.22
22. 'Clues to an Understanding of Mind and Body' *The Scientist Speculates*, ed I. J. Good, NY Basic Books, 1962
23. *Knowing and Being* p.221
24. *Meaning* p.47
25. *Knowing and Being* p.223
26. Karl R. Popper and John C. Eccles. *The Self and Its Brain* Springer International, Berlin, New York, 1977

CHAPTER X

WHAT IS A PERSON?

When Knowledge is Everyman's friend, he can be fully himself.

When Science turns her cold gaze on him, he disintegrates as a person.

If he is not a person, he cannot know — so what becomes of Knowledge?

POLANYI has dared to say that there is no impersonal test of truth. Our knowledge rests on the responsible and skilled judgment of persons. So what is a person that truth can rest on him? The scientific world view, imposing its rules about what is to be allowed as valid knowledge, has made it impossible to recognise persons in their full reality, and impossible to understand how persons can know.

"It is simply this sort of mechanical reductionism that is the heart of the matter," says Polanyi in a passionate outburst.[1] "It is this that is the origin of the whole system of scientific obscurantism under which we are suffering today. This is the cause of our corruption of the conception of man, reducing him either to an insentient automaton or to a bundle of appetites. This is why science denies us the possibility of acknowledging personal responsibility. This is why science can be invoked so easily in support of totalitarian violence, why science has become the greatest source of dangerous fallacies today."

If you look back at the scientistic assumptions mentioned in Chapter I, you can see how the world view underlying them all makes persons unreal. Man is an accidental result of physical events, they say; man is a machine which can be superseded by better machines; sanity and insanity are equally irresponsible since all thought is determined; religion is incredible because physical necessity rules; persons can only be known by analysing and classifying which destroys them.

The results of this depersonalising are seen not only in the suicide or despair of sensitive and intelligent people, in violence and nihilism or in cynical triviality. They create a climate in which the needs of persons can be overridden with 'scientific' justification, in the interests of bureaucratic convenience or tyrannical whim. The only basis for respecting persons is that they are sentient, responsible, creative beings, and if with 'scientific' authority this can be denied, the respect and sensitivity must fade. The use by governments of such barbarities as psychiatric prisons for political dissidents, or any of the modern abuses of state power, gets 'scientific' validation, and so do the many lesser kinds of bureaucratic disregard of persons. Behaviourist philosophies can be used to justify cruelty, for how can we know that other people suffer? They weep or grimace, but we have no proof that they feel pain, just as we have no proof that any brutalising public spectacle in debasing humanity really harms people. No moral statement can be proved or disproved by experiment, so an outlook which accepts only what can be proved must lead to disregard of persons as moral beings. Art is trivialised, morality and justice are shams, if the reality of persons is thus denied.

Some may admit that this is so, but may think it unavoidable. Personal reality cannot be saved by saying or shouting it with however much passionate conviction. The enterprise of re-establishing Everyman as a sentient, creative, responsible person cannot be done easily. We cannot just return to the state of innocence in which we believed that man was something quite apart from the animal and physical world. Science has made that impossible. Nor is it enough to say – 'The scientific world view is depressing and causes suicides, let us give it up'. Many depressing things are true, and the authority of science comes in part from its claim to speak the truth however dismayed anyone may be by it. If faith in our personal reality and responsibility is to carry conviction, the scientific world view has to be shown to be in this respect *not true*, in spite of the truth of so much that science has revealed about man. Man *is* related to the apes, man *is* in some respects a machine, man *is* part of the universe known by physics and chemistry. He *is* often ruled by pressures he neither understands nor can control, driven to action by animal instincts or economic forces he does not recognise. We have to admit all that science has opened our eyes to, and still maintain that the conclusions of the scientific view are wrong and that persons are real.

This challenge Polanyi accepted. He asked – "Does the nature of man as a material system, as a machine, as a centre of appetites, and as part of a society subject to coercion by predominant interests, permit him to make any truly independent choices?"[2] His answer is yes, and his account of the way we know offers a kind of world and a kind of knowledge which does not drive us to the futility of abolishing in the name of knowledge the persons who alone are capable of knowing.

Arthur Koestler once arranged a gathering of distinguished scientists to discuss, under the title 'Beyond Reductionism', their views about any reality that could not be reduced to the stuff of physics and chemistry. He warned in his opening words that an easy solution would be useless. "Nothing would have been easier," he said, "than to collect in this room a bunch of amiable cranks to concoct a 'New Philosophy' . . . if a new synthesis is to emerge, it will emerge from within the laboratories."

It is the same sort of warning that Ernest Gellner gives when he speaks of dehumanisation as the price of the advance of knowledge.[3] In reaction against this disturbing dehumanisation Gellner discerns a 'Movement for the Preservation of Man', to which he is not very sympathetic, since he thinks the dehumanisation is a price we have to pay. "The more we can explain the world, the more we are ourselves explained." He agrees some of our humanity should be retained, but not too much and not too easily.

Polanyi would agree that a real 'preservation of Man' must *take account* of the laboratory; it cannot be done by pretending science has not happened. But perhaps he would not agree that man's salvation can *start* in the laboratory. He knew and respected the laboratory, but he started from a rockfast belief in the reality of persons, a belief acquired through living among them, sharing and recognising their responsibility, understanding and creativity. Then he looked in the laboratory for any reason why we may not believe in such beings, and found on the contrary that we must, if we are to believe in the laboratory. In his experience they *were* the laboratory, in their disciplined, co-operative and responsible pursuit of truth; the rules and equipment of the laboratory were simply their tool kit, and tool kit instructions cannot prove the tool users unreal.

We all in some degree start from our conclusions, as Polanyi said he did. Bertrand Russell started from the conclusion that the rules and methods of the laboratory rule out persons, and was stoically prepared to be ruled out in theory, though in fact he went on illegitimately being there. Quine[4] starts from the same conclusion; the methods of physics are so successful that we must not go outside them; he is prepared to pour mind and meaning down the laboratory sink in order to "preserve the closed character of the physical world". Gellner is more tenderly disposed towards persons[5] but would reduce them a good deal to fit laboratory requirements. Polanyi starts from the other end, from knowing persons and never doubting their entire reality, finding them decidedly more real than atoms. He looked full in the Gorgon face of this 'Science' whose rules of knowledge turn man to matter, and found it to be a false mask, for the real face of science is discovery, and discoveries are made by persons, not by rules. And the reality that persons know is, like persons, recognised as real because it can be known but never fully known; it draws and leads us by having always more to reveal, unforeseeable but in character.

Polanyi's ideas of tacit knowledge and the many-level world

transform the possibilities for recognising persons in their full humanity, without rejecting the scientific knowledge of the physical world. Human thought is the highest level known to us, and all through the range of knowledge of ascending levels of reality we have seen how the higher level is the authoritative level, because only in our perception of the higher level can we see what the items of a lower level really are. For instance when we recognise apparently random marks on a page as features of a face, or scattered bits of metal as parts of a machine, our recognition of the whole, the meaning, changes the appearance of the parts. Or when we look down from an aeroplane and see the outline of a prehistoric site in what had seemed from the ground to be random hillocks, the same transformation occurs. Our tacit integration of particulars on the lower levels changes the particulars, although it does not upset the laws by which they are governed on their own level.

Each level of reality, as we saw, relies on but is not fully determined by the level below it; can be crippled or destroyed by failure of the lower level, but cannot be explained in its successful working by the laws of the lower level. The higher controls the lower by imposing boundary conditions on the area left undetermined by the lower level laws.

Thus a person, existing on the highest level of reality, also exists on many other levels and can be studied on each level; as a physical and chemical structure, as a machine, as an animal body, but only fully as a person who exercises free choice. The studies of the lower levels are valid; it is perfectly possible and legitimate to study a man on any of these levels as long as it is recognised that these lower level studies are studying an abstraction. It is the person, the highest level, that gives the particulars of the lower levels their joint meaning and their full reality, which will never be arrived at by focussing on the lower level particulars and then adding up the results. The higher levels, and indeed all levels involving life, cannot be recognised without the concept of achievement and possible failure. They have to be grasped by a tacit integration, an indwelling knowledge. Now can the reality and freedom of the person be ruled out by laws discovered on the lower level, since the lower level laws only determine what happens when they are not harnessed by a higher level imposing boundary conditions.

There are various ways in which the reality and value of a person is reduced by the scientific outlook with its insistence upon completely explicit knowledge. The neurological approach reduces him, as we saw in Chapter IX, to the sum of his brain programs. Behaviourist psychology reduces him to bits of behaviour. Both if consistently applied rule out the possibility of personal freedom and responsibility. Both achieve their only plausibility by relying on the tacit knowledge they deny.[6] But perhaps the most powerful modern myth in devaluing persons is that of artificial intelligence, for instance, the myth of "cheap computers no larger than a portable typewriter" that will be able shortly to "solve almost any problem faster and more efficiently than we can".

Polanyi argues from the unspecifiable nature of much of our tacit knowledge that this vision's fulfilment is logically impossible. While, he says, "all arts can be performed automatically to the extent to which the rules of the art can be specified, no unspecifiable skill or connoisseurship can be fed into a machine".[7] He also argues that a machine is necessarily the tool of the person who uses it, and who in programming and reading the results of its operation can supply the tacit elements of interpretation. "A man's mind can carry out feats of intelligence by aid of a machine and also without such aid, while a machine can function only as an extension of a person's body under the control of his mind . . . Since the control exercised over the machine by the user's mind is – like all interpretations of a system of strict rules – necessarily unspecifiable, the machine can be said to function intelligently only by the aid of unspecifiable personal coefficients supplied by the user's mind."[8]

"There is," he says,[9] "a school of thought today which passionately pursues this mechanical conception of all vital adaptive functions, including the activities of human intelligence." It is sometimes claimed that a machine could develop conscious thinking, but if this were possible, Polanyi says, the consciousness would be simply an accompaniment to mechanical operations which it would not affect. If this were taken as a true model of a person's mind, "we shall have to imagine for example that Shakespeare's conscious thoughts had no effect on the writing of his plays; that the plays were subsequently performed by actors whose thoughts had no effect on their acting; while successive generations of audiences flocked to see the plays without being impelled by the fact that they enjoyed them". None of this is strictly inconceivable, but it is such a distortion of life as we know it that we are driven to acceptance of a different system of belief, which Polanyi's reasoning shows to be legitimately open to us, which acknowledges persons as responsible centres of originality, and Shakespeare's plays as "a massive demonstration of a creativity which cannot be explained in terms of an automatic mechanism".[10]

"Our capacity for knowing things either focally or subsidiarily is decisive here," Polanyi says.[11] "Mind is not the aggregate of its focally known manifestations but is that on which we focus our attention while being subsidiarily aware of its manifestations. This is the way . . . by which we acknowledge a person's judgment and share also other forms of his consciousness . . . According to these definitions of 'mind' and 'person', neither a machine, nor a neurological model, nor an equivalent robot, can be said to think, feel, imagine, desire, mean, believe or judge something. They may conceivably simulate these propensities to such an extent as to deceive us altogether. But a deception, however compelling, does not qualify thereby as truth."

We saw that Polanyi's idea of the tacit domain of thought, on which this argument relies, has much more to do with Piaget than with Freud. Built up and patterned by a person's active achievement of skill and sensory knowledge since the beginning of his life, it provides an orientation, a sense of probabilities, it is the source of hunches and dim fore-knowledge of where to look for a solution to a problem. Piaget's explanation of the 'schema' thus helps in understanding Polanyi's meaning about persons.[12]

Piaget's 'schema' was a growing integrated body of tacit knowledge and skill, developed through the child's active and interested dealings with the real world, and becoming his means of relating to his environment. Piaget showed how the child's sense of space and time, his bodily skills and later his logical and moral understanding, all grow in this same way; and we have seen how like this is in some ways to Polanyi's idea of how we *indwell* in our body and our tacit knowledge, using it as a tool for further exploration; an extension of ourselves. But I am thinking in a more general sense of a schema not only of one activity but of the whole person, where it would mean the coherence built up from all the elements; heredity, experience and active striving for meaning. Each person's 'schema' needs to be both strong and flexible, strong to hold the knowledge already gained together in a real unity and prevent it being confused by a welter of unconnected facts; flexible so as to assimilate new knowledge and modify itself to include the new facts meaningfully. My schema enables me to learn and grow, it also limits my learning and growing: it cannot be too open or it ceases to digest the new knowledge, ceases to be the organic whole which is the only thing that *can* know. I have to rely on my 'schema', to dwell in my body of knowledge, accepting its power and its limiting functions, so that it becomes a tool for knowing more reality and enlarging itself. And in this I am supported and limited by a community which has the same sort of organic body of knowledge, the same strength and power of self-renewal.

A rigid schema will not allow one to absorb any new idea unless it fits exactly into the pattern that is there already. "If I tell my granny anything," says a girl I knew, "she either says Nonsense, or she says Of course, I knew that before you were born." Granny was suffering from ossification of the schema, it had become so rigid that everything was rejected except pieces that exactly slotted in and seemed always to have been there.

On the other hand the weak schema will let anything in, but will not integrate it with the rest, like the White Queen believing six impossible things before breakfast. The new ideas will then knock around loose and probably fall out again; they will not make sense with what is there already, and the whole thing will be a ragbag of miscellaneous items, often mutually contradictory.

But a personal schema that is in good health will try out a new idea, introducing it to the ideas which are there already and seeing how they get on. It will grow while keeping its wholeness and self consistency. It will react to contradictions, but not necessarily by rejecting the new ideas unexamined; possibly by reorganising itself in a more satisfactory pattern in which the contradiction is resolved.

Eddington once described a scientist as a man working at a jigsaw puzzle; you come along one day and ask him how it's going and he says – "Fine! All this blue is the sea and this dark bit is a boat." You come along the next day and ask again, and he says "Fine! It turned out to be upside down; the blue was sky and the boat was an umbrella . . ." A well exercised schema can accept such drastic changes of arrangement if they give a more satisfying picture of reality. A confident and supple schema may be happy to let contradictory ideas live together within it for a time, if there is a sense that both the new and the old idea have claims and that they will be reconciled some day in a deeper insight. But such a contradiction is a challenge to the healthy schema. Contradictory items will not just lie around inert in it, but will be held in a lively tension. It is this tension from which discoveries often spring.

Polanyi's view of knowledge is an organic one[13] and he expressly extends biology into theory of knowledge.[14] Knowing is a biological function which in man has risen to the level of a search for objective reality. As a biological function it can only work by the two means, building up a structure and adapting it. Polanyi often turned to the logic of Gödel for illustration and support. I make no claim to understand this deep and difficult logic, but through Polanyi's interpretation it conveys to me that the infinity, the inexhaustible depth of reality of which he spoke, is anchored in the very structure of our universe. Polanyi often said, "We know more than we can tell" – and in Gödel's work he found a recognition that we also tell more than we know, for within any fully articulated system of knowledge we make statements whose full implications we cannot be sure of. These may lead to undreamed of new knowledge; they may also lead to contradictions or unanswerable questions, questions which can only be resolved or answered by moving into a richer system. So reality leads us on, and it is in such a universe that poetry, art and religion can give us knowledge, and that persons can be real.

Polanyi's insistence on the personal character of all knowing now becomes more definite. This person, this I that knows, is the unique self built up since the beginning of life, the whole self including the body and all that the person dwells in and extended itself into. All of it, the whole active knowing self with its unique store of tacit knowledge, is involved in this process of building up and innovating. Its growth is like that of science, which Polanyi says, "is constantly revolutionised and perfected by its pioneers while remaining firmly rooted in its traditions".[15] Thus knowing changes a person, since in committing ourselves to a new view of reality we accept a reorganisation of our schema or person. But the schema may not be abolished or destroyed, since without its strength and continuity we cannot be aware of meaning, we cannot be an integrated self.

It is a very un-Cartesian view, for in it there is no separate immaterial intelligence looking out at a purely material world. Persons exist on all levels of reality and can identify themselves from time to time with different levels. All the levels have their material aspect but all can be drawn into a higher level whole, where meaning becomes more important than material.[16] Instead of a person being 'himself' on the lower level as the 'naked ape' school of thought implies, he is most himself when the highest level meaning informs and integrates all the levels. All levels have their validity, but in man they are partial, not totally real, until shaped by the highest level. The highest level is however never finally defined, it is always a frontier with further horizons glimpsed but not completely known.

The 'schema' pattern shows all a person's learning as a combination of two opposite tendencies, the building up of frameworks to which new experience is assimilated, and the adaptation of these frameworks to accommodate new experience. These two tendencies appear in many forms, such as Kant's 'concepts and intuitions', the distinction of 'classical and romantic', 'rigour and imagination', 'convergent and divergent'. 'Dwelling in and breaking out' Polanyi calls the two tendencies. The reality of a person, his relation to truth, depends on these two movements being held together in him.[17] "The manner in which the mathematician works his way towards discovery, by shifting his confidence from intuition to computation and back again from computation to intuition, while never releasing his hold on either of the two, represents in miniature the whole range of operations by which articulation disciplines and expands the reasoning powers of man."

Indwelling in the knowledge or skill he has made part of himself, a person can focus his attention away from its particulars on to their joint meaning, then he can turn back and focus on the particulars. This temporarily destroys their joint meaning, but the movement is held in control by the person, who can keep the other focus in mind too and go back to it. This is the way in which skills and many kinds of knowledge advance, and the same dual power appears in all discovery, where a dimly sensed pattern draws the seeker on, and he can then turn back and scrutinise the facts again in the light of the pattern he has sensed.

Only in a person can these two ways of perceiving work upon each other. Thus a person has to be an open and closed system, and in this duality he is like the scientific community. We saw how the community of science has its closed aspect of authority and tradition, not readily admitting new insights, while this very sternness enables it to accept the new insights which it can incorporate and which will change it profoundly.

The Blot and the Diagram was the title of an article by Lord Clark about modern art[18] in which he cited Leonardo as an artist for whom science, measurement and geometric form were of supreme importance, so that he seemed to be on the concept, classical side. Yet Leonardo urged artists to look at blots and stains, at fire and water and such inchoate free forms, for inspiration. Leonardo held the two tendencies together and believed that art involved their interaction. He would not have been impressed by the kind of painting that pursues blots for their own sake, a reduction to meaninglessness like the reductionism of the scientific outlook. Blots are useful because they liberate our perception from a dominant meaning, a framework that has become a prison. In itself a blot is nothing; it is only valuable because our perception thus liberated can find a truer orientation.

I once knew a painter who had the disconcerting habit of stopping suddenly while walking along, to stoop down and look at the landscape upside down between her legs. This liberated her from the constriction from which artists always suffer, of knowing so well what things are that they can't actually see them. Upside down, things lose their identity, get out of their conceptual frames, and become more like the baby's world of pure sensation. As Polanyi says – "the loss of meaning caused by the unusual posture is compensated for by increased sensory vividness".[19]

There is a similar story about an artist travelling in a train with a small boy. They saw from the window a white horse grazing in shadow, while behind it was a hillside in strong orange light. The boy exclaimed, "Oh look at that blue horse!" The artist commented – "The privilege of seeing a blue horse is lost to those of us who know that horses are not blue". Artists, he said, have to strive consciously to get back to the child's pure vision; to break out of their concepts. Yes, but remember that the privilege of seeing a blue horse is also denied to babies, for instance, who do not know that it *is* a *horse*. So concept and intuition, rigour and imagination have to wrestle together, and the total victory of either makes us lose touch wtih reality.

This blue horse story has an interesting parallel in science, in a story about Einstein's discovery of relativity. The discovery was made by a rational intuition about the real world – yet Einstein admitted his great debt to Ernst Mach, who like Karl Pearson maintained we cannot know about a real world, only about our sense impressions. How could Einstein owe him anything? A. J. Ayer mentions this in his discussion with Brian Magee.[20] "Since our knowledge of scientific facts comes through our senses, Mach reasoned that in the last resort science must simply be a description of sensation. The Vienna Circle took this over . . . Einstein had been affected by Mach – I heard it from his own mouth that he owed a great deal to Mach." So the Logical Positivists saw Einstein's work in the theory of relativity as a vindication of their approach. But Polanyi, who quotes the Einstein-Mach connection, shows it in a different light. What Ernst Mach did by rigorously sticking to sensation was to liberate us from compulsive misinterpretation of our sense impressions. We cannot help interpreting, and we have an inbuilt urge to see movement against a background which does not move. It was this inbuilt urge which made Newton postulate an absolute immovable space against which movement can be measured. Mach managed to free himself from this urge, insisting that all we actually *see* is one thing moving in relation to another. Mach meant to cut out *all* interpretation, as though my painter friend had insisted that the upside down view was the only true view of the landscape. But what he actually did for Einstein was to cut out a misinterpretation, and so free Einstein, standing right way up again, to make a truer interpretation. Mach thought Newton's interpretation of space was meaningless; Einstein saw that it was not meaningless but wrong, but he could not have seen that if Mach had not shaken his vision free from interpretation to clear the way.

The change from diagram to blot or from blot to diagram can liberate us in this way. Sometimes a theory or concept liberates, sometimes its destruction liberates. Ayer said in the discussion quoted above[22] that Logical Positivism had turned out to be almost entirely mistaken, but he insisted it had been very liberating. Quine says much the same about behaviourism[23] – it liberates us from misconceptions. A simplified framework does liberate, just as the London Underground map with its simple diagrammatic form liberates us from all the distracting details and enables us to see much more clearly how to get from A to B. All these liberations by theories, concepts, styles in art, diagrams, or blots are very important, very essential for knowing, *as long as, on condition that,* we realise they are abstractions, and we continue to be persons, able to use the other way of seeing too. London Transport does not maintain that places not shown in the diagram do not exist. We have to realise that philosophers like Ayer and Quine are making useful little diagrams like the Underground map, very liberating, very helpful, but abstractions – not the whole story. The whole of modern physics is an abstraction; such a successful one that it has dominated our thinking ever since. In Arthur Koestler's discussion of reductionism, Paul Weiss said that physics is exact because it excludes so much of the wealth of reality.[24] Physics decided not to concern itself with individuals – but biology, he said, must retain the courage of its own insights. It need not deny the difference of living things from inanimate things because this does not show up on the physicists diagram. But philosophers do not talk modestly about their diagrams as useful simplifications, they give the impression that if you are not in that diagram, you are as good as non-existent. Quine in his discussion with Magee spoke of the physicist insisting on a closed system of physical causes for physical events; and "the successes in natural science have been such that we must take its presuppositions very seriously".[25] So wishes, emotions, feelings, decisions, thoughts and so on *are* micro-physical changes, he declares, in order to fit into this pattern. He would find it uncongenial, he said, to allow anything that broke this rule.

When I was a child there was a medicine called Iron Jelloids which advertised itself on enamelled metal plaques, appropriately rusting round the edges, affixed to the steps of the railway bridge. Their message ran –

> Take Iron Jelloids now and then
> The tonic for women, the tonic for men
> (and children).

This lamentable failure to fit the content into the form used to worry my brother and me. We did not, like Quine, want to consign the children to oblivion because they did not fit the closed system of the writer's chosen verse-form. It was clearly important that if children would indeed be benefited by Iron Jelloids, this should be said. But we found it extremely 'uncongenial' (in Quine's words) to have them hanging loose, unintegrated into the artistic whole, which in itself quite pleased us in spite of a certain galloping rhythm necessary in reciting the second line. We even felt this change of rhythm might be intentional, conveying the sense of revival and joie de vivre in the women and the men as the Jelloids got to work. But those poor children! We solved the problem to our own satisfaction by lifting the whole thing into another dimension – music. If sung to the tune of 'Ye watchers and ye holy ones' it went quite well, the alleluyias at the end accommodating the children, and even raising them into their proper priority. The railway bridge rang with our alleluyia chorus of "A-and children, A-and children, A-and chil--dren".

So physics, as well as behaviourism, logical positivism, and all such abstractions, diagrams, styles or models, are enormously useful but cannot rule out the children, or the persons that do not fit in. Physics, if it does not want Life hanging unconnected outside its system, will have to allow another dimension in which persons may take their rightful place of pre-eminence.

Suppose then that our right to believe in persons without disowning science is admitted. Of course in practice everyone believes in persons to some extent since life could hardly go on without such belief. But scientism has pushed us into the position of believing half-heartedly and apologetically as we might believe in ghosts or astrology, and this allows us to abandon the belief when it is inconvenient or embarrassing, without shame, indeed with a sense of scientific rectitude. But if we agree that we do believe with full commitment, in what are we believing?

We could try to answer by looking with some Polanyi insight at the ways we think about persons as we actually know them.

1. First, the persons we know are individuals, each one different though they have much in common. Inanimate objects may be different from each other but they are not individuals, and plants are hardly so; higher animals have more individuality, but only persons are fully individual, with their own intelligible active coherence. Yet they are unmistakably members of the human race, although altogether lacking in the uniformity strict classifiers require.

"Common law," says Polanyi, "makes the crime of murder, and punishment for murder, dependent on the human shape of the individual whose death has been caused. It demands that through all its variations – caused by difference of age and race, by malformations and mutilations, or by ravaging disease – we should always identify the presence of the human shape. Nor does this demand seem excessive, since no case is known in which an accused has pleaded failure to recognise the human shape of an individual he had killed. Yet it would seem impossible to devise a definition which would unambiguously specify the range over which human shape may, and beyond which it may not, vary, and it is certain that those who recognise this shape are not in possession of any such explicit definition."[26]

2. These persons we know recognise each other as individuals of the same kind by empathy or 'indwelling', by the kind of power used for generating a focal awareness of a comprehensive entity from a subsidiary awareness of its parts. They recognise each other's individuality in thought and action as personal, and as valid – that is, bearing on reality. This is true whether what they recognise is the creativeness of an artist or the originality of a great scientist, or the intuitive wisdom and goodness of ordinary people. Two sane and responsible persons recognise in each other a unique relationship to

the same reality to which they themselves relate. Polanyi calls this mutual recognition a 'convivial' relationship, only possible where the two persons recognise the same frame of truth by which they can judge their own and each other's thoughts.

In ordinary life we accept that only a person can know a person, and that emotions are involved as well as intellectual understanding. Only a person who suffers and rejoices, loves and fears and hates, can know another person. Polanyi speaks of the passions necessarily involved in the pursuit of truth, intellectual passions; he does not have so much to say about more ordinary human feelings, but they are also implied in the argument. Machines cannot feel, so cannot know persons.

3. The persons we know are funny, honest, exasperating, delightful, obstinate, loving, wise or stupid – such adjectives are endless but they all imply some autonomy and freedom, imply that to some extent the person chooses to be so and could be otherwise. Other words we use about persons categorise them as in various ways *not* free to choose. They state something about the person that he is not responsible for; it is a condition he finds himself in; it is the hand that life has dealt him, for good or ill. He is tall, handsome, black, Welsh, deformed, intelligent, a Brahmin or an untouchable or an old Etonian. This 'given situation' of persons may be hard or easy, but we reckon they all have some power to make something of it; they are not entirely helpless. But, even if one does not accept the cutting down of man to fit the diagram of physics, must we not agree that personal knowledge is limited and subjective because we are all so largely determined by our environment? Each of us may build his own schema but he has to build it from the materials available, and the way each of us knows the world is coloured through and through by the tacit assumptions of the culture we grew up in. As Polanyi puts it – "Every mental process by which man surpasses the animals is rooted in the early apprenticeship by which the child acquires the idiom of its native community and eventually absorbs the whole cultural heritage . . . Our believing is conditioned at its source by our belonging".[27]

How then can persons know objectively? Surely all their knowledge must be tainted by the parochialism of their setting? Polanyi uses a curious word for this situation; he talks of our acceptance of these inevitable limitations as our 'calling'. This word has a religious connotation, but Polanyi uses it to mean that each person's obligation to the truth is from his own particular setting, whose particular advantages and disadvantages are his own path to truth. This is what gives each person his unique contribution to make and his special responsibility, as each sees the truth from his own unique reservoir of tacit knowledge. The objects of our knowledge, being real, can be perceived from many different angles, just as a real live model sitting for a life class can be truly represented by quite different shapes drawn by students seeing her from different angles. The truth of their representations depends on the faithfulness and skill with which each draws what *he* sees, while believing that he is drawing a real person who exists in the round. There can be no true representation that is drawn from no particular place.[28]

4. It is a very old belief that a person has an immortal soul; this belief has persisted in many forms through centuries and civilisations. It may not be so much consciously held now, but at times of crisis, or at the end of life, it has some resonance still in most minds, as a question if not as an affirmation. Yet it seems bound up with the idea of a separate soul or mind inside a material body. If we accept the idea that 'the mind is the meaning of the brain', that a person exists on many levels, that his mind extends itself into whatever it uses to know with, that the mind can only be expressed in body and matter – is it possible to think any more of a person as an immortal soul?

Perhaps it is not possible then to believe in a literal 'life after death', a continuation of individual consciousness. But it could be, all the same, that such a naive belief is nearer to truth than the 'scientific' view of a person as a meaningless collocation of atoms. Polanyi found the Genesis story a truer account of the origins of the universe than the science story of atoms and chance, because it does at least recognise significance in the emergence of man.[29] And in this significance, in the achievement of personhood and meaning by the human race, he sees the creation of a new fabric of life not centred on individuals and transcending the natural death of individuals. Such hints do not add up to the new idea of immortality but they perhaps open the way towards it.

To believe that persons simply go on endlessly in time may be a sort of pre-Copernican misunderstanding of something much greater which we cannot at present grasp, but can trust, in the same sort of way as a scientist can trust the intimation of reality given by intellectual beauty and profundity. Human life can attain to meaning, and this meaning is not an arbitrary invention of our own but is part of reality and in some sense outside time.

In the last section of *Personal Knowledge* Polanyi set human personhood in a cosmic perspective of evolution, seen as emergence and achievement. He reminded us that living things cannot be known without recognising that they achieve or fail to achieve, and these ideas of achievement and failure are not known to physics and chemistry, they do not show up on the 'diagram' of these subjects. Thus evolution as a grand panorama of achievement of ever higher levels of meaning, culminating in human thought, can simply not be seen or recognised by physics, just as the creative leap of discovery cannot be recognised by looking at discoveries from after they have happened. This comparison goes deep, for Polanyi quotes again Hans Spemann's words (see p.173) that the suitable reaction of a germ fragment in an embryonic 'field' was more comparable to mental processes than to chemical reaction. He uses the idea of a 'field' of emergent meaning in which persons are active centres. The 'field' does not compel, but offers opportunities. This kind of interpretation involves the claim that evolution, seen in long enough perspective, shows itself as a progressive achievement, a creative process. Admitting that natural selection can account for short term variation such as protective colouring, Polanyi denies that it could possibly be sufficient to account for the long term movement towards ever more meaningful form, the development of consciousness and responsibility and creative thought or action.

Polanyi has cleared a way for belief in persons which leads back to where he started, for it makes possible and justifies the free society.

In Chapter VI we saw persons in a community – scientific, or moral – a community which derives its freedom from its progressive response to reality. The persons in it are imbued with its values, conform to its traditions and yet are able to achieve the freedom of creative dissent by seeing more deeply the truths which the tradition partially embodies. Men in a community, such as the scientific community, learn respect for truth from the society which cultivates it, but "a man who has learnt to respect the truth will feel entitled to uphold the truth against the very society which has taught him to respect it".[30]

Such a community can only exist if the persons in it also have this freedom, this power of choice and personal judgment to seek and recognise truth. But we have seen how the 'scientific world view', imposing rules about what is to be allowed as valid knowledge, has made it impossible to allow to persons their full reality, their freedom and responsibility, and thus undermines belief in the free community and opens the way for totalitarianism. Unbelief in persons leads to the unfree society.

"Our theory of knowledge is now seen to imply an ontology of the mind. Objectivism requires a specifiably functioning mindless knower. To accept the indeterminacy of knowledge requires, on the contrary, that we accredit a person entitled to shape his knowledge according to his own judgment, unspecifiably. This notion – applied to man – implies in its turn a sociology in which the growth of thought is acknowledged as an independent force. And such a sociology is a declaration of loyalty to a society in which truth is respected and human thought is cultivated for its own sake."[31]

Since writing the above I have read a novel which illuminates the two ways of seeing a person.

A Child Possessed by R. C. Hutchinson tells the story of a father's relations with his idiot daughter, a child so dreadfully deformed in body and mind as to be scarcely human. The clever doctors at the hospital explain to him the principles on which each of their patients is placed in the appropriate class and grade of deficiency, and try to persuade him to permit one of their operations to be done on his daughter to make her more docile. They assure him that it makes no sense to talk of personality in such a case. Unimpressed, he takes the child away to share his sordid lodging and his rough life as a lorry driver. There is no great breakthrough; the story is not sentimental. But his absolute conviction that there is in that misshapen body and brain a person, who feels suffering and joy as he does, evokes slight but unmistakable signs that it is so, and that she knows him as a person. These clues to her personhood would never have been noticed in the hospital, indeed they would not have appeared. Yet the analytic approach of the clever doctors, with all its impersonality, has its place in medicine which can bring relief to many kinds of suffering. It is only when the other way, the convivial knowing of a person, is forgotten, that knowledge goes wrong.

Notes to Chapter X

1. *Meaning* p.25
2. *The Study of Man* p.63
3. *Men of Ideas* p.292, 296
4. *Ibid* pp.172–176
5. *Ibid* p.292
6. See *Personal Knowledge* p.370–373 for a critique of Behaviourism, psychological and logical.
7. *Personal Knowledge* p.261
8. *Ibid* p.262
9. *Ibid* p.336
10. *Ibid* p.336
11. *Ibid* p.263
12. see pages 58, 59, above
13. *Personal Knowledge* p.373
14. *Ibid* p.374
15. *Science, Faith and Society* p.56
16. *Personal Knowledge* p.301
17. *Ibid* p.131
18. Kenneth Clark 'The Blot and the Diagram', in *Encounter*, Jan 1963
19. *Personal Knowledge* p.197
20. *Men of Ideas* p.120
21. *Personal Knowledge* p.11
22. *Men of Ideas* p.131, 132
23. *Ibid* p.175. *cf* M. Polanyi, letter to C. C. Gillespie 1966 – "Science itself is liable to be misled when it accepts some temporarily useful fiction as the scientific world view, to be violently protected against criticism. A science that in the practice of its fictions becomes contemptuous of manifest truths is in constant danger of losing its way to the truth".
24. *Beyond Reductionism* p.42
25. *Men of Ideas* p.172
26. *Personal Knowledge* p.348
27. *Ibid* p.322

28. Compare Polanyi's research on the structure of white tin. Two researchers discovered apparently quite different atomic structures until they realised that one was described along lines forming an angle of 45 degrees to the other. (See *Knowing and Being* p.124)

29. see above p.47

30. *Science, Faith and Society* p.61

31. *Personal Knowledge* p.134

CHAPTER XI

THE POET'S EYE

"Take off your spectacles sometimes!" says Beauty to Science. "There are other ways of seeing the world."

"But how will Everyman know if he is seeing true if I do not tell him?" asks Science.

"No-one can tell him for sure, but together we can help him to find the way."

REMEMBER Karl Pearson and the Grammar of Science[1] – "The scientific method is the sole path by which we can attain to knowledge. Other methods may lead to fantasy, to belief or superstition, but never to knowledge."

Polanyi, we have seen, denied this claim and showed first that science cannot attain the impersonal certainty Pearson imagined; then that we can make our way through other fields, history, poetry, art and religion towards the understanding of reality. This needs the same basic powers, disciplined by the same responsibility and showing the same relation of creativity to discovery. Knowledge of life and mind needs deeper personal indwelling than physics, but there is no sharp separation of science from the rest as a guaranteed certainty. Polanyi's work is dedicated to the validation of all man's creative and responsible approaches to reality, for "Science can no longer hope to survive on an island of positive facts around which the rest of man's intellectual heritage sinks to the state of subjective emotionalism".[2]

To look at one area, that of imaginative literature, let us take one of those who have approached from their side to the same sort of understanding. The writings of the English critic F. R. Leavis illustrate the recognisable common features of truth in literature and in science. Leavis admired and quoted Polanyi, finding many of his principles of literary criticism paralleled in Polanyi's science-based philosophy.

One point is their common belief in a living tradition, both authoritative and developing, within which individual creative discovery can grow. Polanyi wrote for instance in *Science, Faith and Society* about a general authority such as prevails in science. "A General Authority relies for the initiative in the gradual transformation of tradition on the intuitive impulses of the individual adherents of the community, and it relies on their consciences to control their intuitions . . . Such a regime assumes that individual members are capable of making genuine contact with the reality underlying the existing tradition and of adding new and authentic interpretations to it."[3]

Compare with this Leavis's words about Jane Austen.[4] "Jane Austen, in her indebtedness to others, provides an exceptionally illuminating study of the nature of originality, and she exemplifies beautifully the relation of 'the individual talent' to tradition. If the influences bearing on her hadn't comprised something fairly to be called tradition she couldn't have found herself and her true direction, but her relation to tradition is a creative one. She not only makes tradition for those coming after, but her achievement has for us a retro-active effect: as we look back beyond her we see in what goes before, and see because of her, potentialities and significances brought out in such a way that, for us, she creates the tradition we see leading down to her. Her work, like the work of all great creative writers, gives a meaning to the past."

Elsewhere Leavis wrote of the "full necessity of a living creative literature, of the cultural continuity without which there can be no criteria of the humanly most important kind".[5] Again he wrote of "that continuous collaborative renewal which keeps the heritage of perception, judgment, responsibility and spiritual awareness alive, responsive to change and authoritative for guidance".[6]

Leavis and Polanyi both link creativity with personal responsibility to reality, and base on this link the objectivity of personal judgment. So Leavis writes – "The Blakean sense of human responsibility goes with . . . realisation that without creativity there is no apprehension of the real, but that if experience is creative, the creativity . . . is not arbitrary, it is self-dedication to a reality that we have to discover".[7] "The artist in his creativity is conscious of being a servant."

Polanyi calls this 'the paradox of dedication', when "a person asserts his rational independence by obeying the dictates of his own conscience, that is, of obligations laid down for himself by himself. Luther defined the situation by declaring – 'Here I stand and cannot otherwise'. These words could have been uttered by a Galileo, a Harvey or an Elliotson, and they are equally implied in the stand made by any pioneer of art, thought, action or faith. Any devotion entails an act of self-compulsion".[8]

Polanyi and Leavis agree that the principles to which an artist or scientist is dedicated are not fully explicit. Polanyi says this in the appendix on the Premisses of Science in *Science, Faith and Society*. "The premisses of Science cannot be explicitly formulated and can be found authentically manifested only in the practice of science as maintained by the tradition of science." He had said elsewhere that the principles of an art are more truly embodied in its practice than in its maxims; and we recognise that this is so when we agree that we can learn more about golf from a good golfer, more about music from a musician, more about mothering from a good mother, than from the instruction books of any of these skills. Polanyi wrote too[9] about universal standards in artistic creation, and how we rely on ultimate criteria in forming a judgment, yet often do not fully realise what these criteria are until we have tacitly relied on them.

Leavis too finds general principles involved in criticism, but principles that can only be grasped through using them in judgment. His method is to take a range of examples and set them out so that the principle of judgment becomes apparent. We can compare Polanyi's account of the recognition of symptoms by a doctor, for instance the accentuation of the second sound of the pulmonary artery. "He must personally know that symptom and he can learn this only by repeatedly being given cases for auscultation in which the symptom is authoritatively known to be present, side by side with other cases in which it is authoritatively known to be absent, until he has fully realised the difference between them."[10]

Reading Leavis one is not left with the impression that literary criticism is less rigorous or responsible, less concerned with reality than science; and his methods often beautifully illustrate Polanyi's thought, confirming the similarity of ways to truth in their respective disciplines.

In the series of lectures which now form the central chapters of *Meaning*, Polanyi set out to extend his ideas about tacit knowing into the field of aesthetic experience and beyond; first applying them to the understanding of metaphors, symbols, painting and poetry, then to myth and ceremony, and lastly to religion, ritual and belief.

In science, as in everyday perception, our knowledge depends on tacit awareness of clues which are not entirely specifiable but are integrated into our focal awareness of the object to which we attend from them. In the kind of knowledge we get through art and poetry, he thought, there is a difference; it is not factual truth about things here and now, yet it is *truth*, it can tell us things about reality that we cannot reach in any other way. He thought that a work of art calls on our imaginative fusion of *contradictory* clues; the awareness of the flat canvas in a painting contradicting the illusion of depth in the landscape depicted on it; the stage 'frame' of a theatrical performance contradicting the reality of the murder taking place in it; the rhyme and rhythm of a poem framing and detaching the content from immediate reality. The great religious myths are accepted by the same imaginative fusion of incompatibles, to give us a truth which could not be expressed in explicit prose statements of the separate elements. In poetry and ritual the words and symbols are a more integral part of the meaning than in prose, and cannot be changed without loss of meaning.

The argument of these chapters seems sometimes ambiguous and not entirely convincing. Yet the point about the imaginative fusion of opposite or contradictory clues to give a special sort of truth, peculiar to art, is interesting, and it led me to an area in which I found a demonstration, which to me is more convincing, of the kinship of poetic with scientific truth.

Polanyi in these chapters argues against a view of art as an imitation of reality. He points out the triviality of an art (like Madame Tussaud's) whose products could be mistaken for real objects. There may be representation of real objects in art, but there are clues, too, pointing away from reality, framing and distancing what is stated in the work of art, so that it stands out as something greater, more universal, than everyday reality. In the course of this argument there is a statement, three times repeated, that Coleridge was mistaken in thinking that art requires 'a willing suspension of disbelief'. We do not, and are not expected to, believe factually what we see or hear in a work of art; if for instance we thought an actual murder was taking place on the stage, the effect would not be a work of art but something quite different. This is true, but I was jolted by the remark about Coleridge, having a fairly firm conviction that Coleridge would not be mistaken on this subject; a conviction which became more obstinate with every repetition of the accusation. So I looked up Coleridge's phrase in its context.

"During the first year that Mr Wordsworth and I were neighbours," Coleridge wrote,[11] "our conversation turned frequently on the two cardinal points of poetry; the power of exciting the sympathy of the reader by a faithful adherence to the truth of nature, and the power of giving the interest of novelty by the modifying colours of imagination." From these talks between the two poets sprang the joint enterprise of the 'Lyrical Ballads' in which, says Coleridge, "it was agreed that my endeavours should be directed to persons and characters supernatural, or at least romantic, yet so as to transfer from our inward nature a human interest and a semblance of truth sufficient to secure for these shadows of imagination that willing suspension of disbelief for the moment which constitutes poetic faith. With this view I wrote the Ancient Mariner".

The comment in *Meaning* is "We do not appreciate a work of art . . . by suspending our disbelief in its prose content". But it is quite clear from Coleridge's statement and from the 'Ancient Mariner' that Coleridge did not mean that. It would be ridiculous to suppose that he expected a reader of the poem to believe the story as a factual account of what actually happened. 'Suspension of disbelief' clearly means acceptance within the terms of the poem. Coleridge explained further – "The incidents and agents were to be, in part at least, supernatural, and the excellence aimed at was to consist in the interesting of the affections by the dramatic truth of such emotions as would naturally accompany such situations, supposing them real".

So in fact Coleridge meant something very like what Polanyi is saying in these chapters. If we look again at Wordsworth and Coleridge dividing up the work of the 'Lyrical Ballads', Wordsworth was to write about familiar subjects, Coleridge about unfamiliar and supernatural. "The principal object which I proposed to myself in these poems," Wordsworth wrote in the Preface, "was to choose incidents and situations from common life, and to relate them as far as possible in a selection of the language really used by men, and at the same time to throw over them a certain colouring of imagination, whereby ordinary things should be presented to the mind in an unusual way."

Thus the pattern of their intentions was symmetrical; Wordsworth to lift common things out of the common by imaginative colouring, Coleridge to bring uncommon things within the grasp of the common imagination by emotional truth. In fact, to use Polanyi language, both were intending to provide contradictory sets of clues to be integrated into a poetic experience, but opposite ways round; Wordsworth's subject matter and language belonging to the everyday world, his 'frame', which would distance and detach it, being the 'colouring of imagination' – and the verse form. While Coleridge made the subject (strange and supernatural), his distancing frame, and the contradictory content, the everyday reality of human feeling involved.

There is a relevant book about Coleridge which I read years ago – *The Road to Xanadu* by Livingstone Lowes. He shows how the magic quality of *The Ancient Mariner* arises from Coleridge's success in just this; that the supernatural elements of the story and the strange eerie setting fuse with what is within our emotional compass, the deep and universal human feelings invoked, the vivid homely language steeped in the actual experience of the early explorers, and the inwardly cohesive logic of the poem's structure. It is all compelling and convincing within the experience of the poem, just as a play can carry us away in its own terms.

Now this is not at all incompatible with what Polanyi is saying, and is indeed very close to the explanations in *Meaning* of how we grasp the meaning of a work of art or a play or ritual by imaginative integration of conflicting clues, which does assume a 'suspension of disbelief' within the artistic experience. Without this we could not be moved by the experience, as Polanyi recognises we are by a fine metaphor for instance. He quotes Shelley as saying that poetry reveals 'the wonder of our being' by purging our usual chaotic experience of the film of familiarity – this was Wordsworth's aim; and he admits as something involved in the acceptance of a work of art that – "the 'story' part of such works must have some degree of plausibility. It must strike us, the audience, that a man like Hamlet might kill a man like Polanius, under the circumstances presented in the play . . . the requirement is slightly different from the merely cool objective judgment of its logical possibility. As Aristotle pointed out, a convincing impossibility in a play is better than an unconvincing possibility".[12] Surely this is just what Coleridge means by "willing suspension of disbelief", and the Ancient Mariner is a classic example of a convincing impossibility.

Having convinced myself that Coleridge and Polanyi were on the same side, I turned to the workings of Coleridge's poetic imagination as described in *The Road to Xanadu*, and found this a vivid illustration of tacit knowledge.

The Road to Xanadu begins from Coleridge's notebooks with their strange farrago of facts and phrases. Livingstone Lowes followed the tangled trails of these jottings back to their sources in Coleridge's voracious reading, and on to their places in *The Ancient Mariner*. This part of the book has all the fascination of a good detective story. But if that were all, it would be of limited interest. What concerns us is the study that follows of the ways of the poetic imagination. Livingstone Lowes was fascinated by the problem of what happened to this vast reservoir of knowledge in Coleridge's mind – "the amazing throng of images"; and of what transmuted the hoarded nuggets of fact into the pure poetic imagination of *The Ancient Mariner*. He shows how in some earlier poems Coleridge used some of the material raw, so to speak. He calls this 'joiner's work', for Coleridge was fitting together pieces of his material in verse, unmodified by imagination. But when Coleridge and Wordsworth talked together in a state of heightened poetic excitement, and the right subject appeared, to power the thrust of the creative imagination, the throng of latent images was drawn out from the 'deep well' of the subconscious where they had mingled and coloured each other. They were no longer bits of Coleridge's reading, but pure poetry.

In trying to understand the process, Livingstone Lowes came very close at times to talking in Polanyi's terms. It is interesting that they both quote Henri Poincaré's account of the process of scientific discovery and point out its similarity to the process of imaginative creation in the arts. There is first the intuitive search for a good problem. As Polanyi puts it – "At the inception of an inquiry, intuition predominates. Imagination enters at this stage only by keeping intuition alert to the sensing of a problem . . . The whole course of the quest is filled by laborious efforts of the imagination, broadly guided by a questing intuition, which also continues to select from the fragments mobilised by the imagination those which promise to become part of the solution".[13]

The quest for a problem in science becomes the quest for a subject in poetry. Coleridge's reading was not random but guided by an intuitive feeling for a possible subject; he gathered his material with insatiable curiosity along the lines that drew his interest. At this stage he did not know what the subject would be; for some time 'A Hymn to the Sun, Moon and Elements' was in his mind; but the vague intuition of a subject guided his reading, while the material he gathered in turn shaped the search for a subject. When he did the 'joiner's work', one could say that he was still viewing focally the material he had gathered; but when the thrust of the imagination came, the garnered images had fallen into subsidiary awareness and were able to become part of a rich new imaginative meaning.

Livingstone Lowes' analysis of the verses in the Ancient Mariner about the water-snakes is particularly interesting.[14] It might have fallen under Polanyi's criticism of such analysis of poetry, that it destroys the poetic vision by focussing on the separate elements, but it begins and ends with such feeling for the imaginative truth and beauty of the verses that it does not have this effect; and in showing the multitude of sources which have coloured and enriched these few, simple, perfect lines, it illustrates beautifully Polanyi's words – "This rich and delicate pattern of subsidiaries imbues a poem with the quality of a distinctive artifact. It lends the poem harmonies that no other speech possesses, and establishes its claim to be received for its own sake . . . A poem's story is thus exempted from being heard as a mere communication of facts and asks instead to be heard by the imagination. Therein lies its independence as a work of art".[15]

Compare with this Livingstone Lowes' comment – "It is as if the separate images from Coleridge's reading had carried with them into their new environment a shadowy penumbra of other images with which they had once been joined, or as if each focussed within itself subtle potentialities of suggestion caught from associations which it had before the poem was ... The rich suggestiveness of a masterpiece of the imagination springs in some measure from the fact that infinitely more than reached expression lay behind it in the shaping brain, so that every detail is saturated and irradiated with the secret influence of those thronged precincts of the unexpressed".[16]

Having been thus led to think about Polanyi in connection with Coleridge and Wordsworth, I found that I went on pondering Wordsworth and Polanyi together. It seemed an unlikely connection; the poet and the scientist, one Hungarian-born, the other essentially English. I remembered that I once quoted to Polanyi some lines from the *Excursion* in which Wordsworth seemed to anticipate the arguments of Polanyi's critics –

"But what is error?" "Answer he who can" –
The Sceptic somewhat haughtily exclaimed.
"Love, Hope and Admiration – are they not
Mad Fancy's favourite vassals? Does not life
Use them, full oft, as pioneers to ruin,
Guides to destruction? Is it well to trust
Imagination's light when Reason's fails?"

But at that time I had not thought much about any connection between these two, except my reverence for both. Now I find a coherence appearing in the experience and thought of the two men, which is compelling and in many ways illuminating.

Wordsworth, like Polanyi, grew up and developed his great imaginative powers and his idealistic spirit in a time of comparative political quiet, was deeply stirred in early manhood by violent political upheavals and the turmoil of ideas that accompanied these, and disenchanted by the violence and tyranny to which high ideals had led. Shattered for a time, he then recovered his essential vision and faith in man, with deeper strength than before and wider sympathies, and bent all his powers to the task of seeing with his own eyes and telling with his own voice the truths about man in thought and action which he believed had been disastrously obscured by a false idea of knowledge. Wordsworth's experience thus has parallels to Polanyi's, but Wordsworth was more emotionally shattered by it than Polanyi seems to have been, the political changes having first appeared to him as a realisation of his own ideals. It is well known how he was carried away by the high hopes of the French Revolution –

"Bliss was it in that dawn to be alive,
But to be young was very heaven."[18]

It seemed to the young Wordsworth that all idealists – "those who have fed their childhood upon dreams" now at last had scope to build their dream worlds –

"Not in Utopia, subterranean fields
Or some secreted island, heaven knows where,
But in the very world, which is the world
Of all of us, in which in the end
We find our happiness, or not at all."[19]

The lines in which he tells of his subsequent disillusionment and moral confusion are less well known; they give a vivid picture of a mind of great sensitivity and imaginative strength nearly broken by the corruption of hope and by the rationalist scepticism into which the disaster drove him for a time. It was the same scepticism which Polanyi found so destructive; it taught that nothing, no moral faith or transcendent belief, can stand that cannot be proved. It was in the form of Godwinism that Wordsworth encountered it, a philosophy of determinism and of individual reason without emotion and without tradition. Godwin's *Political Justice* was published in 1793, just at the time when Wordsworth was most vulnerable to its coldly rational view of man, after the shock to his moral being of England's declaration of war on France. "His intense love for England and belief in her as a stronghold of liberty came into violent conflict with his faith in France as the deliverer – no less – of humanity. This faith in turn was to be rudely overthrown. In Paris a despotic government had been supplanted by a tyranny yet more cruel . . . Wordswoth's feelings were 'soured and corrupted upwards to their source' . . . he sought succour in a creed which banished feeling and took its stand on reason."[20]

He described later the state into which he was thrown at that time.[21]

"Thus I fared
Dragging all passions, notions, shapes of faith
Like culprits to the bar, suspiciously
Calling the mind to establish in plain day
Her titles and her honours, now believing,
Now disbelieving, endlessly perplexed
With impulse, motive, right and wrong, the ground
Of moral obligation, what the rule
And what the sanction, till, demanding *proof*
And seeking it in everything, I lost
All feeling of conviction, and, in time,
Sick, wearied out with contrarieties,
Yielded up moral questions in despair,
And for my future studies, as the sole
Employment of the enquiring faculty,
Turned towards mathematics and their clear
And solid evidence –"

How like this is to the state of mind that Polanyi describes as having led so many young idealists to nihilism or to a ruthless totalitarian creed. Polanyi set out their dilemma in prose, but it is essentially the same – "Proving or disproving has a proper meaning in science and the law courts, it has no bearing on the beliefs which sustain our existence as moral beings. We must resolutely teach ourselves once more openly to hold these beliefs as an act of faith.

"This is very difficult because it evokes the danger of obscurantism and of an arbitrary suppression of free thought. If we repudiate the absurdity of dealing with our own responsibilities by the methods of science, can we avoid setting up an anti-scientific attitude which endangers the legitimate position of science?"[22]

Polanyi too has told of the free and hopeful air of his youth, so soon polluted by war, terrorism and revolution.[23] He has not recorded any such violent upheaval in his own emotional life, or that he himself ever saw his ideals embodied in a revolutionary programme or was ever tempted into rationalist scepticism. Thus he may have avoided the worst element of Wordsworth's suffering, the conflict of trust and disillusionment. But he too felt intensely the shock of the descent into violence, and was driven by it to search his own faith and reason for a philosophy that could stand up to the destructive alliance of extreme rationalism with irrational violence. For both men it was an agonising question how abstract ideals of liberty and justice could produce chaos, oppression and cruel tyranny.

Both were able, Wordsworth only by the skin of his teeth, to hold to a deep faith in man and in his powers of knowing his world. Both set out to search the roots of this faith within themselves, and to develop it through a long discipline of thought and feeling into a more reliable understanding of man's relationship with the world; a theory of knowledge which would not destroy its own foundations.

I do not want to force this comparison of their experience and its effect, but to compare the answers reached by the poet and the philosopher scientist as remarkably congruent visions reached by different paths.

Both saw the danger of the exaltation of the critical and analytic method into a whole philosophy, with its separation of intellect from emotion; both felt a mission to 'unstop our ears' and save us from the crippling restrictions of this philosophy. Wordsworth wrote –

"The estate of man would be indeed forlorn
If false conclusions of the reasoning power
Made the eye blind, and closed the passages
Through which the ear converses with the heart."[24]

and his passionate belief in the truths which reach the heart through ear and eye rings through his poetry.

Polanyi's arguments against the view, that to analyse anything into its least elements is to understand it, were often summed up in his attack on the proposition of Laplace, that if we could know the position of every atom and the forces operating on it, we could have a complete scientific knowledge of the whole universe and everything in it.

Actually we would by this means know nothing of any interest at all, Polanyi showed.[25]

Wordsworth, telling with passionate feeling of the true knowledge and understanding of the world that primitive or pagan man often had, lamented the lesser wisdom of the great scientific discoverers. Was it ever meant, he asks –

"That we should pore, and dwindle as we pore,
Viewing all objects unremittingly
In disconnection dead and spiritless,
And still dividing and dividing still
Break down all grandeur, still unsatisfied
With the perverse attempt, while littleness
May yet become more little, waging thus
An impious warfare with the very life
Of our own souls!"[26]

This destruction of the very life of his own soul was what he felt
had happened to him in the crisis which soured and corrupted his
power of feeling. He had lost his admiration for his heroes, his
feeling of continuity with the great and noble men of other times –

> "for it seemed
> That their best virtues were not free from taint
> Of something false and weak which could not stand
> The open eye of Reason –"[27]

So history was deadened for him, poetry withered, even Nature
lost her power to move him. He had felt intensely the effect which
Polanyi so often described, when the critical faculty, out of control,
has killed the power of indwelling and feeling the reality of the
intangible things, so that service to them becomes hypocrisy and we
are left without reverence. "We need reverence to perceive
greatness," Polanyi said, "even as we need a telescope to perceive
spiral nebulae." "By recognising our heroes and masters we accept
our particular calling."[28] Or as Wordsworth put it –

> "We live by Admiration, Hope and Love – "[29]

But when our moral passion for perfection is cut off from faith and
feeling so that we lose the reality of moral qualities, we see failure
and hypocrisy in all human endeavour. Any greatness can be
criticised and analysed away; we have to learn to revere it in faith.
Wordsworth felt that he had 'unsouled' by logic the 'mysteries of
passion' which make 'one brotherhood of all the human race'.[30]
Polanyi wrote – "We need a theory of knowledge which shows up the
fallacy of a positivist scepticism and authorises our knowledge of
entities governed by higher principles".[31]

Wordsworth found no theory, that was not his business as a poet,
but he found a poet's answer, as Polanyi found a philosophic one.
Both went back to what was most real for them, what they were sure
of, and started from there.

For Wordsworth that meant going back to the intense life of the
senses he had lived as a child. Through the healing influences of
Coleridge, and of his sister Dorothy, he was able to find his way back
to that experience and work from it. He was always sure that his
intense sense experience in childhood and youth had never been
simply sensuous but a revelation through the senses.

"It is the full intense life which he lived through his senses as a child and youth that he first tries to recapture and record; and the quality of that life that makes it invaluable – this is the surprising thing – is its sheer, unquestionable spirituality. Most of us are moved at some time by some beautiful aspect of Nature . . . What is the meaning of this sense that Nature gives me of a life beyond sense, this feeling of an extraordinary beauty and mysterious power? Is there an ultimate spiritual power, and have I a spirit that can unite with it? Wordsworth never asks the question. The eternal spirit was revealed to him through his senses, and his spirit was aware of it from the first."[32]

So he went back to his own sure and clear experience of Nature and also of man, finding in the ordinary undistinguished men that he knew, whose lives were close to nature, the greatness and nobility of feeling that he had lost, and he learnt that the recognition of the worth and dignity of man comes through feeling and convivial understanding, not through abstract reason.

In fact what Wordsworth recaptured was, was it not, tacit knowledge, and though he had no theory of it, he came near to describing it when he wrote of 'the glorious faculty which higher minds bear with them as their own'.[33]

> – "they build up greatest things
> From least suggestions, ever on the watch,
> Willing to work and to be wrought upon,
> They need not extraordinary calls
> To rouse them, in a world of life they live,
> By sensible impressions not enthrall'd,
> But quicken'd, rous'd, and made thereby more apt
> To hold communion with the invisible world."

Then he has that wonderful description of the moon in the mountain scene as an image of imagination; the highest intellectual power; which works through the senses and creatively transforms the objects of sense. "And the effect of this is not elaboration and variety but the drawing into intense significance of the simple and ordinary . . . Imagination perceives and creates unity."[34]

Polanyi's understanding of beauty as a clue to significance is akin to this, for instance when he remarks on the acceptance of great new theories in science – "We cannot truly account for our acceptance of such theories without endorsing our acknowledgement of a beauty that exhilarates and profoundity that entrances us".[35]

For Polanyi, too, the renewal of vision came through going back to what he knew with the sureness of feeling; his convivial knowledge of the men he had worked with; his understanding of what it was they had been doing in their scientific discovery. He often, too, appeals to common sense, to what we all know to be the case when we are not blinded by a theory; for instance our knowledge that consciousness is something actual, however psychologists deny it; that body and mind are not the same thing, that freedom and moral obligation are real. Often he appeals to our knowledge of the least scientific skills, the skill of a boy on a bicycle, a wine-taster, the half literate Stradivarius making violins that we cannot emulate with all the resources of science, the unconscious skill by which we see the objects around us, the carpenter's use of a hammer – all skills dependent on our native faculties and on the traditions in which we grow up, not on logical proof or scientific test. His answer to the question how we can know the intangible realities without which we cannot live or know anything, is, in the same way as we can have these unformalised skills, through tacit knowing, the imaginative power which integrates the particulars of sense into their meaning, and which involves us as feeling, responsible persons.

So what Polanyi worked out intellectually Wordsworth worked out poetically. Wordsworth saw himself as dedicated to a true understanding of what his early experience had been and what it implied; he had disciplined himself in the service of truth to his feelings just as much as Polanyi had in the service of true understanding.[36] Of course there is no complete separation of the two worlds, and Polanyi's understanding involved feeling just as Wordsworth's feeling involved reason. For neither of them was the choice seen as Bertrand Russell saw it, honest scepticism or dishonest faith in our feelings. So often the scientific method is contrasted with feeling, emotion, intuition, as if these were something whimsical and anarchic. But Wordsworth does not leave us with the impression that the pursuit of truth in imaginative insight is easier, less demanding or less objective than that of the 'minute analysis' of science or philosophy. It requires the cultivation of the most delicate discriminating moral awareness and sense of truth; it involves, like science, both humility and daring in the sensing of new coherences, and what it discovers, like a new theory in science, shows its reality by casting unforeseen light not only for ourselves but for other minds with other problems.

The comparison of Wordsworth and Polanyi leads on to the religious dimension of Polanyi's thought. For Wordsworth's rediscovered vision was religious in the sense that it was a direct apprehension of the divine through the world of the senses and the feelings, a passionate intuition of –

"a motion and a spirit that impels
All thinking things, all objects of all thought
And rolls through all things."[37]

It was God revealed through the majesty of Nature and the greatness of man's mind. When in later life he lost this direct intuition and could not recover it, Wordsworth turned to orthodoxy and the Anglican church. This later religion was not insincere, but it was never integrated into his poetic vision as the direct intuition had been. It did not come from the heart of his experience. In its narrower light he revised and changed many of the words in which he had expressed his former vision; they now seemed to him too pantheistic. But was it pantheism? The divinity of which he was so directly aware was seen through the senses but was not any of the objects of sense. His experience was a transformation of the here and now by indwelling it so as to see its meaning. It was like Polanyi's description of the religious mystic's relaxation of the intellectual control by which he usually categorises his experience, so that he sees things "not focally but as part of a cosmos, as features of God".[38] It has surely something in common with the apprehension of intellectual beauty which he says guides the scientist to areas of important meaning.

Another element in Wordsworth's vision is hinted at by one word in the lines just quoted; the word 'impels'. His intuition was always of direction and movement:

"So build we up the being that we are;
Thus deeply drinking in the soul of things,
We shall be wise perforce; and while inspired
By choice, and conscious that the will is free,
Shall move unswervingly, even as if *impelled*
By strict necessity, along the path –
Or order and of good."[39]

"This is the paradox; to live according to the order of Nature is to be free."[40] We may compare this with Polanyi's words about Luther; his connection of freedom with commitment to truth.

Polanyi speaks in tones like Wordsworth's when he expresses his profound belief in man's dignity and worth. Towards the end of *Personal Knowledge* he has brought biology and philosophy to a confluence where, he says –

"Man stands rooted in his calling under a firmament of truth and greatness. Its teachings are the idiom of his thought; the voice by which he commands himself to satisfy his intellectual standards. Its commands harness his powers to the exercise of his responsibilities. It binds him to abiding purposes, and grants him power and freedom to defend them.

"And we can establish it now as a matter of logic that man has no other power than this.

"He is strong noble and wonderful so long as he fears the voices of his firmament; but he dissolves their power over himself and his own powers gained through obeying them, if he turns back and examines what he respects in a detached manner. Then law is no more than what the courts will decide, art but an emollient of nerves, morality but a convention, tradition but an inertia, God but a psychological necessity. Then man dominates a world in which he himself does not exist. For with his obligations he has lost his voice and his hope, and been left behind meaningless to himself."[41]

Notes to Chapter XI

1. see p.21 above
2. *Personal Knowledge* p.134
3. *Science, Faith and Society* p.59
4. *The Great Tradition* p.13, 14
5. *The Living Principle* p.49
6. *Nor Shall My Sword*
7. *Ibid* p.12
8. *Personal Knowledge* p.308
9. *Meaning* p.103
10. *Personal Knowledge* p.54
11. *Biographia Literaria*
12. *Meaning* p.158
13. *Ibid* p.96
14. *The Road to Xanadu* p.59
15. *Meaning* p.80
16. *The Road to Xanadu* p.59
17. *The Excursion* IV. 766–72
18. *The Prelude* X. 693 (1805 text)

19. *Ibid* X. 724
20. Darbishire – *The Poet Wordsworth*
21. *The Prelude* (1805) X. 890
22. Polanyi 'Science and Faith' in *Question V*, Winter 1952
23. see Ch. 1, p.2 above
24. *The Excursion* IV. 1152–5
25. see *Personal Knowledge* p.139–40
26. *The Excursion* IV. 940
27. *The Prelude* XI. 64–67
28. *The Study of Man* p.98
29. *The Excursion* IV. 763
30. *The Prelude* XI. 80–
31. 'On the Modern Mind' in *Encounter* XXIV. 1965 p.9
32. Darbishire – *The Poet Wordsworth* p.46
33. *The Prelude* XIII. 90
34. *The Poet Wordsworth* p.118
35. *Personal Knowledge* p.15
36. *The Prelude* XIII. 126
37. 'Lines written above Tintern Abbey'
38. *Personal Knowledge* p.198
39. *The Excursion* IV. 1264–70 (my italics)
40. *The Poet Wordsworth* p.165
41. *Personal Knowledge* p.380

CHAPTER XII

A MEANINGFUL WORLD

OUR starting point at the beginning of this book as Polanyi's diagnosis of the sickness of the modern world as 'the dissonance of an extreme critical lucidity and an intense moral conscience –' the latter an inheritance from Christian aspirations torn from their religious setting. And now at the end of Chapter Eleven we saw Polanyi showing us 'man left behind meaningless to himself', if by critical examination he dissolves the reality of what he respects – law, art, morality, tradition, God. The underlying aim of all his work has been to show that man can legitimately believe in such meanings; that he is not doomed by his faithfulness to reason to be left meaningless to himself. But the conviction may grow on us in reading Polanyi that a *final* meaning is unattainable for man; there will always be further horizons to lead him on. We shall not go back to the old relationship of religious faith to reason.

At the end of *The Tacit Dimension* Polanyi wrote of the tragic situation of man, bound by all his limitations and by the fatal flaws that seem inevitable in his societies, yet needing "a purpose which bears on eternity". "Perhaps," he says, "this problem cannot be resolved on secular grounds alone. But its religious solution should become more feasible once religious faith is released from pressure by an absurd vision of the universe, and so there will open up instead a more meaningful world which could resound to religion."

The religious dimension of Polanyi's thought is a stumbling block to some, who may go along with much of his reinterpretation of science, but are taken aback to be pointed finally in a religious direction. For so long religion has stood, in the scientific world view, as the barrier to free enquiry, the dogmatism that has to be discarded. Not that the authority of religion is feared any longer, for it is science that now has the unquestioned authority which used to belong to religion. Rather, religion is regarded with contempt as an unjustified escape from the rigours of philosophic debate, or as an ostrich-like posture in the bleak reality of the universe revealed by modern science. So to philosophers and scientists the religious element tends to discredit Polanyi; it seems a kind of cheating, like 'vitalism'. While from the other side, although some theologians (such as Professor T. F. Torrance) were among the first to recognise the importance of Polanyi's thought, and to see its relevance to their own work, there are many religious people who hold their religion as a quite separate kind of truth, to be accepted on authority, and who may feel threatened by his incursion. In claiming that religion and science are talking about the same world, and that knowledge has essentially the same meaning for both, he opens them up to each other in ways that demand a change of outlook in both. He appeals, from both science and religion as they are, to both as they ought to be. But religious people who are not prepared for change may either claim him as an eminent scientist who – 'look – supports religion!' as if one could go straight from *Personal Knowledge* to the Athanasian Creed: or they may say he was not religious at all. For instance Father Terence Kennedy, who has lately written with great understanding about Polanyi and his significance for theology, finds it necessary to comment on the ambiguity of his religious stance. "Honesty demands that we acknowledge that Polanyi was not religiously committed, nor did he have religious faith as this is understood in Christian theology."[1]

I do not believe we know how far he was religiously committed, it was something he kept veiled even from his friends. Perhaps he did not know. Who does know for sure how deeply he is committed, unless he is tested to the limits of endurance and so discovers his deepest beliefs? Perhaps Polanyi only differed from some, more apparently committed, in knowing that he did not know. But if not committed to a particular creed, he was entirely committed to reality, and it is impossible to doubt that his vision of reality had an element of deep religious, Christian feeling.

Remember Polanyi's hero Christopher Columbus, committing his reputation and his life to a new idea of the world which others only held theoretically – sailing out westward to find the East[2] – getting it considerably wrong but finding a new world. Polanyi's religious commitment was like that. But what is often thought of as religious commitment is more like having a detailed map of the country we say we believe in, agreeing that the map is perfectly correct and just as tradition has handed it down, but having no intention of taking the risk of actually going there.

Once I wrote to him about an article he had sent me to read. I commented that although it did not mention religion it seemed to point to a religious meaning. He replied, "I am of course aiming at the foundation of religious faith. Have been doing so since I started thinking about matters in general twenty-five years ago. But I became increasingly reticent about this as time went on".

Why, if his aim was the foundation of religious faith, should he become more reticent? Possibly because the dangers from both sides which I have mentioned grew clearer, and made him feel that if he was to be taken seriously he must be wary. So he was careful to disclaim religion *as a platform* and after, for instance, writing about the role of tradition in science he added, "I am not reasserting traditionalism for the purpose of supporting dogma. To argue, as I do, that confidence in authority is indispensible for the transmission of any human culture is not to demand submission to religious authority. I admit that my reaffirmation of traditionalism might have a bearing on religious thought, but I want to set this aside here. Modern man's critical incisiveness must be reconciled with his unlimited moral demands, first of all, on secular grounds. The enfeebled authority of revealed religion cannot achieve this reconciliation, it may rather hope to be revived by its achievement".[3]

Although Polanyi's personal religious position is thus veiled, and may be left so, it is justifiable to look at the salient facts that we know. His family was of Jewish origin, but Jewish religion had no explicit part in his upbringing or belief. He said that it was through reading *The Brothers Karamazov* in 1913 that his religious interests were awakened, and for some years he was 'a completely converted Christian'. He was baptised in 1919 into the Catholic faith, a choice which seems to have been made more for practical than religious reasons. Later, in England, he developed a great admiration for Protestant Christianity and most of what he says about religion applies to Protestantism. In 1934 he wrote to a friend who had sent him Catholic papers –

"I do not doubt that science and Catholicism can be united in one mind. Quantum mechanics are certainly more difficult to believe than Catholic faith. But I bring myself to believe quantum mechanics. I need them. I think I should believe them. I have not the same feeling, the same urge towards Catholicism. Not now. In my country Catholicism has associated itself with an unfair treatment of the Jews; that may be one reason. The other probably the history of the Spanish Inquisition. Many things that I love and hope for in this world have been born in deadly struggle against that power. All this I admit might be a prejudice, but it represses any possible urge in the direction of belief. Also I do think that the task of *thoughts* (Science) and *inventions* is not clearly perceived by Catholicism. The whole adventure of practical reasoning, I feel, is only tolerated by the Church. I think it is a vital mission of humanity to push on this adventure. If you forgive me, I would say, God has ordained this adventure to us."

In a paper written in 1948 on *Forms of Atheism* he spoke of the horror of religious fanaticism which animates the rationalist form of atheism, and added, "I am myself very responsive to this kind of horror" – He went on to criticise fundamentalism and dogmatism as liable to turn into a claim to infallibility. This he contrasted with the faith required in science and in all knowledge, which claims universal validity for beliefs, while yet realising that they may appear to be contradicted by other aspects of reality. "I hold it to be fully consistent with my belief in the transcendent origin of my beliefs that I should be ever prepared for new intimations of doubts in respect to them."[4]

New insights in science led him to new approaches to religion. As he explored the reality of scientific discovery as he knew it in his own experience, and struggled with the false scientific outlook which had distorted the understanding of science, he came to see very vital connections between the scientific search for truth and the religious. He returned many times to two great masters of Christian thought, St Augustine and St Paul. Their formulations of the Christian scheme seemed to him to express most truly the faith on which science also rests. "Unless you believe, you will not understand" – the saying which Polanyi called Augustine's fourth century inauguration of the first post-critical philosophy[5] – firmly placed faith before reason, as Polanyi came to feel it had to be placed in science. The fundamental premisses of science have to be accepted in order for a scientist to work at all. Augustine's order of priority held until the seventeenth century, when demonstrable knowledge was promoted to the first place and faith reduced to subjective belief; an unsatisfactory stopgap where knowledge had not yet reached. The priority of faith imposed by Augustine had indeed held up scientific progress, but when it was overthrown the opposite imbalance took its place. Believing in the necessity for faith *and* reason in science and in all knowledge, Polanyi wanted to restore the balance.

For so long, since science became powerful, men have tried to bring all kinds of knowledge closer to the pattern of what they supposed science to be, and those kinds of knowledge which could not be so treated have been demoted and devalued. By going back to Augustine's ordering and showing faith prior to reason *in science*, Polanyi changed the situation. The 'science' of measurement, experiment and doubt to which other knowledge was to be made to conform, in fact rests on a foundation of faith in what cannot be proved, in skills and imaginative powers that cannot be formalised, and in tradition by which alone such skills can be passed on. This change opens the way to accepting the validity of the truths that can only be explored in myth, poetry and ritual, hard as this is to accept for men conditioned by the scientific myth and the doubt it casts on all other myths.

Polanyi has the courage to say that the truth of poetry and art, of morality, philosophy and law, is more vital than the truths of science,[6] and to declare[7] that "the book of Genesis and its great pictorial illustrations, like the frescoes of Michelangelo, remain a far more intelligent account of the nature and origin of the universe than the representation of the world as a chance collocation of atoms. For the biblical cosmology continues to express, however inadequately, the significance of the fact that the world exists and that man has emerged from it, while the scientific picture denies any meaning to the world and indeed ignores all our most vital experience of this world". The discovery of meaning in our most vital experience of this world is a function of religion, Polanyi believed. This is not only not incompatible with the truth of science, but is a complementary way of looking at the world, without which science is left meaningless. Imagine an everyday example – you read in the paper that a man jumped into a river to rescue a child from drowning. It would be possible to construct a 'scientific' account of this event in terms of the weight, volume, direction and rate of movement of all the physical components without mentioning man, child, or purpose; this account could be accurate and not omit any physical change that took place, but it would not only be meaningless in human terms, it would be pointless in any terms except for its reference to the meaning which it omits, and which could not be discovered from reading the 'scientific' account.

"The Christian enquiry is worship," Polanyi wrote.[8] "It resembles, not the dwelling within a great theory of which we enjoy the complete understanding, nor an immersion in the pattern of a musical masterpiece, but the heuristic upsurge which strives to break through the accepted framework of thought, guided by the intimations of discoveries still beyond our horizon. Christian worship sustains, as it were an eternal, never to be consummated hunch, a heuristic vision which is accepted for the sake of its unresolvable tension. It is like an obsession with a problem known to be insoluble, which yet follows, against reason, unswervingly, the heuristic command: 'Look at the unknown!' Christianity sedulously fosters, and in a sense permanently satisfies, man's craving for mental dissatisfaction by offering him the comfort of a crucified God."

"An eternal, never-to-be-consummated hunch" is an unusual definition of religious faith, and is not a description of a comfortable or a static religion. This emphasis on the breaking out and exploring aspect of religion gives a picture which does not fit the public face of religion as we know it, at all. Set forms of worship, which seem to arise even in the religions which start by breaking away from set forms; repetitions of creeds and formal prayers and hymns – all this seems much more concerned with the preservation of things as they are than with any great heuristic upsurge. And the religious movements that do seek a new revelation of meaning, discarding old forms, often seem to lead to much more cruel tyrannies of conformity than the traditional kinds.

But we have to remember how in science Polanyi saw tradition and new discovery, authority and originality, depending on each other. Dwelling in and breaking out of established ways of thought must be both part of the way to truth, in religion as they are in science. He is not attacking traditional forms of religion nor proposing some new abstract doctrine-free synthesis. He quoted with approval a saying of George Santayana[9] that it is as impossible to be religious without having *a* religion as it is to speak language without having *a* language.

The fact that theological accounts of God may appear meaningless from outside the religious frame is not surprising. "The comparatively modest attempt to describe atomic processes in terms of classic electro-magnetics and mechanics has led to self-contradictions which appeared no less intolerable until we eventually got accustomed to them."[10] God's existence can only be known in a commitment, in worshipping him, and religious understanding is a skill, like the skill of mathematics or the appreciation of art or music. Religion is one of the great articulate systems of thought and feeling in which the mind of man can dwell by imaginative integrating of the clues it provides. To those who dwell in it, it reveals meaning in the universe, as do the other great systems. Christian worship and teaching are a system of clues from which a tacit art of comprehension reaches their meaning – faith. "The capacity for such skilful religious knowing seems universal, at least in children. Once acquired, the skill is hardly ever lost, but it is rarely mastered at an advanced age without some previous training in childhood. Divine service can mean nothing to a person completely lacking the skill of religious knowing."[11]

It is what Polanyi has elsewhere called 'our calling'. We learn religious understanding by being brought up in a religion which is meaningful to the people we trust who are practising it, just as we learn language, just as in science we learn by dwelling in a tradition, trusting it and sensing the meaning in it, so that we become able to go beyond it. By dwelling in the forms and rituals of one religion we can thus learn meanings which reach a more universal truth. Polanyi's bringing together of science and religion would involve the religious community becoming more like the scientific community, where respect for tradition and authority are maintained with the purpose of encouraging creative dissent that will change the tradition. In fact a Society of Explorers, rather than rule and dogma, to safeguard the search for truth.

But are the meanings discovered in religion of the same kind as the meanings in science or in daily life? This question can have various implications but perhaps the important one is 'Can men committed to the scientific understanding of the world, commit themselves as fully and rationally to its religious understanding?'

"The assumption that the world has some meaning, which is linked to our calling, as the only morally responsible beings in the world, is an example of the supernatural aspect of experience which Christian interpretations of the universe explore and develop,"[12] Polanyi wrote. The word *supernatural* raises sharply the question we are asking. The supernatural in its usual meaning implies two separate worlds; here in this one things behave according to physical laws, but sometimes another world breaks through, a world in which the laws do not rule. It is arbitrary, anything can happen. Belief in this kind of supernatural is a kind of dualism, and Polanyi probably for this reason avoided the word in later life. If his religion involved this magic meaning of supernatural then it would be open to the charge of cheating and evading philosophic argument. We could not as rational beings commit ourselves to it. But it was not so, for his *supernatural* – we might call it *supra natural* to distinguish it from the other – is the natural world revealing a meaning. The meaning belongs to a higher level in the hierarchy, and may be glimpsed only in a few clues on the natural level, but if it can be grasped it illuminates and can change the whole of every level. This *supra natural* is the meaning of the natural, as the mind is the meaning of the brain; whereas the supernatural as usually understood is an arbitrary abrogration of the laws of the natural world.

The idea of the hierarchy of levels enables us to see man as a morally responsible being, a status to which he has emerged through evolutionary achievement, without ceasing to exist also on lower levels. The explanation of man in purely physical terms (as in *The Selfish Gene*) is then inadequate, but so is the explanation of man in purely spiritual terms such as Darwin's opponents tried to maintain.

Their understanding of man as a completely separate kind of being from the rest of creation made him 'supernatural' but the view of evolution as an achievement sees morally responsible man as supra natural to his lower levels of being.

Thus for Polanyi religion is a tacit integration of clues to a higher level meaning, in a universe which consists all through of a hierarchy of levels. A *supra natural* level but not separate or anarchic, for it is attained by the same tacit process of discovery by which each level in the hierarchy has been attained, from the lowest level of animal awareness upwards. At each level, first living creatures and then men have been able, by passionate striving and commitment to what they can dimly sense but not wholly grasp, to reach to an understanding of the next higher level and to living by its laws. They cannot do this entirely by their own efforts, since the principles of the higher level are not fully discoverable on the lower. There is a creative power in the universe which meets their striving. Polanyi often used the Christian word 'grace' for this power outside ourselves which enables us to solve the unsolvable and to reach towards what is beyond us.

Is not such a power bound to be supernatural in an objectionable sense? Polanyi often spoke of reality having attractive power, leading us on, laying an obligation upon us, as though our discoveries, even in science, are encounters with creative power; with rationality in the universe. But such power is not supernatural if the coherences we discover are real. The same power appears even in our ordinary perception when a pattern or shape begins to attract our attention because it seems to indicate something real; it draws us on to discover what it is. Our ordinary perception is supra natural to the processes on which it relies.

I spoke of Polanyi's deep interest in St Augustine and St Paul, and here it is St Paul whom he often quotes when he speaks of the need for passionate striving in the process of discovery, and the insufficiency of our own striving without this power outside ourselves which meets our efforts. After telling in *Personal Knowledge* how we rise above our subjective condition to achieve personal contact with reality, Polanyi wrote[13] –

"The stage on which we thus resume our full intellectual powers is borrowed from the Christian scheme of the Fall and Redemption. Fallen Man is equated to the historically given and subjective condition of our mind, from which we may be saved by the grace of the spirit. The technique of our redemption is to lose ourselves in the performance of an obligation which we accept, in spite of its appearing on reflection impossible of achievement. We undertake the task of attaining the universal in spite of our admitted infirmity, which should render the task hopeless, because we hope to be visited by powers for which we cannot account in terms of our specifiable capabilities. This hope is a clue to God."[11]

Remember how Polanyi had avoided the dualism of mind and body by showing it is just one instance of duality which occurs at each change of level in the hierarchy of levels. The particulars of each level are both themselves, on their own level, and also can become elements of a higher-level coherent whole. So each level of the hierarchy could be called *supra natural* to the natural of the level below; not 'supernatural' for the higher does not abrogate the laws of the lower level, but supra natural as it controls the lower level by imposing boundary conditions, and makes the lower level laws work for a higher principle. Just as biological laws control without abrogating the laws of physics and chemistry, and the laws of justice or music or morality control the laws of their lower levels, so the laws of a divine level could control and shape the laws of the human level. All through, our achievement of meaning takes this form as we strive to discover in a lower level the clues to a higher level which we can at first only vaguely sense, but to which we commit ourselves, and to which in some way reality helps us as it leads us on, tests and judges what we have discovered.

In *Science, Faith and Society* Polanyi described a pattern or rhythm of discovery, the same in science, in artistic creation, in diagnosis and recognition of species, and even in the prayerful search for God. "All these processes of creative guesswork," he said, "have in common that they are guided by the urge to make contact with a reality which is felt to be there already, waiting to be apprehended."[14] He suggested then some element of extrasensory perception and spoke of 'the spell of a potential discovery striving to emerge into actuality[14] but later the image of a morphological field helped to integrate the idea with biology, as the idea of Grace integrated it with religion.

The theologian with whom Polanyi was most in agreement at one time was Paul Tillich. But later he argued against Tillich[15] when Tillich said that science and religion bypass each other, as they talk about different domains and so cannot come into conflict as long as each keeps to its own domain; that of science being strictly detached knowledge while that of religion is the domain of unconditional commitment. Polanyi says no, they are talking about the same world; there is no strictly detached knowledge, although to recognise the higher levels of mind and human responsibility needs more indwelling and commitment than physics. And the leap of imagination by which the religious level is reached, like the primitive daring by which the first steps in knowledge were taken, attests the creative power in the universe that enables human understanding to surpass itself. This power imposes an obligation "to strive for the impossible in the hope of achieving it by divine grace" – another reference to the Christian scheme of redemption set out by St Paul.

Thus science, truly understood, does not rule out the meanings religion can reveal, and these meanings, when seen, change our vision of all the rest, just as shapes once revealed as features of a face cannot be seen again as separate meaningless marks. Polanyi once described the highest mystical vision as a letting go of the categories of our normal seeing, so that we see all things as features of God.[16] And things that have been so seen can never be seen in quite the old way again.

In all this, Polanyi's vision of the wholeness of knowledge has exhilarating meaning for religion. It liberates religion, as Polanyi said was his intention, from an absurd view of the universe; it unstops our ears from the false and deadening scientism which has enfeebled religion and opens up important realms of meaning for man to explore.

The interpretation I have been trying to make is what I think emerges from the whole of Polanyi's main line of thought. But sometimes, particularly in later life, he expressed himself in words which were ambiguous and capable of being interpreted in very different senses. This has emerged clearly in discussions between

Harry Prosch, who collaborated with Polanyi on his last book, *Meaning*, and Richard Gelwick, who also worked closely with Polanyi in those years. I have to try briefly to state the difference.[17]

Professor Prosch in reviewing Professor Gelwick's book *The Way of Discovery* has argued that Gelwick was mistaken in interpreting Polanyi. Prosch denied that Polanyi meant to say the meanings found through religion refer to realities existing independently of us like the realities dealt with by science. Prosch says that Polanyi made a sharp separation between the discoveries of science, which can be verified, and deal with an external reality, and the discoveries of art, myth and religion which do not bear an outside reality and cannot be verified, only 'validated'.

Certainly in the book, *Meaning*, there is much emphasis on metaphor, myth and symbol, less on a reality that is reached *through* symbols, and much that can be interpreted either way. Gelwick, interpreting it in the light of the rest of Polanyi's thought, finds no difficulty in accepting it all as consonant with Polanyi's reconciliation of science and religion. Marjorie Grene understood it as Prosch does, and called it "tragically misguided, a betrayal, in its separation of art and science, of his (Polanyi's) own best insights".[18]

It is not possible to be sure how far Polanyi wavered or changed his mind, how far he failed in later life to express his views clearly. In his letter to me he did not say he had become unsure about religion, only more reticent. This is not the place to argue the question; it is enough to say that Harry Prosch in spite of his very definite denial of Polanyi's intention to allow religious knowledge a bearing on reality, said in the discussion that, "although there are these different notions of reality in science and in art and religion, both nonetheless fit Polanyi's often expressed definition of reality as that from which we expect indeterminate properties to arise in the future, properties of which we have not yet dreamed – that they have as it were a life and development of their own which we can neither control nor anticipate, that they are not products of our subjective whims or fancies". So what are they, one may ask, if not an apprehension of reality? Prosch seems to have reverted to the cobblestone definition of reality which Polanyi in his whole work expressly repudiated because it could not allow the reality of the higher intangible things.

The crucial question is the relation of symbol to reality. An article by F. W. Dillistone[19] quoted a headline "Down the slippery slope of symbolic representation" and protested at the idea implied in it that what really matters is the bare fact; simply objects as they are, or events as they actually happened. He says, as Polanyi did, that there are no *bare facts*, for interpretation enters into all knowledge. "The word 'incarnation' is a symbol, so is 'resurrection' ... A symbol is that which holds or draws two things together . . . It always serves to maintain a two way relationship, between the seen and the unseen . . . The slippery slope is downwards to a view that would regard everything as no more than lifeless mechanism. The upward leap is towards an exhilarating ascent of symbolic interpretation opening out new vistas."

This is true; there is a slippery slope down to an atomism which related nothing to anything else. As Polanyi says, "Sartre's Nausée' contains the classic description of the process. You can destroy meaning wholesale by reducing everything to its uninterpreted particulars, we can eliminate all subsidiary awareness of things in terms of others, and create an atomised, totally depersonalised universe. In it the pebble in your hands, the saliva in your mouth, and the word in your ear all become external, absurd and hostile items".[20]

But turning from the 'slippery slope' to the 'exhilarating ascent', it is also possible to lose meaning by an exhilarating leap into symbolic interpretation which lets go of the real world altogether. There are no bare facts, it is true, but there are facts. The Resurrection is symbolic or it would have no meaning for us, but it would also not have its Christian meaning unless it *happened*. It is this delicate balance between meaning and fact that Polanyi so often pointed out, explaining how a scientist has to judge, when he senses a new meaning, whether an awkward fact which does not fit can be disregarded or is significant. In our imaginary example of the man jumping into the river to save a child, as I said, the account of the happening in purely physical terms, though accurate, would be meaningless, but the account in human terms would lack force if it did not in fact happen.

In the discussion of religion in *Meaning* it seems sometimes that the significance of symbol and metaphor is exaggerated and separated from a reality being symbolised, so that whether an event happened is unimportant. For instance in the account of the rite of Holy Communion there is only the symbolic meaning of the breaking of bread together and other elements of metaphor, reinforced by "the myth that this rite was ordained by a god".[21] Christians would not agree that this description was sufficient; they would surely feel that at least the element of commemorating an event that actually happened, and a person the disciples actually knew, must come in.

It is clearly a very difficult line to draw, but it is essential to Polanyi's insight that religious truth is continuous with scientific and historic truth.

Professor W. T. Scott in his summing up of the discussion ends by saying, "I am convinced both that he (Polanyi) considered the Christian religion at its best to involve an encounter with and surrender to a pre-existing reality, and that he must have had some vision himself, however ineffable, of this reality".

I think it is clear that Polanyi's main line of thought is expressed for instance by Professor Torrance, who sets out the differences between belief in science and in religion, and then says, "Within these important differences, however, religious belief remains essentially the same as scientific belief in that it is the direct bearing of the mind upon reality in a basic act of cognition and acknowledgement, and as such is the ground of knowledge".[22]

Insofar as Polanyi did waver and become ambiguous, which I think one must admit he did to a certain extent, he had in some way lost sight of his essential vision, for this sharp separation of science from imaginative truth is contrary, as Marjorie Grene implied, to the whole direction of his thought; his hierarchic view of reality in which the highest levels are the most real; his understanding of the daring and imagination needed in all discovery, his ideas of indwelling. Certainly he recognised the difference between the truths of science and the truths of art and religion. The difference was not that science deals with a reality existing independently of art and religion, rather it was a difference in the degree of personal involvement and in the obligation that these higher truths lay upon us.

In comparing Polanyi with Wordsworth in Chapter XI I said that Wordsworth had recovered his vision by going back to two things, to the immediate apprehension of the divine which he had received through the senses in childhood, and to his reverence for the strength and greatness of man's mind as he found it in the most humble and unremarkable men. I said that Polanyi too had gone back, for a defence against destructive rationalism, to two things, to his experience of discovery, and to reverence for ordinary things he knew and trusted, such as common sense, our animal powers, personal judgment, skills and the innate sense of beauty and order. Wordsworth's vision faded in old age – was it a fading of vision that turned Polanyi aside into the pursuit of a symbolism that symbolises nothing real? We don't know; the important thing is to judge, with all the skill and sensitivity we can, where his greatest insight leads, and to follow that.

I am no theologian, but all of us, like Everyman, have to understand as best we can and judge the truth of that to which we commit ourselves, and I find the framework of Personal Knowledge very revealing when applied for instance to the miraculous element of the Christian gospel.

We can admit that many of the miracle stories may be due to man's inveterate habit of mixing up the levels, taking an event which was special and moving because it revealed a glimpse of spiritual meaning, and making it special on the material level; sticking a material halo on it, so to speak, and thus making it 'supernatural' not supra natural. This disregards the structure of tacit knowing, by trying to put the revealed meaning on the same material level as the clues to it. Too often, wishing in this way to mark the spot where the wonder of the divine level showed itself, we distort both levels. We find it difficult to hold on to the fact that divinity shone out from ordinary events, and we have to change the event into something that somehow broke the laws of nature. Attention thus becomes concentrated on the anomaly in the material world and not on the revelation of divinity. Meaning is lost either way, whether by insisting that nothing special could have happened because material laws cannot be changed, or by insisting that they *were* broken and losing sight of the spiritual meaning which transfigured without destroying them.

We tend to put a marker at the spot where spiritual power showed itself, and then to take the marker for the revelation. The real miracle is the transformation of the natural by a higher level meaning. We cannot always and do not need finally to decide how far such spiritual power actually made nature behave differently, but remembering how life transforms the action of physical laws, how the recognition of a face transforms meaningless shapes, we have to use the indwelling imagination to see that 'here the power of meaning showed itself and was recognised'. The real miracle is meaning and power embodied in ordinary facts and transforming them, revealing unforeseen possibilities within them.

Because of the clouds of religiosity and anti-religiosity that swirl around the Christian gospel it is risky for an ordinary Everyman to venture on this ground. But I venture, for although Polanyi did not, for reasons we have partly explored, carry his philosophy explicitly into this area, he certainly hoped that others would do so. And doing so one finds a new light thrown upon the Jesus of the gospels as a great discoverer, revealing a higher level meaning in the universe congruent with each of the levels we have progressed through in the course of our evolution. This would be a level supra natural to the natural of the level below it, as each higher level is, but not supernatural in the magic sense. This higher level transforms the facts of the lower level – redeems them – as has happened at each step, but at this level the personal involvement is more complete and the personal obligation to the higher level meaning more compelling, in the real world of action and history.

For as Professor Ronald Hall has said,[23] "Religious encounter within history is not primarily an aesthetic experience . . . has no artificial 'frame', it really does occur in the everyday experience of human action in concreto. Moreover religious encounter within history does not lead to personal disappearance as in science and art; rather history becomes the very space of human and divine appearance in concrete revelation through word and deed".

What we miss in *Meaning* and what Polanyi's whole thought could lead us to, is this actuality; the effect in the lives of ordinary suffering men of what actually happened in the life and death of Jesus, and of the meaning for them that these events revealed. Of course symbol and ritual come into religion, and they help to keep the meaning alive, but without the point of reference of what actually happened, symbol and ritual would not have their power.

When Polanyi wrote about the Hungarian Revolution he said – "Its typical utterances . . . manifest the deep emotional upheaval caused by recognising once more that *truth, justice and morality have an intrinsic reality*, and that this is the decisive fact".[24] And he put religion in the same category when he says – "Religion, considered as an act of worship, is an indwelling rather than an affirmation. God cannot be observed, *any more than truth, beauty or justice can be observed*. He exists only in the sense that he is to be worshipped and obeyed, but not otherwise – any more than truth, beauty or justice exist as facts. All these, like God, are things which can be apprehended only in serving them".[25] And this does not apply only to the truth of religion, for Polanyi has said elsewhere that truth can only be thought of by believing it,[26] and that the scientific standards to which the scientist submits only exist in his submission to them.[27]

It is actuality like that of the Hungarian Revolution that we find in the Gospels, for it was the power of God seen in the lives of men and women who knew Jesus which convinced others of his divinity and has become "the decisive fact" for many. It is not a question of whether Polanyi's religion is orthodox; that is irrelevant. It is from the point of view of his whole philosophy that one feels he could, had he wished, have gone straight from his faith in discovery and in man's mind to the Jesus of the Gospels. I have come to think so from going back to the Gospels in the light of Personal Knowledge and finding how much illumination results. This is much too great a subject and I can only indicate a few areas in which this is so, to show what I mean.

1. The relation of tradition to new vision. The Jesus of the Gospels is shown deeply aware from his youth of the great tradition of his people. That tradition had been, through the long years of Jewish history, reinterpreted by the prophets, who saw, each in his time, a deeper truth in the tradition which called for a change in its form. From being a tribal god, a god of violence and vengeance, their God gradually emerged purified, universalised and merciful. In this creative conflict of insight and tradition Jewish religious history was like science, and Jesus like a Newton or an Einstein, bringing its supreme fulfilment and its deepest challenge in the name of its true meaning. His challenges never questioned the need for a continuing tradition, and indeed always assumed the continuance of tradition, but his life and teaching was a constant questioning of the tradition where it had settled down and lost meaning. And in turn the new insights which Jesus brought have often been turned into dogma which has lost meaning and has to be challenged. It is an inevitable process, as every society needs to build walls round its insights to keep them from being dissipated and lost, but needs constantly to guard against the tendency to make the walls so strong and permanent that *they* become the thing that is guarded, and new insight cannot grow.

2. *Discovery*. Jesus as the rectifier of tradition was also the great discoverer, pointing always beyond himself, revealing the reality of a moral universe. The story of the Temptation is a story of discovery which, like the stories of scientific discoveries, has been distorted by looking at it from after it happened. Before the choice was made, it must have seemed indeterminate and open, not just a struggle to do what was clearly right, but the search for the right answer. (Denis Potter's play, *Son of Man*, brings out this discovering aspect.)

Jesus knew he had a mission to fulfil, but what was the way to go about it? Was it bread – the satisfaction of material wants? Was it the supernatural, flouting the laws of nature? Was it worldly power? And from the way he led his life we can see that the answer he found was none of these, it was *meaning*. The power, and the transcending of physical law, and the bread, would flow from this, but this must come first. The history and traditions of his people had a meaning, and so had the lives of the human beings he knew, and there were clues in them to tell what the true meaning was. His teaching and life were revelations of this meaning in ordinary human relationships.

3. *The insight of the discoverer.* The stories of Jesus show him to have had the artist's eye; the deepest and most lively intuitive insight through imaginative sympathy into the hearts of men and women and the springs of human action, and into the laws of the moral universe. To make this power *magically* divine is to make it less, not more divine than to understand it as a higher power of an insight that we all have in some degree – the power of tacit knowing. The parables in which Jesus taught show this quality. An illuminating small book[28] points out how the parables have often been distorted by making elaborate allegorical interpretations, whereas the true mystery "consists precisely in the fact that the natural and earthly, faithfully observed and truly understood, do really illustrate the heavenly and spiritual . . . A genuine parable, by its truth to nature, reveals a real relation between the natural and spiritual order . . . Its heavenly meaning is not really grasped until it is seen also as the understanding of earth itself". These parables are the opposite of the moral stories often used to drive home a lesson. In such stories the moral is quite definite, though the story may be unconvincing. But in Jesus' parables the story has never a false note; it is absolutely true to earth and life, but "there is generally a thought-provoking doubt about the moral".

4. *The relation of the different levels.* The idea of the hierarchic structure of the universe, and of our knowing, helps in seeing the relation of the kingdom of heaven to the world. It is not a separate region; it is this same world but seen by an imaginative fusion of clues. 'Seek first the kingdom of heaven' does not mean turn away from this world, but so dwell in its particulars that their joint meaning shines out. 'Look at the unknown' – seek the meaning, do not focus on the particulars. Other Gospel sayings light up with the illumination of this pattern. 'The deceitfulness of riches' takes on a wider meaning than simply that of money and possessions. 'Riches'

is the multiplication of separate things or items of knowledge, which may overwhelm their possessor so that he cannot pick out the clues to meaning. We have to become as little children to enter the kingdom, and simple people can have true understanding of spiritual reality, because from few clues we may more easily glimpse a joint meaning.

5. One of the most misquoted sayings of Jesus is – 'Judge not that ye be not judged'. Of course a Christian has to judge; like the scientist, his personal judgment has to be trained, sensitive, discriminating. Jesus was always saying, 'Look! Judge! Can't you see what this means?' The 'Judge not' saying seems, at least in one of its senses, ironical, meaning Be careful how you judge because your judgment judges you. If you say Shakespeare is a pretty poor poet, it is not of Shakespeare men will think less, but of you.

The judgment needed in moral and religious questions is like that of science but more personal, more involving of the whole person. And if the highest meaning of the universe is in some sense personal, this is surely what *Personal Knowledge* has led up to in tracing the ascent of man into meaning.[29]

What then in the end has Polanyi done to free us from the choice that Bertrand Russell left us with – the choice between honest scepticism and dishonest hope?[30] This was the choice that Polanyi saw as the root of so much of the despair and violence of the modern world, leaving men as it does with no honest hope, yet with moral passions that must find an outlet.

Polanyi's work was not to produce any once-for-all solution. It was more like clearance work in that 'high country of mind'[31] to find and clean up some of the springs of thought. The cleaner water will take time to flow. But when it begins to reach us without its poisons, our native powers can revive and start to work.

He has shown how our faith, imagination and personal judgment, so long paralysed by the poison of sceptical doubt, in fact run right through all our knowledge. Without faith in a real universe and in our own powers of getting hold of some direction and sense in it, there is no knowledge at all. Science relies on these same powers and stands or falls with them. The sceptics cheat by relying on powers which they cannot admit to be real; if things are as bad as the sceptics say, then they are *much worse*, for there is no sense anywhere, even in scepticism.

There is no guaranteed certainty for man; that has been a will-o-the-wisp leading him astray. But there is a sureness of direction and of faith which can be found in many different kinds of knowledge as well as in science. This faith is not irrational nor subjective. We have to believe in our own powers, but we have to train them, use them and discipline them as the scientist does his faculties. The truth of feeling, of moral sense, and of art need as much skill and dedication as the truth of science. It is not our every emotional whim that is to be trusted, any more than our abstract impersonal science, but the best judgment and discrimination that we can attain through self-discipline and through apprenticeship to the masters of our art, who speak to us with authority because we recognise in our hearts that they speak the truth.

Man has an awesome responsibility, but not the agonising and impossible responsibility of the existentialist creed, in which man makes his own values and has no reason to trust them. The truth we pursue has its reality in the universe, and meets our endeavours, and if evolution is the gradual emergence of meaning, then man's daring and suffering, questioning and faith, are not meaningless.

Notes to Chapter XII

1. Thesis – The Morality of Knowledge. Terence Kennedy CSSR. Rome 1979
2. see p.65 above
3. *The Tacit Dimension* p.62
4. Unpublished paper written for 'The Moot' in 1948
5. *Personal Knowledge* p.266
6. *The Tacit Dimension* p.84
7. *Personal Knowledge* p.284
8. *Ibid* pp.281, 199
9. *Meaning* p.179
10. *Personal Knowledge* p.282
11. *Ibid* p.282
12. *Ibid* p.285
13. *Ibid* p.324
14. *Science, Faith & Society* p.35
15. 'Science and Religion – Separate Dimensions or Common Ground?' in *Philosophy Today* VII, Spring 1960, p.4–14
16. *Personal Knowledge* p.198
17. American Academy of Religion Consultation on the thought of Michael Polanyi, November 1980. The papers

read at this consultation, together with Professor
W. T. Scott's 'adjudication' appear in *Zygon*.
The debate sprang from Prosch's review in
Ethics Jan 1979 of Gelwick's book *The Way of
Discovery*

18. Journal of the British Society for Phenomenology, Oct 1977
19. Article in *The Times* 28.1.78
20. *Personal Knowledge* p.199
21. *Meaning* p.153
22. *Belief in Science and in Christian Life*, p.12, 13
23. Paper delivered to the Consultation on the Thought of
    Michael Polanyi at the American Academy of
    Religion, Nov. 1980
24. *Knowing and Being* p.35, 36
25. *Personal Knowledge* p.279 (my italics)
26. *Ibid* p.305
27. *Ibid* p.302–3
28. Quick – *The Realism of Christ's Parables*
29. *The Study of Man* p. 67 "only by staking our lower interests
    can we bear witness effectively to our higher
    purposes".
30. see p.8 above
31. see p.2 above

BIBLIOGRAPHY

Books mentioned in the text or suggested for further reading

ARBER, AGNES *The mind and the Eye*, CUP, Cambridge 1954

BEVERIDGE, W. I. *The Art of Scientific Investigation*, Heinemann, London 1950

BRONOWSKI, J. *Science and Human Values*, Hutchinson, London 1951

BUTTERFIELD, HERBERT *The Origins of Modern Science*, Bell, London 1949, Macmillan, NY 1960

COHN, NORMAN *The Pursuit of the Millenium*, Paladin, London 1970

COLLINGWOOD, R. G. *Autobiography*, OUP, Oxford 1939

COLLINGWOOD, R. G. *The Idea of History*, OUP, Oxford 1961

CURIE, EVE *Madame Curie*, Heinemann, London 1938

DARBISHIRE, HELEN *The Poet Wordsworth*, Clarendon Press, Oxford 1950

DAWKINS, RICHARD *The Selfish Gene*, OUP, Oxford 1976, Paladin, London 1978

EINSTEIN, ALBERT *The World As I See It* (trans A. Harris) p.125, *Mein Weltbild*, Europa Verlag, Zurich 1934, p.168

EVANS PRITCHARD E. E. *Witchcraft, Oracles and Magic among the Azande*, OUP, Oxford 1957

GELWICK, RICHARD *The Way of Discovery*, OUP, New York 1976

GIBSON, A. B. *The Religion of Dostoievski*, SCM Press, London 1973

GRANT, PATRICK *Six Modern Authors and Problems of Belief*, Macmillan, London 1979

GRENE, MARJORIE *The Knower and the Known*, Faber and Faber, London 1966

GRENE, MARJORIE *The Understanding of Nature*, D. Reidl, Boston 1974

HARDY, ALISTER *The Living Stream*, Collins, London 1965

HOLBROOK, DAVID *English for Meaning*, National Foundation for Educational Research 1980

HOLBROOK, DAVID *Lost Bearings in English Poetry*, Vision Press 1977

HOLBROOK, DAVID *Education, Nihilism and Survival*, Darton Longman and Todd, London 1979

HOYLE, F. and WICKRAMASINGHE *Evolution from Space*, Dent, London 1980

HUDSON, LIAM *The Cult of the Fact*, Cape, London 1972

HUTCHINSON, R. C. *A Child Possessed*, Michael Joseph 1977

KENNEDY, TERENCE CSSR, *The Morality of Knowledge*, Academia Alfonsiana, Rome 1979

KOESTLER, ARTHUR *The Ghost in the Machine*, Pan Books, London 1970

KOESTLER, ARTHUR *The Sleepwalkers*, Hutchinson, London 1968

KUHN, THOMAS *The Structure of Scientific Revolutions*, University of Chicago Press, Chicago, London, 2nd ed 1970

LAGERLOF, SELMA *Jerusalem*, Heinemann, London 1903

LANGFORD and POTEAT *Intellect and Hope*, Duke University Press, Durham N.C. 1960

LEAVIS, F. R. *The Great Tradition*, Chatto and Windus, London 1948

LEAVIS, F. R. *The Living Principle*, Chatto and Windus, London 1975

LEAVIS, F. R. *Nor Shall My Sword*, Chatto and Windus, London 1972

LOWES, J. LIVINGSTONE *The Road to Xanadu*, Constable, London 1927

MAGEE, BRIAN (ed) *Men of Ideas*, BBC, London 1978

MARRIS, PETER *Loss and Change*, Routledge and Kegan Paul, London 1974, paperback 1978

MERLEAU PONTY, M. *Phenomenology of Perception*, Routledge and Kegan Paul, London 1962

MEYER, FRANK *The Moulding of Communists*, Harcourt Brace, New York 1961

MITCHELL, BASIL *Morality, Religious and Secular*, OUP 1971

MONOD, JACQUES *Chance and Necessity*, Collins, Glasgow 1972

OPPENHEIMER, J. R. *Science and the Common Understanding*, OUP 1954

PEACOCKE, F. R. *Creation and the World of Science*, Clarendon Press, Oxford 1979

PEARSON, KARL *The Grammar of Science*, Macmillan, London 1896

PIAGET, J. *The Origins of Intelligence in the Child*, Routledge and Kegan Paul, London

PIAGET, J. *Psychology of Intelligence*, Routledge and Kegan Paul, London

PIAGET, J. *Judgment and Reasoning in the Child*, Routledge and Kegan Paul, London 1928

PIRSIG, ROBERT *Zen and the Art of Motorcycle Maintenance*, Bodley Head, London 1974, Corgi Books 1976, William Morrow & Co, New York

POLANYI, MICHAEL *USSR Economics*, Manchester University Press 1935

POLANYI, MICHAEL *The Contempt of Freedom*, Watts, London 1940, Arno, NY 1975

POLANYI, MICHAEL *Science, Faith and Society*, OUP 1946, Chicago University Press 1946, Phoenix Edition, Chicago 1964

POLANYI, MICHAEL *The Logic of Liberty*, Routledge and Kegan Paul, London 1951, Chicago University Press 1951

POLANYI, MICHAEL *Personal Knowledge*, Routledge and Kegan Paul, London 1958, Chicago University Press, Torch Books 1964

POLANYI, MICHAEL *The Study of Man*, Routledge and Kegan Paul, London 1959, Chicago University Press 1959

POLANYI, MICHAEL *The Tacit Dimension*, Routledge and Kegan Paul, London 1966, Doubleday, New York 1966

POLANYI, MICHAEL *Knowing and Being*, Routledge and Kegan Paul, London 1960, Chicago University Press (All Michael Polanyi's books also from Phoenix Books, 1964)

POLANYI, MICHAEL and PROSCH, HARRY *Meaning*, Chicago University Press 1975

POPPER, KARL *The Logic of Scientific Discovery*, Hutchinson, London 1959

POPPER, KARL and ECCLES, JOHN *The Self and Its Brain*, Springer, New York 1977

RAMSAY, IAN *Religious Language*, SCM Press, London 1973
RUSSELL, BERTRAND *The Scientific Outlook*, Allen and Unwin, London 1937
RUSSELL, BERTRAND *The Impact of Science on Society*, London 1952
RYLE, GILBERT *The Concept of Mind*, Penguin, London 1970

SKINNER, B. F. *Beyond Freedom and Dignity*, Penguin, London 1973
SUTTIE, IAN *The Origins of Love and Hate*, Kegan Paul Trench Trubner, London 1956

THORPE, W. H. *Science, Man and Morals*, Methuen, London 1965
TORRANCE, T. F.(ed) *Belief in Science and in Christian Life*, Handsel Press, Edinburgh 1980
TOULMIN, S. *The Philosophy of Science*, Hutchinson, London 1953

WADDINGTON, C. H. *The Nature of Life*, Allen and Unwin, London 1961
WATSON, J. B. *Behaviourism*, Kegan Paul Trench Trubner, London 1928
WATSON, J. D. *The Double Helix*, Penguin, London 1970
WEIZENBAUM *Computer Power and Human Reason*, W. H. Freeman, London 1977
WHEWELL, W. *On the Philosophy of Discovery*, Parker, London 1860
WHITEHEAD, A. N. *Adventures of Ideas*, Cambridge University Press 1933
WOODHOUSE, A. S. F. *Puritanism and Liberty*, Dent, London 1975
WORDSWORTH, W. *The Prelude*, 1805 text, ed E. de Selincourt, OUP 1933
WORDSWORTH, W. *The Excursion*, Poetical Works of W. Wordsworth

YOUNG, J. Z. *Programs of the Brain*, OUP, Oxford 1978

In the full list of Michael Polanyi's published work there is a flood of articles on scientific subjects up to 1940, then this gradually lessens and the number of articles on economics, science and society, and philosophy increases. This list is a selection from the latter.

The Growth of Thought in Society – *Economica* VIII Nov 1941
Science and Faith – *Question* V Winter 1952
The Foolishness of History – *Encounter* IX Nov 1957
Science Academic and Industrial – *Journal of the Institute of*

Metallurgy LXXXIX 1961
The Unaccountable Element in Science – *Philosophy* Jan 1962
Science and Religion, Separate Dimensions or Common Ground?
Philosophy Today VII Spring 1963
Science and Man's Place in the Universe – in *Science as a Cultural Force* ed H. Woolf 1964
On The Modern Mind – *Encounter* XXIV May 1965
Contribution to *Mid Century Authors* 1966
Logic and Psychology – *American Psychologist* XII Jan 1968
On Body and Mind – *The New Scholasticism* XLIII Spring 1969
The Determinants of Social Action – *Roads to Freedom*, Festschrift for F. A. von Hayek ed Streissler, Routledge and Kegan Paul 1970, Chicago University Press
What is a Painting? – *The American Scholar* vol.39 no.4 Autumn 1970, *The British Journal of Aesthetics* vol.X no.3
Science and Man – *Proceedings of the Royal Society of Medicine* LVIII pp.969–76 Sept 1970
Genius in Science – *Boston Studies in the Philosophy of Science* XIV 1972

Articles by other writers relevant to Polanyi

TORRANCE, T. F. The Place of Michael Polanyi in the Modern Philosophy of Science – *Ethics in Science and Medicine*, vol.7, Pergamon 1980
TORRANCE, T. F. The Open Universe and the Free Society – *Ethics in Science and Medicine*, vol.6, Pergamon 1979
E. P. WIGNER and R. A. HODGKIN Michael Polanyi 1891–1976 – *Biographical Memoirs of Fellows of the Royal Society*, vol.23 Dec 1977
Journal of the British Society for Phenomenology – special number on the Philosophy of Michael Polanyi, vol.8 no.3 Oct 1977
SCOTT, W. T. A Bridge from Science to Religion, based on Polanyi's Theory of Knowledge – *Zygon*, vol.5, no.1 March 1970, University of Chicago
SCOTT, W. T. The Personal Character of the Discovery of Mechanisms in Cloud Physics – T. Nickles (ed) *Scientific Discovery*, Reidl Publishing Co 1980
SCOTT, W. T. Tacit Knowing and *The Concept of Mind* – *Philosophical Quarterly* 21, Jan 1971. Also in

Interpretations of Life and Mind, M. Grene (ed),
    New York Humanities Press 1971
Pre/text, an Interdisciplinary Journal of Rhetoric, special number on
    Michael Polanyi, guest editor Sam Watson 1981
Zygon, Journal of Religion and Science vol.17 no.1, March 1982.
    The American Academy of Religion discussions on
    Polanyi and Religion
GRENE, MARJORIE Sociobiology and the Human Mind, in
    Sociobiology and Human Nature ed Gregory, Silvers
    and Sutch, Jossey Bass, San Francisco 1978
PROSCH, HARRY Cooling the Modern Mind – Polanyi's Mission
    Skidmore College Bulletin, Aug 1971
SILONE, IGNAZIO The Choice of Comrades, *Encounter*, Dec 1954
CLARK, KENNETH The Blot and the Diagram, *Encounter*, Jan 1963
HOLBROOK, DAVID Are We Only DNA's Way of Making More
    DNA? Poetry and Science, *New Universities
    Quarterly*, Winter 1978
WOOD, MICHAEL The Four Gospels, *New Society*, 18 Dec 1969

INDEX

The extracts from Michael Polanyi's books are quoted by kind permission of the publishers: Routledge and Kegan Paul and the University of Chicago Press for *Personal Knowledge* and *The Study of Man, Knowing and Being;* Routledge and Kegan Paul and Doubleday for *Tacit Dimensions;* The University of Chicago Press and the Oxford University Press for *Science, Faith and Society;* the University of Chicago Press for *Meaning* by Michael Polanyi and Harry Presch.

For permission to quote from J. Z. Young *Programs of the Brain* I thank the Oxford University Press; from Eve Curie *Madame Curie,* William Heinemann; from Agnes Arber *The Mind and the Eye,* the Cambridge University Press; from A. S. P. Woodhouse (ed) *Puritanism and Liberty,* J. M. Dent and Sons; from Robert Pirsig *Zen and the Art of Motor Cycle Maintenance,* The Bodley Head; from Hilaire Belloc 'A Moral Alphabet' in *Cautionary Verses,* Duckworth; from Ignazio Silone 'The Choice of Comrades' and Michael Polanyi 'On The Modern Mind', *Encounter.* (Details in Bibliography, p. 200.)